LIFE IN RIVERFRONT:
A MIDDLE-WESTERN TOWN SEEN
THROUGH JAPANESE EYES

LIFE IN RIVERFRONT: A MIDDLE-WESTERN

TOWN SEEN THROUGH JAPANESE EYES

MARIKO FUJITA

and

TOSHIYUKI SANO

HARCOURT BRACE COLLEGE PUBLISHERS

Fort Worth   Philadelphia   San Diego   New York   Orlando   Austin   San Antonio
Toronto   Montreal   London   Sydney   Tokyo

Publisher	Earl McPeek
Acquisitions Editor	Lin Marshall
Production Manager	Andrea E. Archer
Marketing Strategist	Katie Rose Matthews

ISBN: 0-15-506421-5

Address for Editorial Correspondence: Harcourt Brace College Publishers, 301 Commerce Street, Suite 3700, Fort Worth, TX 76102.

Address for Orders: Harcourt Brace & Company, 6277 Sea Harbor Drive, Orlando, Florida 32887. 1-800-782-4479, or 1-800-433-0001 (in Florida).

Printed in the United States of America

0 1 2 3   039 9 8 7 6 5 4 3 2 1

For Hosaki & Yuzuki

ABOUT THIS CASE STUDY

This book is a case study of a town in middle America — in central Wisconsin, to be exact. This town is not a particularly unusual place. Anyone would recognize it as an American town, or a city, according to the census. The location has an ethnic mix that is almost exclusively European, predominantly Polish, and it has the thriving University of Wisconsin, which brings in more than 9,000 strangers each September.

What is most unusual about this case study is not the research site but the researchers — two Japanese anthropologists. Mariko Fujita and Toshiyuki Sano both graduated from Stanford University with a Ph.D. in anthropology. Dr. Sano did his dissertation research in "Riverfront City," the pseudonym used for the town they studied for 2 years. Dr. Fujita already had her degree and did further research on preschool care and the care of the aged, special interests of hers, in Riverfront City.

They have used their Japanese cultural origins wisely in the interpretation of life in Riverfront City. Reflexivity has a new meaning in their treatment of the ethnographic data they collected, for they respond to it not only as skilled, trained observers but also as Japanese. Finding a place to live and raising a child (a son born during their fieldwork), along with the everyday experiences they had as field-workers accepted in the mainstream of life in their research site, are all seen and interpreted through Japanese eyes, as well as by their anthropological vision. These factors give the case study an unexpected dimension, one that informs in ways that standard interpretations cannot equal.

Mariko and Toshiyuki explore nuances of American culture as displayed in Riverfront City and do so in ways that are profoundly stimulating. For instance, they examine dependence and independence, pivotal areas of American life, in the contexts of the care of the aged and the care of preschool children. Independence and dependence as understood in American culture is quite different than the way it is understood in Japanese culture, and they make the behavioral manifestations of both abundantly clear.

The reader looking for a solid ethnography of an American community will not be disappointed. The authors let informants speak for themselves, but they never relinquish their interpretive voice. The authors' behavioral observations and ethnographic data are plentiful and appropriate, providing a well-rounded understanding of Riverfront City.

This case study will join the ranks of outstanding studies of American life written by both native observers and foreign workers.

George Spindler, Editor
Case Studies in Cultural Anthropology

ABOUT THE AUTHORS

Mariko Fujita is professor of anthropology and American studies in the Faculty of Integrated Arts and Sciences, Hiroshima University. She received her Ph.D. in anthropology from Stanford University in 1984. In her dissertation, she explored how talk, cultural ideas, and action combine to shape the daily experiences of middle-class, elderly European Americans in the San Francisco Bay Area. From 1984 to 1987, as a Spencer Fellow, she conducted postdoctoral field research in central Wisconsin in collaboration with her husband, Toshiyuki Sano. This book is based on that research, which is part of a larger investigation into American conceptions of individual life stages and how these affect processes of socialization and enculturation. As a means of comparison, she has conducted similar studies in Japan with Toshiyuki. A second area of her interest is the relationship between gender and society — how feminist theory has affected women's efforts to balance job and family, both in the United States and Japan. She focuses on working women with preschool children and on women who take care of elderly parents. Mariko is currently studying social, cultural, and historical factors affecting the career patterns of female scientists in the United States and Japan in the 20th century.

Toshiyuki Sano is professor of anthropology in the Faculty of Human Life and Environment, Nara Women's University. After receiving his master's degree in physical anthropology from the University of Tokyo, he shifted to cultural anthropology by entering the graduate program at Stanford University, where he received his Ph.D. in 1990. As a master's student, he conducted fieldwork from 1978 to 1979 at a day-care center in Tokyo, observing children's nonverbal behavior patterns and social interactions. Some of the methods used in that study were later used in the American day-care center research on which the present book is based. Toshi conducted this research collaboratively with his wife, Mariko Fujita, in central Wisconsin from 1984 to 1987. Based on this fieldwork, he wrote his dissertation on ethnicity, cultural identity, and concepts of caring for others and how individuals apply these concepts to their everyday lives. Currently, he is analyzing historical changes in caring patterns in the Riverfront area between 1850 and 1980. He is also interested in the role of cloth in Japanese, American, and other cultures.

Preface

Our intention in writing this ethnography is not to present a definitive picture of people's lives in Riverfront but to attempt to understand the culture of the Riverfront area by reflecting on American culture in the light of our own Japanese culture. The impressions presented here were shaped by the encounters we had with particular individuals whom we met during our stay on the outskirts of the city between October 1984 and March 1987. We used our own cultural perspective to interpret our experience in Riverfront. Instead of trying to escape from our Japanese cultural background, which we believe is impossible, we constantly invoked Japanese culture during our fieldwork. Given a particular situation, what would be the equivalent in Japanese society? How might Americans be treated in a similar situation in Japan? What would our mothers say in this context? In other words, we continually go back and forth between American and Japanese cultures. When these two cultures are juxtaposed, different interpretations of the same phenomena emerge. We use these differences as keys to understanding the culture of Riverfront and its environs. Hence, the interactions between ourselves and Riverfrontans comprise a dialog between Japanese and American culture. It is a dialog about how we perceive them and how they perceive us using our respective cultural sensors.

We would like to express our gratitude to the people of Riverfront and its surrounding area. Many local institutions were also helpful and cooperative in our research. We are especially grateful to the people of Maple Child Day Care Center, Jefferson Center, and the local campus of the University of Wisconsin. These individuals and institutions appear in this book under pseudonyms. We are grateful to George and Louise Spindler, who have been helpful to us not only as teachers but also as colleagues and friends. Louise passed away while we were finishing this ethnography, and we deeply regret that we were unable to share the final version with her.

Teachers and friends provided valuable comments on our work. We are especially grateful to Harumi Befu, Lee Coleman, the late Frank Dubinskas, Charles O. Frake, Estelle Friedman, Roy Hamilton, Joseph J. Lauer, Jerry Marr, the late Michelle Rosaldo, Renato Rosaldo, Harold Stevenson, Ann Swidler, Sharon Traweek, and Sylvia J. Yanagisako for the discussions we had. We gratefully acknowledge the editorial assistance that Jerry Marr offered us. He helped bring our English closer to the norm and clarify ambiguous statements without changing our ideas.

Finally, our family, both directly and indirectly, helped us in this study. Hosaki, our eldest son, was an excellent research assistant during fieldwork. Moreover, he and our second son Yuzuki, who was born in Japan after we finished our fieldwork, presented us with situations back home comparable to our field experiences and enriched our cultural dialog. Our parents, Fujita Hisajiro and Toyoko and Sano Torakichi and Sachiyo, inspired us. We often thought of them while conducting research and writing this ethnography and wondered how they might react to similar situations in Japanese contexts.

This study was supported in part by a Spencer Fellowship from the National Academy of Education, awarded to Mariko (1984–1987); a Monbusho Fellowship awarded to Toshiyuki during his stay in the United States (1989); a Monbusho Grant-in-Aid to Mariko and Toshiyuki for the census analysis (1994; 1995–1997); and an Ishizaka Foundation Scholarship to Toshiyuki for the first 2 years of graduate work at Stanford.

Contents

Introduction

This book is an ethnography of the everyday lives of Euro-Americans in a midsize town and its environs in central Wisconsin through the observations and interpretations of two Japanese anthropologists, Mariko Fujita and Toshi Sano. The town is located along the Wisconsin River, and because the river is so important to the development and life of the town, we gave the town the fictional name "Riverfront." Riverfront is a multiethnic community with a population of 22,000. Its residents are nearly 100% European American, their ethnic composition being generally Anglo-Saxon (called "Yankees" by the locals), Irish, Scandinavian, German, and Polish. Riverfront became a city in 1856, and since then its major industry changed from logging to furniture manufacturing to paper mills. More recently, service industries such as an insurance company and a university have become major employers.

One of the main tasks of anthropologists is to make the strange familiar and the familiar strange. What seems exotic and enigmatic at the beginning will become understandable, sensible, and eventually familiar once we know what it means to the natives. Simultaneously, trying to make sense of their culture will enable us to see our own culture in a new light. We realize that what is taken for granted is also culturally constructed. Our anthropological inquiry is a constant dialog between *their* culture and *our* culture (Spindler & Spindler, 1990).

For us, Riverfront is enough of an exotic place to make us aware of *our* existence as distinct from *their* existence. In terms of the many indicators commonly used in a social scientific inquiry, such as race, nationality, religion, language, ethnicity and class, we are different from Riverfrontans. When we moved to Riverfront in our early 30s, Mariko had just obtained her Ph.D. and Toshi was about to start his dissertation research. We had been married for 2 years. Although we had been exposed to American culture in California, this was our first experience living in the Midwest. Our Californian friends assured us that Midwesterners were very different from Californians.

With this in mind, we moved to Riverfront, acutely aware of the differences between ourselves and its residents. First, they are Americans, and we are Japanese. They are of European descendants, and we are not. Although there is a Japanese restaurant in town, only a few Asians live in Riverfront, and most of them are associated with the local university. Most Riverfrontans are of the Christian faith, and we are not. Their native language is English, whereas ours is Japanese. Having graduate educations meant we would be classified as "highly educated" and perhaps "middle class." However, without steady employment, we were not certain how we would be classified. The size of the town was also important to our initial perception. Riverfront was far smaller than any other place we had ever lived. We had believed that a "small town" was conservative, rigid, and closed to outsiders. Mariko had an additional apprehension: she was not sure how people would regard and treat a woman aspiring to a professional career. She did not wish to be seen as a housewife who merely accompanied her husband to assist in his research. To be sure, we were both quite nervous when we started our fieldwork. We felt as though everything we would do would stand out.

In understanding the culture of Riverfront and its environs, we wanted to function as a mirror. Riverfrontans, in accepting us into their daily lives, would use their own cultural perspective to make sense of our existence; that is, they must place us in their system of classification. How they perceive us, what questions they ask us, and how they react to what we do would reveal their concerns and their world view.

One of the strangest things about Riverfrontans for us was that they were constantly distinguishing themselves from each other. People commonly made statements about themselves such as, "I am not a typical American," and "I have been living in Riverfront since I was born, but I am different from other people." These kinds of statements surprised us because we tended to see Riverfrontans as being very much alike. The reasons people gave for being atypical included: "I am not a churchgoer"; "I'm a teetotaler. I don't drink you know"; "I'm a farmer. I don't like living in town"; "Well, I am a Catholic"; and "I am Polish." Although we expected to encounter divisions between Riverfrontans and ourselves, we did not expect Riverfrontans to draw boundaries around themselves as well.

The fact that Riverfrontans differentiate themselves from each other does not mean that the community is on the verge of collapse. There are many community-wide events in which people collaborate. Many try to bridge the differences and to create unity. When Riverfrontans differentiate themselves from others, they are essentially defining who they are. In Barth's terms, statements of differentiation establish personal identity by making boundaries between the individual and others (Barth, 1969). A key to understanding the culture of Riverfront is to ask how people define themselves and how they relate to each other in their daily lives.

To answer these questions, we examine the events, episodes, and encounters that we experienced in Riverfront. We pay particular attention to those incidents that we believe revealed the nature of Riverfront culture, either because we found them strikingly different from Japanese culture or because people in Riverfront were very involved and concerned. We call these incidents "critical tales" (Van Maanen, 1988). After describing the tale, we ask why it is an issue, what is at stake, and how the people involved deal with it. The critical tales work as tools for us to analyze the cultural assumptions embedded in people's day-to-day lives. In this volume, the chapters are organized according to the critical tales and cultural questions we experienced in conducting our fieldwork. Our search for answers to these questions led us to further questions. In this sense, this ethnography is a biography of our inquiries to be a "good" ethnography presented by Marcus and Fisher (1986, pp. 24–25).

Conventionally, chapters of an ethnography are organized according to domains of social structures, such as geography, history, political organization, economy, religion, and so forth, or according to ethnic groups, such as German, Irish, Polish, or Yankees. This book, however, does not follow these conventions. Social structure is not something observers can see as a rigid framework. Rather, it emerges as we explore various aspects of people's daily lives. Therefore, we portray the process of how we came to grasp the social structure rather than presenting only the conclusions of our analysis. Also, we describe several events that crosscut conventional domains of social structure. For example, a dispute in a political meeting was attributed to people's different religious backgrounds even though no one was discussing religion at the time. By depicting such events, we demonstrate the interconnectedness of various social domains in day-to-day lives.

Likewise, we do not organize chapters according to ethnic groups although ethnicity is, as we shall see, an important factor in understanding the Riverfront culture. The reason for not doing so is that a people's ethnic identity is essentially contextual. We agree with Anya P. Royce's view that an ethnic group is "a reference group invoked by people who share a common historical style (which may be only assumed), based on overt features and values, and who, through the process of interaction with others, identify themselves as sharing that style" (1982, p. 27). For instance, a man may identify himself as Polish in the context of talking about his cultural heritage, but he may identify himself as a Catholic in the context of choosing a marriage partner. For that reason, it is important that his marriage partner is a Catholic but not necessarily Polish. If we were to organize the book chapters according to ethnic groups, we would risk presenting a more static and rigid picture of Riverfrontans than is actually the case.

Another reason for depicting the development of our inquiry is that we want to incorporate three transitions into our account. First, the town's long-term historical change is an important element to consider; whatever we saw during our fieldwork must be set in historical context. For this reason, we collected individual life histories and also investigated archival materials (see Chapters 3, 4, and 5). Second, our relationships with Riverfrontans were not static. As time passed, we transformed from strangers to acquaintances and even friends to some people. The nature of our experiences changed accordingly (see Chapter 6). Third, the transitions people undergo in their lives are important to consider (see Chapters 7, 8, and 9). Paying attention to these transitions enabled us to understand that cultural boundaries are not fixed but changeable over time.

Because we have chosen such an unconventional way of organizing our ethnography, we would like to explain in further detail how and why the chapters are organized as they are.

Our original intention in doing fieldwork in Riverfront and its environs was to learn about "authentic" American life and to study ethnic diversity among European Americans. We had some expectations beforehand about doing fieldwork in a Midwestern town (see Chapter 1). We thought we would find some examples of "authentic" and "typical" American life because we would be in the heartland of the nation. Also, we were told that Riverfront is a Polish town and this, too, stimulated our curiosity about the area. In addition, not far from Riverfront, as we were told, is a town called Pulaski, so named because it was settled by Polish immigrants. To us, this sounded exotic.

We knew very little about Poland or Polish culture. When we left California, we decided we would dine at a restaurant in the Polish section of town as soon as we arrived in Riverfront. We thought that experience would surely introduce us to Polish culture. To our disappointment, there was no Polish restaurant in Riverfront nor even a Polish section of town, and Pulaski was no different than any small, rural town. It was essentially a residential area in the middle of farmland. There was a sizable Catholic church with a cemetery, a grocery store, and two shops that dealt with agricultural machinery. We had imagined an ethnic enclave in a large urban area, such as Chinatown in San Francisco, and we were hoping for some tangible ethnic signs. Our search was in vain.

In retrospect, we realize that our understanding of ethnicity, at the beginning of fieldwork, was based on what anthropologist Isaw called an objective definition of ethnicity (Isajiw, 1974). We thought an ethnic group would be distinguishable from others by its culturally distinctive characteristics, such as a common ancestral origin, shared customs, religion, racial or physical characteristics, and language. Therefore, we looked for signs of these characteristics. It took several incidents to realize that ethnic identities are essentially contextual.

At the very beginning of our fieldwork, we were puzzled by several experiences (see Chapter 2). For instance, when we were looking for a place to live, one of the owners asked us the question: "Which church do you go to?" We were astonished by this question because asking one's religion seemed not only a highly private matter but also inappropriate in the context of house-hunting. The same woman, when asked about her ethnic background, abruptly became silent after mentioning that her grandfather was a Norwegian. Another time (see Chapter 3), a man described to us how, in the past, the town had been divided into ethnic enclaves. The next time we saw him, he made sure that we did not think that he was prejudiced and discriminating against Polish people. We were surprised at his reaction because the issue of discrimination did not even occur to us. These incidents told us that ethnicity was a sensitive issue. It concerned one's privacy, but so did religious belief and affiliation. Why were they vocal about religious difference but reticent about ethnic difference?

These incidents also taught us that although ethnicity and religion are important factors in understanding the culture of Riverfront, they are subtle and embedded in people's daily lives. We needed to examine how these factors are invoked in daily life and to inquire as to their meanings in the contexts of these day-to-day interactions rather than merely seeking out their outward signs.

To gain a better grasp of the region's religion and ethnicity, we first turn to the history of Riverfront (see Chapter 3). Because many people mentioned that the town used to be more divided according to ethnic and religious lines, we asked people in their 70s to tell us their life histories and how they viewed Riverfront as they were growing up in the 1920s and 1930s. We saw different experiences between Anglo-Saxon and Polish people.

While collecting life histories, we heard that the northern section of the town was thought to have been a "Polish territory" in the past. We searched archival materials such as the U.S. census (original schedule), historical records, and city directories to discern the relationship between movement patterns and ethnicity (see Chapter 4). Marriage announcements in a local newspaper were consulted to discern changes in intraethnic and interethnic marriage patterns among Polish people.

Riverfront is by no means a town isolated from the rest of the world. During our fieldwork we could see evidence of major historical changes that started throughout the nation in the mid-1970s. As we describe in Chapter 1, because of a revitalization project, the downtown was transformed from an old commercial area to a large modern shopping mall. Human service programs for senior citizens and children were available, and generally cultural and ethnic revitalization was taking place. Although the town lacked ethnic restaurants or enclaves, there were many occasions during which ethnicity was manifested during our fieldwork. These were mostly community and church-sponsored events such as a Polish festival, a Norsk dinner, church picnics, and a Polish Christmas dinner called *Wigilia* (see Chapter 5).

Anthropologists in the field often experience a point at which the nature of the relationship between themselves and their informants changes drastically. The most dramatic turning point for us was the birth of our son (see Chapter 6). The change in relationships was most noticeable with the elderly people at Jefferson Center, where we had been volunteering. The birth of a baby is, of course, a universal experience that we all can share, and it certainly helped us to set closer to our interviewees. However, the birth of our son meant more to them than just getting closer. Like them, our son is an American citizen by birth — a "border-crosser." In a sense, he is one of "them" and can be a bridge between "us" and "them."

The birth of our son also shed powerful new light in our effort to understand Riverfrontans. As a neophyte of American culture, people consciously and unconsciously tried to educate him and also his parents, especially his mother (see Chapter 7). We were witnessing a cultural transmission in action. Many core values and symbols, such as "independence" and "sharing," emerged in their advice. However, what they taught us was not uniform. We could therefore see diversity along ethnic, gender, religious, and class lines.

The cultural transmission processes to which our son was subjected made us pay more attention to the various stages of people's lives. How do people become self-sufficient and independent, and how do they create relationships with other people at different life stages? We focused on the two ends of the life cycle, young children and senior citizens, and chose a day-care center and a senior center as the places where we could witness a variety of people interacting (see Chapter 8). Again, we could see many core cultural values and symbols, such as "independence," "caring," "sharing," "visiting," and "family," emerge in their daily conversations. (Part of this chapter is adopted from Fujita and Sano [1998] and from Chapter 4 of Sano's dissertation [1989].)

Inquiring about people's concepts concerning birth, child-rearing, and caring for the elderly, we tended to circulate among women because women traditionally have been caregivers. We wanted to understand more about men's life histories, especially their career-building processes (see Chapter 9). Are "caring," "sharing," and "family" important values for men as much as they are for women? Or, since men have traditionally been breadwinners, do they stress "independence" and "hard work" as their primary values and relegate "caring" and "sharing" to women? Judging from our Japanese cultural perspective, we expected to see just such a dichotomy of these values along gender lines. To our surprise, men's life histories revealed that family relationship and "caring for the family" as well as "independence" and "hard work" were central values by which they organized their lives; they even adjusted their career patterns to uphold these values.

Now we begin our story by recounting what we *expected* to see in "middle America" before starting our cultural journey in Riverfront.

CHAPTER 1 / What Is "Middle" America and Riverfront?: Our Expectations and Reality

Central Wisconsin, the location of Riverfront, did not evoke much for us when in April 1984 Professor Frank Woodland suggested the area for our ethnographic fieldwork. Although we had lived in the San Francisco Bay Area for several years, we had not learned much about Wisconsin or other Midwestern states. According to the 1980 census, Riverfront was a "city" and the Pine County seat; however, its population was too small to be a city in our estimation. We both had lived in metropolitan areas most of our lives and imagined that Riverfront would be like a rural town or village, even though it was administratively a city. As anthropologists we thought that Riverfront's size would be advantageous for our research because it was small enough to allow us to learn how people's activities were locally organized, practiced, and managed.

Further talks with Professors Elinor and Frank Woodland inspired us. Frank Woodland was born and raised in Riverfront but had left the town when he entered college. In later years, he and his wife would drive through his hometown many times in their professional lives. They told us about the town of Pulaski, which is near Riverfront. We were intrigued when they told us that the citizens of Pulaski were Polish-Americans, as the name suggested, and we became interested in meeting these people and learning about their lives. Although we had known that American society is ethnically diverse, we tended to associate ethnicity with racial minorities such as African-Americans, Hispanics, and Asians and tended to see European-American people as of a uniform ethnicity. Throughout our fieldwork we hoped that we would gain a better understanding of ethnic diversity among European-American people in America. We also hoped to understand the discourses and dialogs of laymen and professionals on diversity and unity in American culture, specifically European-American culture, as European ethnic identities are said to be in the process of transformation (Alba, 1990).

The map of Riverfront and its surrounding area that was available at our home university's library shaped our image of Riverfront. (It was the U.S. Geological Survey's map [scale 1:250,000] dated 1955 with limited revision in 1967.) This map indicated major roads connecting Riverfront to other towns and also many smaller roads crossing each other — many more than we had expected. From this map, we assumed that Riverfront was not an isolated rural town. This was encouraging to us not because we disliked isolation but because we would be able to drive around easily to see people in the surrounding communities.

To develop our images of Riverfront and to situate them in larger geographical contexts, we decided to drive from California to Wisconsin. On the way, we traveled through the Southwest, Deep South, and Mid-South to Midwest. According to another regional classification (Garreau, 1982), we moved from "Ecotopia" through "The Empty Quarter," "Mexamerica," "Breadbasket," "Dixie," to "the Foundry," and finally the "Breadbasket" again, missing the Islands and New England. In 1989, 2 years after we left Riverfront, we stayed both in eastern Texas and in Wisconsin and traveled between them. The two areas have similar outlooks of communities and farms, and thus we are convinced that Garreau rightly lumped them together in his classification, "Breadbasket."

Seeing American regional differences while moving to Riverfront was helpful to our prospective research. We consulted guidebooks and other materials about the regions we were going to pass through. Among our sources was J. and M. Stern's Goodfood: *The Adventurous Eater's Guide to Restaurants Serving America's Best Regional Specialties* (1983). This book was especially useful because we wanted to know about regional differences using our five senses. It gave the names and addresses of eating establishments where specific regional foods, by J. and M. Stern's definition, were served. The authors described the atmosphere of each place and the quality of the food. By testing the authors' interpretations, we could create our sets of experiences and interpretations of the different regions.

An advantage of this kind of traveling was that it allowed us to experience a transitional feeling, in other words, to reframe our social status from one of students studying at school to one of scholars conducting independent research. Although Riverfront lay within the United States, we imagined it to be another world. This was our fantasy as anthropologists who wanted to write about a different world and its people. In our cultural tradition, traveling has a symbolic meaning related to an individual's life course; it is associated with freedom and independence. Traveling on foot with one of his students into Japan's deep north for 6 months in 1689, Matsuo Basho, a great poet of Japan, desired to experience time and space. He wrote:

> Days and months are travelers of eternity. So are the years that pass by. Those who steer a boat across the sea, or drive a horse over the earth till they succumb to the weight of years, spend every minute of their lives traveling. There are a great number of ancients, too, who died on the road. I myself have been tempted for a long time by the cloud-moving wind — filled with a strong desire to wander (Matsuo, 1966, p. 97).

For Matsuo Basho, traveling and writing along the way freed him from the various constraints in urban life. We undertook our travels across America based on Matsuo's model.

Driving north from Kentucky to Ohio, through part of the Midwest, or "The Foundry," we felt, at first, disenchantment. This feeling stayed with us until we escaped from the urban landscapes and ventured into northern Michigan, where we passed rural towns and summer tourist spots. These sights lifted our spirits, but every time we encountered landscapes full of buildings and freeways, our good feelings again sank. We were becoming concerned that Riverfront would be like the urban centers we were passing along the way. The popular image of Wisconsin as a dairy land, as displayed on its automobile license plate, affected our image of the state. After listening to elderly Riverfront residents talking about their work experiences at factories beyond the local area, mostly around Lake Winnebago, Green Bay, and Lake Michigan, we gradually came to understand that the Midwest was heavily industrialized.

From upper Michigan to central Wisconsin, forests and small lakes were replaced by farmland. Although agriculture is considered dairy in this part of the upper Midwest, people have long raised potatoes in Pine County and recently have developed strategic land use for cash crops — ginseng in the county north of Pine County and beans and cucumbers in the south. Nevertheless, from central Wisconsin to the southern end of the state, dairy farmlands predominate.

While on a major freeway on the way to Riverfront from northern Wisconsin, we decided to stop in Janesville, a city that was larger than our destination, for comparison. Following the road signs marked "Business," we easily found the city center, saw a national department store, and spotted several churches. We soon realized that JC Penney was part of a downtown shopping mall. Leaving downtown, we drove south for awhile, seeing houses, stores, and business offices along a major boulevard. We then came to a shopping zone, which consisted of gas stations, fast-food restaurants, and a K-Mart (a large discount department store). Entering this area meant that we were coming to the end of the road marked "Business." In fact, we soon reentered the Interstate freeway, passing farmlands with silos on both sides of the highway, more than before, and a few swampy areas and lakes.

On taking the Riverfront exit and leaving the freeway, we found a shopping area just like the one we had seen in the previous town. A national chain hotel, restaurants, fast-food restaurants, gas stations, and a discount department store were along a major street. We knew that we were entering a town because in the American landscape such shopping zones are commonly located just off the Interstate. We usually came to the city center by taking a road marked "Business." However, the lesson that we had learned from other towns was not true of Riverfront. We could not find the city center along the "Business" road. We thought we were lost, or perhaps misled, because we had assumed that the downtown area was the center of the town and where the busy streets converged. It turned out that the downtown area lay on an east-to-west main street and not on the north-to-south street we had chosen.

The city center of Riverfront had existed at the same location from the town's beginnings in the mid-19th century, continuously extending toward the east along Main street. The west end of downtown faces the Wisconsin River and used to be a railroad freight yard, which served the town since 1871 and disappeared as late as the 1950s. The dates inscribed on the buildings around the public square were those from the early 1900s. Most of Riverfront's old buildings remained; however, much demolition and construction of buildings were under way, and some streets had been rerouted when we first arrived. Old buildings on both sides of the main street were preserved, but relatively new buildings at the east end of the street were being demolished to make parking space for a new shopping mall, which was to be built on the north side of the old downtown complex. Some houses were relocated, if worth preserving, such as an entire building on the north side of the public square that had been picked up and moved about 10 feet to the west. Because of such relocations and the rerouting of a major street, a street to the north side of the public square disappeared completely.

The construction of a downtown shopping mall was not unique to Riverfront but part of a trend seen in American communities. In fact, neighboring towns also had shopping malls in their downtown areas. Some were successful, some were not. Such malls usually changed a town's appearance and transformed the city's center from the oldest section of the town to the newest (Figures 1 through 4). However, in Riverfront, old buildings were preserved to maintain a historical depth and a "hometown" image, challenging our preconceptions that American towns generally have a shallow history. On the other hand, a new shopping mall represents wealth and comfort that such towns had achieved, thus supporting our preconceptions of American life in the modern and postmodern eras. The coexistence of the old and the new in Riverfront's city center suggested to us that its revitalization was shaped by compromise of different interests among Riverfront residents, thus embodying many voices to attract people with different desires and expectations to the renewed landscape.

Figure 1. The public square in October 1984 just before the new shopping mall was constructed. A Catholic church, originally built in North Side by Polish immigrants, can be seen in the distance.

Figure 2. Work in progress downtown. The JC Penney store had closed, and its building was about to be demolished. A new JC Penney reopened at the west end of the new shopping mall (see Figure 3). (Photograph taken in October 1984.)

Figure 3. The public square just after the new shopping mall was built. (Photograph taken in May 1985.)

Figure 4. Farmers' market relocated in June of 1985. The market soon returned to its original location, the public square. (Photograph taken in July 1985.)

CONDITIONS AND ENVIRONMENTS OF THE PLACE WE LIVE

The Riverfront Area was the term that caught our attention the most when we started reading local newspapers. It forced us to reframe our image of Riverfront and the surrounding area. The use of this term was relatively new, and "area" suggested that the official city limits were blurred to include residents living on the "border" between farm and town. In other words, dichotomies of rural and urban and countryside and city became less descriptive. In fact, as the downtown was losing its original function and meaning and as residential zones were expanding outward, there was no center and no boundary for everyday life. Two villages south of Riverfront, Hope and Bishop, were considered to lie within the Riverfront area, and they formed, together with Riverfront, a business district along the road marked "Interstate Business." The relocation of factories of various kinds from downtown to suburban industrial parks and residential suburbanization coincided with similar changes in many other cities nationwide.

Superficially, our image of Riverfront being surrounded by pastoral countryside was not betrayed (Figure 5). Many dairy farms still exist, along with the woodland in which small animals and deer live, cornfields, and silos. Such dairy farms can be seen in the northeastern part of the county, nestled among numerous hills and lakes. However, Pine County is geographically diverse. Land use in the countryside varies according to soil type, and farming practices have been developed to use differing conditions. For example, the southwestern part of Pine

County is marshy, which is suitable only for cranberry farming. There is also a relatively large prairie chicken preserve. Because of past glaciers, sand and stones are prominent features of the county's land, whether flat or hilly. However, sand and stones are seen less in the farmland near Riverfront, and sand is seen even less than stone. Large irrigation facilities on potato fields are an indicator that the sandy land does not retain water. Farmers and major food companies use such land for planting cucumbers and beans on a large scale. The produce is processed in factories built along highways to the south of Riverfront.

Underground water in the Riverfront area was said to be abundant; however, during our fieldwork, contamination of underground water was occasionally reported in the local newspaper, *Riverfront Daily Journal*. The sandy area suffered because of the large-scale deforestation and use of fertilizers for the development of agricultural enterprises. Because our house was located outside of the city water system, we had an electric pump in the basement to supply drinking water from a well. The water was not drinkable without first being cleaned in two filtering tanks, so an employee of a water company in Riverfront came every 3 weeks to service the tanks. The owner of our house told us that he did not need such cleaning devices because his well was deeper than ours. The problem of water pollution had affected only a limited number of people who used underground water for daily life. Nevertheless, we were surprised to see such problems occurring not only in large cities but also in midsized cities and their surrounding areas.

Figure 5. An interviewee's family at their farm. (Photograph taken in June 1985.)

The Wisconsin River, which runs from the north of the county and passes through the Riverfront area, is now well controlled (Figure 6). In fact, the only conspicuous waterway, a slough that divided the north side from the downtown area, was covered in the 1920s. The mouth of the slough was still open when we first came to town, but 2½ years later it was covered, and the waterway disappeared entirely from the city scene. Before the rivers were controlled in any way, floods from the Wisconsin River were sometimes so serious that two of them, one in 1880 and the other in 1911, were re-reported in detail in the *Riverfront Daily Journal*'s special centennial edition (1958). Major floods have not occurred since 1911, and residents enjoy fishing, boating, canoeing, and feeding water birds on the river. Tragically, a fatal accident occurred on the river 2 years after we left. Three members of a family we knew well drowned when they encountered high water and rough waves while riding a boat on the river. Although the problems associated with the river have been largely controlled, water accidents still can happen.

People in Riverfront talked about the weather in greeting much more than we expected. Californians do not usually mention the weather as part of their greeting or even in casual conversation, probably because the California climate is mild throughout the year. Riverfront has, people say, four clear seasons. Newspapers, TV weather reporters, and newscasters often use seasonal terms. The newspaper's community section presents pictures of seasonal sights, and its columns touch on seasonal weather changes and activities, such as raking, snowplowing, mowing, winterizing cars and houses, summer festivals, gardening, watering, tornado-

Figure 6. A view of Wisconsin River from a senior housing project near downtown Riverfront. (Photograph taken in July 1985.)

watching, deer-hunting, strawberry-picking, and whatever seasonal produce is available at the farmer's market.

During our first summer, the lowest temperature was 57°F, and the highest was 82°F. In December during our second winter, the lowest temperature was (1.1°F, and the highest was 18.7°F. The highest temperature of any winter day did not rise above freezing from late November to early March. (The lowest temperature of any day did not rise above freezing from early November to early April.)

For us, winter seemed to last too long. We had no idea how to spend our time in subzero temperatures and heavy snow. We bought only a shovel to be stored in the car and some winter clothes. As long as we stayed in the house, we had no problems. The heating system was adequate; hot water circulated from the basement water heater through pipes connected to radiators in every room. Outside of the house, however, we had serious problems. Our car had to be parked outside, so the battery was easily weakened by extremely cold temperatures. To start a cold engine was so difficult in the morning that we often thought that we should have rented a house with a garage.

Another problem we encountered was thick snow on a 100-foot-long driveway. After we tried a few times to shovel the snow to get our car out of the driveway, we gave up the idea of doing it by ourselves. We hired a person who had a large pickup truck equipped with a snowplow in front who did snowplowing as a seasonal job for $10 to $20 each time. Our first winter was relatively mild and not as snowy as the average year, but the second winter was more severe.

Such weather conditions demand that people spend much time and energy clearing snow from around their homes and offices; therefore, snow removal meant seasonal employment. City government trucks with snowplows cleared streets within the city limits. Chester Stanski, one of our informants, did this job in the 1930s (see Chapter 9). Townships in the county contracted with individuals who could use their pickup trucks to plow snow from driveways of families needing assistance. Nominal fees were paid to the township government for this service. A Riverfront resident who lived several blocks from downtown told us that boys came and asked to be hired to shovel snow from the doorway and driveway, and even from the roof if it snowed too much on it.

Winterizing machinery, especially the car, was a new concept for us. Rebecca Johnson, whom we stayed with during our first few weeks in Riverfront, advised us to winterize our car before the true cold weather came. She referred us to a mechanic who operated a small garage downtown, and she kindly called him to make an appointment for us. It was an old garage with only two pumps, regular and nonleaded, and everything looked old in shape and color. The mechanic, in early middle age, seemed to have a thriving business. In fact, although competing with several other larger garages, his one-man operation had several steady customers. While he worked on our car, several customers pulled up, and he would have to stop and operate the pump for them.

From his garage, we had a view of North Second Street, which had originally been a major north-bound route through a part of the city called "North Side." Toward the south, we saw people working on the roof of the shopping mall building. Although the garage had escaped being relocated by the downtown revitalization project, we wondered how long it would survive.

Wisconsinites have pride in being good winter drivers. The *Riverfront Daily Journal* pointed out that Wisconsin drivers were skilled and could manage on the roads under any condition. They compared themselves with people in southern states who have many car accidents when unexpected heavy snow hits. Learning ways to cope with cold weather conditions was a real rite of passage for strangers like us. We were lucky not to have had a serious accident, although we were scared by several skids. Through such experiences, we realized that we were getting used to winter road conditions.

Life during such cold winters is often depressing or boring. However, people seemed to enjoy both outdoor and indoor activities. Among these was drinking liquor and alcoholic beverages, which we found most striking. Signs of taverns first caught our eyes at the public square, and we saw them scattered along county highways outside of the Riverfront area. Even most of the eating places, except family restaurants, had a lounge and cocktail bar, and both men and women are said to be strong drinkers.

Summertime in Wisconsin is relaxing, peaceful, and healthful. The city and county host many enjoyable events, such as the county fair at the fairgrounds and the Dairy Festival at a farm, as Prosterman (1995) vividly described (Figures 7 and 8). Summertime visitors might view life in Riverfront as comfortable, refreshing, and enjoyable with abundant fresh vegetables and other produce, but at the same time, they might find that life here is too quiet.

Given that the town does not provide young people with enough opportunities, it is natural that they would want to leave Riverfront. Interestingly, older people whose families belonged to a group of early immigrants also expressed, explicitly or implicitly, that life in Riverfront was boring. Other older people who grew up

Figure 7. Pine County Fair, July 1985.

Figure 8. Pine County's "Dairy Festival" held at a private farm, June 1986.

here but whose families had belonged to a group of later immigrants (especially Polish) seemed content with town life. The most recent migrants inevitably accepted life there to survive.

Only older people, Polish and non-Polish, knew that long ago, North Side was considered "Polish territory" and "a rough neighborhood." In fact, one winter we found a sandbox marked "PIASEK," the Polish word for sand; it was still being used at an intersection in North Side (Figures 9 and 10).

The image of Riverfront as predominantly Polish had been held by many local people. Even so, strangely enough, there was no Polish restaurant in North Side, although there were quite a few eating places for a town the size of Riverfront. Some people told us that there used to be a Polish restaurant at the north end of the town. Until recently, even Polish ethnic activities such as festivals had rarely been practiced. These facts suggest that ethnicity is not necessarily tied to food and special events, but rather it is related to expressive artistic forms and storytelling. In fact, there were ethnic paintings on the walls of buildings at the public square, which depicted Scandinavian design motifs and eastern European dancing figures in costume. Ethnic food and customs were occasionally reported in the *Riverfront Daily Journal.*

A county librarian told us that Riverfront had been a Yankee town long ago. She showed us a city map from the 1930s, noting that the name of one subdivision on the map was her father's. Names on this map that indicated the city's subdivisions or land additions were primarily Anglo-Saxon. The same was true for the town's street names. Some of them were well-known local family names and still remained as the names of local manufacturing companies.

Figure 9. A neighborhood in North Side. The Polish Catholic church can be seen on the left. (Photograph
taken in November 1986.)

*Figure 10. An old box bearing the Polish word for sand, is still used in winter and sits at a street corner in
North Side.* (Photograph taken in December 1985.)

"Yankees" were pioneer settlers in this and other towns. However, Protestant churches were established in the early 1850s only a few years before Catholic parishes were founded. Among the first churches organized in Riverfront were the Episcopal Church of the Intercession (Anglican) in 1852 and the First Baptist Church (American Baptist, Protestant) in 1855. The Methodists conducted services among themselves in 1845, and their church was formally organized in 1857. The Presbyterian Church, organized in 1865, used German language for worship until 1915, when they began using English. Although Scandinavian Lutherans were gathering informally as early as 1857, the congregation was established in 1873.

St. John's Catholic Church for Irish immigrants was founded in 1856 and served as the "Senior Catholic Parish" until St. Paul's was established in North Side by Polish immigrants. St. Thomas's was built in 1884 by German-speaking Catholics who came from Trier, Beuern, Giisfeld, Cologne, generally from the Rhein province, Bavaria, Silesia, and Austria-Hungary. St. Ignatius was established for Polish Catholics in 1917 at the northeastern part of the city. Members of the old Polish churches are still predominantly Polish people, whereas many Polish people have become members of other Catholic churches. Once people stopped using ethnic identifiers when they named Catholic churches, and because the restriction against moving from one church to another was relaxed in the 1960s, ethnic divisions in the city for the most part disappeared. Some elders remember a time when the churches had strong ethnic associations, but they assert that they are now mixed and that anybody can go to any church.

Other smaller congregations were established from the 1890s to the 1920s, and a synagogue was formed in 1904. Although the Jewish congregation was still listed in the church section of the *Riverfront Daily Journal,* most of the members had left the area in the 1960s and 1970s. The temple, which is located a few blocks from downtown, was donated to the Pine County Historical Society during our research period.

The structure of the social class and its transformation in the town was of particular interest to us, and we believed that the relationship between social class and ethnicity was important in the context of the town. We felt that it would be easier to concentrate on the Polish-Americans' experiences and to portray the social structure of the town from their point of view. However, because we were concerned with multivocality in this issue, we tried to avoid such concentration and to broaden our perspectives to include interethnic relationships and interactions in this study. It is not our aim to reconstruct the social class structure in this book but to interpret our conversations and interactions with people of different backgrounds and analyze their feelings.

Class conflicts are likely subjects when studying a community and its historical transformations. In approaching this subject, we generally let the residents talk freely during interviews about life in Riverfront. We did not feel that people tried to hide their experiences with class conflict. However, it appeared that people did not know how to talk about such experiences. Almost all of the people we interviewed would not touch on past experiences that they felt were best forgotten. Some well-educated residents seemed to recognize that the town's history might be viewed from a perspective of social class and conflict, but they did not approach these topics by themselves. From the better-educated interviewees, we learned that there had probably been no single incident in which the whole community was involved. Individuals had experienced subtle conflicts with others of different backgrounds, but no one was able to relate such experiences to the larger issue of class structure.

People in central Wisconsin tended to be Democrats. An elderly Polish man, with whom we were acquainted through the Pine County Commission on Aging, had a framed, partly faded photograph of President Kennedy on the wall of his entrance hall. Kataryna Baszka, an elderly Polish woman who had been actively working for the Polish-Americans (see Chapter 5), was eager to talk to a state Democratic congressman at a local Democrat Party's gathering. Thomas Stromborg, an elderly Norwegian professional whose life history appears in Chapter 9, told us that he decided to become a Democrat because of his son's influence. Of course, a substantial number of residents were Republicans. They held their gatherings at more "luxurious" places, a Democrat said jokingly. We did not know who was Republican among our interviewees. Although we had kept a neutral position during interviews, they did not let us know if they were Republican.

At the beginning of the town's history, Riverfront's economic life was closely tied to the timber industry. Pictures taken in the 1880s of rafts and raftmen from towns along the Wisconsin River highlight the centennial issue of the *Riverfront Daily Journal.* An 1874 bird's-eye view of Riverfront depicts the entire town 3 years after the railroad arrived and shows a detailed image of log pools and rafts on the Wisconsin River. Six sawmills can be seen along the river, three on each side. Sawmills were linked to each other by the railroad and then connected to one of Wisconsin's main railroads.

In the 1870s, the surrounding area was not yet developed into farmland, although it was already owned by certain people whose names were printed on an 1876 plot map. People usually owned the land in 40-acre parcels.

Meanwhile, paper mills (one of them, started in 1892, is still operating), cabinet, sash (1893, closed circa 1980), and furniture (1897, still operating) factories and a fishing tackle manufacturer (1896-1986) were built and continued to function through both prosperous and rough times (Figure 11). Among their employees were a number of Polish-Americans. Other major employers include an insurance company (1904, still in business) and the University of Wisconsin-Riverfront campus (1971, still operating). The insurance company recently built a huge, modern headquarters, and Riverfrontans consider it prestigious to work there. However, during our fieldwork, this company announced layoffs, and the remaining employees were anxious about unstable employment conditions. The university was originally Normal School (founded in 1894) but changed its name as it was reorganized to become Teachers College in 1926, State College in 1951, State University in 1964, and the University of Wisconsin in 1971. In addition to bringing a large number of students (about 9,000 in 1984) into the city, it offered miscellaneous college-related job opportunities to Riverfront residents as well as to its students.

The town has not been isolated from the outside world. After the major means

Figure 11. A local furniture factory near downtown. (Photograph taken in March 1986.)

of transportation shifted from the railroad to the automobile (as late as the 1950s), as the federal highway system was developing nearby, and as a local airport 30 miles north of the town had been established, travel became easier from Riverfront to most cities in the United States and the world. The traffic of local, regional, national, and even international business people seemed to become heavier. The insurance company, the university, and the local government hired people from outside Riverfront; hosted conferences and professional meetings in which people from other parts of county participated; and promoted events and activities in which local and outside people could meet. The influence of such institutions provided a variety of experiences and opportunities. During this process, newcomers found Riverfront to be livable for its size and location, and the town grew.

In retrospect, our preconceptions of middle America were based on stereotypes. Like other stereotypes, some aspects turned out to be true; however, we were completely wrong in thinking that life in a midsized town would be simpler. We found it was far from it! Our journey led us to discover and appreciate the complexities of the culture of Riverfront and its environs.

CHAPTER 2 \ "Which Church Do You Go to?": Finding a Place to Live

Our first intimation that the culture was more complex than we had expected came through the mundane task of finding a place to live. This seemingly simple process posed a great deal of worry for us. Of course, we had rented a place in California before, but being students, we had the benefit of university services for house hunting. In Riverfront, we were on our own, wondering where we could obtain information. The town seemed too small to have many rental properties. Nevertheless, we expected that the existence of a university in town might produce rentals for students.

The racial composition of the town also raised some concerns. According to the statistics, 99.9% of the population was listed as European-Americans, whereas the number of African-Americans, Hispanics, and Asians was very small. This percentage made us apprehensive as to what kind of attitude the residents may have toward Asians, and toward Japanese in particular. Could they hold prejudice against us, as some of our Californian friends had predicted? How many people in Riverfront had ever seen Japanese people before? What would we do if their knowledge about Japan was limited only to the attack on Pearl Harbor?

Our concern for racial prejudice in house hunting increased during our conversation with Rebecca Johnson, who kindly let us stay at her house when we arrived. She worked at the university and acted as a liaison between the university and ourselves. During our first night in Riverfront, we asked her about our prospects for finding a place to live. She is not a native, having moved to Riverfront from Illinois some 10 years ago, and thought that people outside the university community were very conservative, particularly the Polish-Americans. She feared that we might run into difficulties in renting a house because of the racial prejudice of some residents. African-American and Native-American students, according to her, often experienced unpleasant incidents renting houses, and foreign students from Southeast Asia also had similar experiences. In the past, so few Japanese came to Riverfront that it was hard to predict what our reception would be. Of course, it is illegal to refuse rentals to people on the basis of race in Wisconsin, but we could conceive of subtle ways in which people might deny us the opportunity. After all, the landlord merely had to say that "the house had been rented already."

Numerous worries, apprehensions, and concerns occupied our minds as we set about to look for a place to live in Riverfront. This fear made us think about foreigners' experiences in Japan. How are American anthropologists treated when they travel to small towns far from metropolitan areas in Japan? Many of our American friends in Japan have spoken about being treated as outsiders: "It doesn't matter how long you stay in Japan, you are always treated as *gaijin* (foreigners). Kids will never stop staring at you!" We sympathized with the plight of our American friends with a renewed sensitivity.

Foreign students at Japanese universities also often complain about difficulties in renting apartments. Landlords are reluctant to rent to foreign students because of difficulty in communication and differences in food preferences and cooking customs, which they fear might result in damaged property. In Japan, universities as an institution often provide guarantees for foreign students and scholars and act as intermediaries between the landlord and the tenant. However, in the United States, we were on our own.

We started collecting information on rental property, and we found the most reliable source to be the classified section of *Riverfront Daily Journal,* in which property owners seeking renters would place advertisements. There were categories for "furnished apartments," "unfurnished apartments," and "homes for rent." Another local paper, *Community Bulletin,* consisted of nothing but classified advertisements, which included various services, garage sales, auto sales, farm auctions, events such as an Amish Quilt auction, and rentals and home sales. This paper was distributed free of charge to each household once a week. Word of mouth is another option people have for finding a place to live. There are also rental agencies that, for a fee, will gather information on one's behalf. We could not rely on word of mouth, because we did not know many people in the community at that time, and we thought we would leave the rental agency as a last resort.

As we were going through the list of apartments advertised in the papers, we noticed a difference between the American and Japanese way of looking for a place to live. Japanese would always turn to a third party. In urban areas most people would consult real estate agents, who act as go-betweens for owners and renters. In rural areas, a potential renter would seek someone who knows the owner. The situation reminds us of an experience a British anthropologist had while doing fieldwork in a rural area of southern Japan. In his book, *Okubo Diary,* Bryan Moeran quotes the advice he received from his friend in the village where he studied:

> It doesn't matter what you do in this valley — whether you're renting a house, buying some land, or looking for a prospective daughter-in-law — you should never do things on your own. Two people talking is anti-social; it smacks of secrecy and double-dealing. What I mean is, never approach anyone directly, but try to get somebody else to act as a disinterested third party on your behalf. Try to involve as many people as possible. That is the first rule of life in the country. That way, you'll have people to support you if something goes wrong. People are a kind of insurance   (Moeran, 1985, p. 22).

If this description fits the Japanese way of renting a house, at least in rural areas, the American way seems to encourage exactly the opposite. The renter is expected to negotiate directly with the owner. The newspaper provides information, but people working at the newspaper do not get involved in the negotiation. The newspaper staff is expected to take very little responsibility in the content of the advertisement; thus, the newspaper, or its parent company, does not function as "insurance." On the other hand, the American way saves the renter time. The direct negotiation method gives both newcomers and long-time residents of the community equal opportunity.

The American way reflects the old American ethos: you are on your own out in the world. It is up to the renter to discover any overstatement or false advertisement placed by the owner, and it is the owner who must judge if the renter is honest and trustworthy. How does the owner determine the trustworthiness of the renter? What are the factors that the owner looks for in a total stranger in order to trust him or her? After all, the owner is risking his or her property. According to the rural Japanese method, the owner can always appeal to the go-between if the renter fails to pay the rent or damages the property. The renter must act prudently to protect his or her reputation and that of the go-between, for the renter is risking the relationship between the go-between and himself or herself. Therefore, involving a third party functions as the "insurance" for both the owner and the renter.

Our house hunting took on new meaning. It was not simply a process to find a place to live but a way to learn how Riverfrontans judged other people. For us to rent an apartment or house, the owner must somehow see us trustworthy. Without having a go-between who could guarantee our good character, owners must find this out by asking us questions while we checked out their properties. Moreover, the questions owners would ask provided us some foresight into their value systems. Thus, we had already begun our research without knowing it.

On a given day, the classified section of the *Riverfront Daily Journal* contained about 30 rental property listings. Rent prices ranged between $200 and $450 per month. Advertisements for apartments usually read as follows:

> 2BR., 1 ba., wall-wall crpt. Lndry facil. AEK. Nr. campus. $315/mo. + deposit. incl. heat. Lease. Sorry, no pets. 357-5310 pm.

After awhile, we were able to figure out the following details: this apartment is unfurnished, has two bedrooms, one bathroom, probably a kitchen and a living room and is carpeted from wall to wall. A laundry facility is located in the apartment complex, and the kitchen, which usually is equipped with a refrigerator and stove, is all electric. The apartment is located near the university. The rent is $315 a month, and a security deposit, often equal to one month's rent, is also required. The security deposit is refunded to the renter at the end of the tenancy if the renter leaves the apartment clean. The cost of heat is included in the rent, although the renter is responsible for electric and telephone bills. The owner requires a contract, called a lease, which obligates the renter to live in the apartment for a certain period (usually a year) and also obligates the owner not to increase the rent for that period. The renter is not allowed to keep pets. The interested renter should call the owner in the evening. Although the advertisement provides such basic information, it does not give the specific location of the apartment, the size, or the condition of each room. Negotiation with the owner begins with the first telephone call.

Some of the listings were rented by the time we called. The first apartment we were able to see was one of four units in an old, large converted house. Advertised as a furnished 1-bedroom apartment for $215 a month, the price was certainly attractive. When we went to see it, the landlady met us in front of the house, which was located in one of the older sections of the town. The apartment was upstairs, and at the entrance there was a screened porch, which would be nice in summer but useless in winter without being glassed in. The living room and bedroom were small compared to California standards. The furniture in the apartment included a double bed and a sofa, which were very old and in poor condition. We learned that furnished apartments, which tended to be more expensive than unfurnished ones, were not necessarily advantageous. We decided we would be able to gather pieces of furniture in better condition at garage sales.

In short, the apartment did not impress us. We told the landlady that we would call her back later, but we never did. Here is an advantage in the American style of direct negotiation. Because it does not involve a third party for the renter, we are not obligated to take the place if we do not like it. Moreover, we do not have to explain to anyone why we do not like it. The situation would be more difficult if a go-between were involved, especially if that person had strongly recommended the apartment. We would have needed some reasonable excuse to decline the recommendation so that he or she would not lose face in relation to the owner. The American owner, however, must have mixed feelings about the direct negotiation method. Although the owner can reach a greater number of people through newspaper advertisements than through friends, he or she must endure transient relationships with strangers who may never return after viewing the property.

The second apartment we looked at, located near downtown in front of St. John's Catholic church, was a second-floor apartment. A heavy-set woman in her early 20s showed it to us. This place was almost the same size as the first apartment. After we saw the apartment, she invited us to meet her mother downstairs, where she and her parents lived. Her mother was also short and heavy-set. We sat in the living room, where there were several young children. A baby was in the crib, the daughter held another one, and two toddlers were playing in the next room. We started discussing the rental conditions more specifically. For example, we asked about the amount of deposit, the parking place, and whether utilities were included in the rent. As both parties relaxed a little bit, we asked whose babies they were. The daughter said she was baby-sitting for others. She had been trained as a beautician, but there were more than 50 beauty salons and too many beauticians for a town of this size. She preferred to baby-sit because she could make more money. We learned that her father was a custodian at St. John's Church.

Then, her mother, who had been quietly sitting beside us, asked, "Which church do you go to?" This question caught us totally unprepared. No landlord in Japan would ask such a question; such matters seemed to be a private issue. We don't remember being asked such a question even in California, neither during house hunting nor in daily conversation. Why did she want to know our religion?

We sensed a moralistic tone in the question, and we felt we should be careful in answering.

Judging by the fact that she said "church," she must have assumed that we are Christians. We are not, but we were not certain how she would view other religions. The worst possible answer may be that we do not go to any church, because then she might view us as untrustworthy. We could say that we were Buddhist, the closest answer to our religious beliefs. But it seemed there was no escape from the impression that "these people do not go to church." We finally answered that we just arrived in this community, and we had not decided which church we would attend. Fortunately, this satisfied her curiosity, and she did not inquire further on the matter.

Next it was our turn to get to know them. We asked the mother about her ethnic background. She said her grandfather on her father's side was Norwegian, and after a pause, she rather abruptly added, "I don't know about my mother's side." She did not say any more. There was an awkward silence, although it probably lasted just a few seconds. As the conversation turned to subjects other than the apartment, we felt that the owner was starting to wonder about our real intentions. We sensed that it was the time to leave. We thanked them for showing us their apartment, and we told them that we wanted to think about it and would call them back. The daughter said, "Well, other girls are interested in the apartment, too." We thought her answer indicated to us that they had reservations about us as much as we had about the apartment.

This house-hunting experience created mixed feelings in us. As anthropologists, we appreciated it as a good opportunity to learn about the town. After all, in what other ways could we actually go into people's houses and observe how they live? On the other hand, as newcomers who were looking for a place to live, the prospect of finding a comfortable place at a reasonable price seemed discouraging. People in Riverfront often have quite sizable houses, especially along Main Street (not downtown) and its parallel, Cowper Street. People often converted these large houses into apartment units for extra income. A problem, however, was that most of them were old, and the heating system, insulation, and lighting in many of apartments were inadequate. We would most likely have had problems in winter when the temperature dropped below the freezing point.

We also suspected that the question of our religious affiliation would come up again and again during our fieldwork. What should we say and how should we act in a predominantly Christian community? We were still wondering the meaning of the woman's question. What does the church affiliation mean to people? What can they tell from your affiliation? Further house hunting might suggest answers to these questions.

The third apartment we looked at was one of four units within a converted Victorian-style house, near the first apartment we saw. It had two bedrooms, although one of them was barely big enough for a single bed. The living room had a nice bay window and a fireplace, and the kitchen was big enough to include a dining area. The monthly rent of $275 was also attractive. Two female university students who were sharing the apartment still lived there and would not be moving out until the end of October.

When we contacted the owner of the apartment, she told us to come to her house first. From there she drove us to the Victorian, which was several blocks away. Although she had told the students we were coming to see apartment, neither of them was present when we got there. However, their stereo was playing music loudly, and even their iron was on. The owner quickly turned off both of them. The apartment was messy; jeans and shirts were strewn on the beds and floor, and the bathroom and kitchen appeared as if the tenants had abandoned the house several months ago. The owner, apparently embarrassed to show the apartment in such a condition, kept saying, "Well, they are in the process of moving out. They must be packing their stuff," even though their actual departure was more than 3 weeks away. Although the apartment advertisement had said "no pets," there was a cat sitting on a chair in the living room. Caressing the cat, we said, "We have a cat, too. We wonder if you would mind?" She said, "Well, a cat is OK. It is dogs that I worry about." How could she have said "No," when the current residents had a pet?

When we returned to her house, the owner asked us what we did for a living. We told her that we were visiting scholars at the university from Japan, and we were in town doing research. "Oh, you are with the university, and scholars! You must be very smart to come here!" She told us that her daughter in Oregon works for a homestay program and lets international students (as foreign students were often called in this community) stay at her house. "My daughter tells me how wonderful an experience it is to live with international students. She convinced me to do the same. In my own house, I have a boarder. He is a bachelor and a professor at the university. I cook for him. I really like this arrangement. I hate to come home where nobody is there." At that point, the telephone rang. We could not help but overhear the conversation. Someone else was inquiring about the apartment. The owner was happy to hear that it was a woman who worked for Brooklyn Insurance, one of the major employers in the area, and she set up an appointment to show the apartment.

After hanging up the phone, the owner came back and asked us, "How do you like the apartment? It would be wonderful if intelligent people like you lived there." She did not hide her enthusiasm, so we asked her how soon it would become available. She said she would ask the current tenants and told us again how much she was interested in having us. As we were leaving, she said she looked forward to hearing from us in the next day or two.

We were certain that the owner found us trustworthy. What were the bases for her judgment? Having steady employment was of primary concern, made apparent by the fact that she was asking the other prospective renter about her occupation too. Thus, hearing the names of the university and Brooklyn Insurance reassured her. In our case, the affiliation with the local university was sufficient. The fact that we were "scholars" rather than "students" indicated a higher educational level, which further reassured her. Interestingly, she became enthusiastic about the prospect of renting the apartment to us precisely because we were foreigners, the factor that we feared would work against us. Because we were exotic and foreign, opening the house to us indicates her generosity, open-mindedness, and hospitality to "other" people.

We found her enthusiasm about having us rather flattering, and we liked the apartment. However, the fact that it would not be available for another 3 weeks would be a tremendous burden for our host, Rebecca Johnson, as well as for ourselves. Therefore, we decided not to take it. Because the owner was so enthusiastic, we felt obligated to call her back and tell her. When Mariko called, the woman immediately recognized her, and her voice sounded excited. Mariko told her that although we liked the apartment very much, we were turning it down because it would not be available until November. To our surprise, she abruptly said, "OK, thanks for calling back, dear," and hung up. We were quite surprised at her terse response. We had expected her to say something more, for example, how disappointed she was, or how much she had enjoyed meeting us, or *something*.

We then surmised there was a tacit rule underlying the direct negotiation method: Only those who are interested in a property would contact the owner, and those who are not would not contact the owner. Hence, the owner hears only from renters who accept and is spared hearing about a rejection. In this way, the owner can remain gracious and welcoming in showing the property to strangers whom he or she will never see again unless the renters accept the offer. The fact that Mariko gave her a call made her anticipate our positive response. Our negative answer was therefore doubly disappointing for her.

Our house hunting came to an end on the fourth day when we found a house advertised as "a cozy home" on one of the major county highways leading to the farmland northeast of town. It was small, consisting of a living room, two bedrooms, a bathroom, a kitchen, a newly-added back room, and a basement. We realized later how small the house was when we put a double bed and a dresser in the bedroom and had barely enough space to walk between them. The house had a large backyard, more than 10 times as big as the house itself. Little did we realize at the time how burdensome cutting grass would be for us. There was a shed, but it was too small to be a garage even for our little sedan. Joe Dobczek and Linda Ronaszak were the owners of the house. Linda introduced herself as Joe's girlfriend, but she soon asked us whether we were legally married. We found it interesting that she would put a higher value on legal marriage than on living together when assessing the trustworthiness of renters. Joe explained that the house was very well insulated and that the previous owner had worked on the insulation himself. Because Joe knew what a good job he had done, they bought the house immediately after it was put on sale. When Toshi said, "I guess there aren't many Japanese people in town," Linda answered, "It's OK. We'll still rent our house." We were not sure exactly what she meant.

We decided to rent this house and signed a lease. Basic rent was $350 per month, and no utilities were included. Water was so hard in this area that it required a special softening device, which cost $15 a month. All together, the house would cost us about $400 monthly. Of course, we could find less expensive places, but we chose this house because it gave us more space both for storage and privacy than an apartment. Living in an apartment, especially one equipped with modern conveniences, definitely seemed easier, but we would have had less exposure to people's daily lives. Doing chores such as mowing the lawns and shoveling snow seemed to be what we were destined to experience. It would help us understand how people lived in this area. Thus, the house on 2659 Highway 55, Riverfront City, Wisconsin, became our residence. Our friends in California chuckled after getting our address. To them, it sounded as though the house was out in the hinterlands.

While we had been house hunting, we learned that the Riverfront community has ample rental properties. Many owners of large houses had subdivided them into apartments. In our house hunting, we often met widows who had subdivided their houses in this way to obtain an additional source of income. Also, developers constructed new apartment buildings, most of which apparently were built to meet the needs of the growing university population in the last 10 or 15 years. It was early October when we were looking for a place to live, and the university semester had begun at the end of August, so most students had already found places to live. Even though we were latecomers, we found many apartments and houses were still available.

At this point, we would like to review the rental process and examine more closely some of the questions the owners asked us, to get an idea of how they judge people. The system is set up so that owner and prospective renter negotiate directly for the property that has been advertised in local newspapers. People do not consider it necessary for a third party to act as a go-between, introducing the owner to the prospective renter and guaranteeing the suitability of the renter to the owner. Indeed, most of the negotiations take place without such a go-between. We were quite surprised to learn that no one during our search required us to present some personal reference, which must mean that the owners prepare themselves for transient encounters with strangers. They judge whether the prospective renter is trustworthy during the brief period when they show the property.

The most common question asked was, "What is your occupation?" or "Where do you work?" This question is quite understandable, for the owners' main concern must be economic, whether the prospective renter can pay the rent. For this reason, having steady employment in a sound occupation is critical. In our case, affiliation with the local university, although we were not employed there, served as a major guarantee for us. The second most common question, "Are you legally married?" indicates that marriage enhances the image as someone who is responsible. It is an interesting question because in the one case in which the question was asked, the person who asked it was not legally married to her boyfriend, with whom she lived.

We were surprised that no one asked where we were from, although we volunteered that we were Japanese. We never sensed that differences in race and national origin were a concern for the owners we encountered. In Japan, owners would be most concerned about whether a prospective tenant is Japanese.

Again, our affiliation with the university must have worked in our favor. The owners could accept the fact that we were neither American nor European because they knew that the university attracted students and scholars from a variety of countries. Our affiliation with the university was sufficient reason for our presence. Also, they probably predicted that our stay would not be permanent, which made it easier for them to accept us. Moreover, we also realized that some people consider renting to non-Americans an enhancement to their status. It implies they are hospitable, open, international, and sophisticated.

However, what does the question, "Which church do you go to?" mean? To us this question seemed irrelevant in deciding whether to rent an apartment. We found this question not only strange but also awkward to answer. In asking ourselves why we found this question to be so awkward, we decided that it is probably due to the way Japanese view religion. Asked their religious affiliation, most Japanese would answer Buddhist, but that does not mean that Japanese "believe in" Buddhist doctrines or have made a "commitment" to Buddhist faith. Religion for Japanese people is something you do rather than something you believe. In general, there is no sense of choosing one's religious faith in Japan. Indeed, the word *commitment* is almost impossible to translate into Japanese. In this sense, *ancestor worship* is a better way of describing affiliation and is more central to Japanese lives than Buddhism. Because Buddhist monks are responsible for conducting death rituals such as funerals and memorial services in Buddhist term, most Japanese are Buddhist at least in this respect. At the same time, most Japanese also can be said to be Shintoists; they go to shrines on New Year's Day to wish for good luck, and they ask Shinto priests to pray for happiness and good luck when, for example, a baby is born. However, Japanese do not have the custom of attending either temple or shrine regularly. When the first woman whose apartment we saw raised the issue of religion, we immediately were at a loss. We didn't think we could explain the Japanese custom to her satisfaction.

Differences in custom aside, the question, "Which church do you go to?" is nevertheless strange, at least to us. The woman who asked it was not trying to find out our religion, for she did not say, "What is your religious belief?" Perhaps she assumed that all people in the world are Christian because she used the word *church,* and not *temple, shrine,* or *synagogue.* She was not interested in knowing whether we are churchgoers because she did not say, "Do you go to church every Sunday?" If she had asked that question, we might have thought that she was testing our moral quality. She wanted to know, of the churches in town, which one were we affiliated with. Because this question was posed in the context of assessing the trustworthiness of prospective renters, church affiliation must be a crucial element for Riverfrontans to situate people in their social map. What can they tell about people from their church affiliation?

The puzzlement of church affiliation reminds us of another incident we encountered at a very early stage in our fieldwork. When we arrived at Riverfront, shortly before the 1984 presidential election, there were many political gatherings. One of the professors we had met took us to a local committee meeting of the Democratic Party. In deciding which resolutions to adopt, there was a heated discussion. This professor proposed that "population control" is strongly recommended in developing countries. Several other members objected to his proposal, saying, "You mean, genocide?" The professor said, "No, I mean birth control." "Well, that's genocide." There was such a sharp division over the interpretation of "population control" that neither side yielded to the other. Finally, the word *health care* was used instead of *population control.*

On the way home, the professor, still very angry over the discussion, said, "You see, they are Catholic. I'm not a Catholic. I'm a Methodist. They don't believe in birth control. Oh, we are going to have population explosion!" We were truly startled by his reaction. As far as we can tell, there was no reference to religion during the meeting. How did he know that his opponents in this discussion were Catholic? Why did he attribute the difference in opinion to the difference in religious faith, among other possible explanations, such as class or age difference? Again, we sensed that religion or religious affiliation is a great concern for people of this town.

Thinking about the meaning of church affiliation, we noticed another aspect of the earlier episode when we met the apartment owner. Although she had no problem asking about our church affiliation, when we asked about her ethnic background, she abruptly became silent after mentioning something about her father. Were we not supposed to ask about people's ethnic background? What was the difference in asking about religious faith and ethnic background? People in this town seem to be quite vocal about religious difference. Are they equally silent about ethnic difference?

Through our experience of looking for a place to live, we encountered various individuals and gained a glimpse of how people view themselves and others in Riverfront. But we also gained more questions. In particular, we could see that ethnicity and religion are important factors in understanding the culture of Riverfront; however, their significance is subtle and embedded in daily life. We needed to examine the contexts in which these concepts are actually used on a daily basis. Because many people mentioned that ethnic and religious differences were more marked in the past, we decided to look into the life histories of people of this area as our next step.

CHAPTER 3 / "In the Old Days Things Were Different": Ways of Growing Up

When interviewing, we always tried to ask people older than 60 years of age to tell us their life histories and what Riverfront was like as they were growing up. Based on the life histories we collected, we will sketch a picture of town life in the 1920s and 1930s.

The life histories that follow are arranged according to ethnic backgrounds, which are divided roughly into two groups: early immigrant families of predominantly white-Anglo-Saxon-Protestant (WASP) background and late immigrant families of predominantly Polish and Catholic backgrounds. In ordinary conversation, people rarely refer to themselves as *WASP* when asked their ethnic background. People usually say, "Well, I'm partly English, Scotch, Irish, and German" or "mostly English, but, my grandmother was a German." Intermarriages between people of different European cultural backgrounds were common. Some individuals refer to themselves simply as an *American*. Others highlight what they are not, for example, "I'm not Catholic," or "I'm not Polish." On the other hand, Polish people readily refer to themselves as Polish. Their life histories are included in the second half of this chapter.

LIFE HISTORIES OF EARLY IMMIGRANT FAMILIES

Frank Woodland (age 65) was born and raised in Riverfront and recalls the town up until the 1930s, when he left to take a teaching position at the age of 21. Although he no longer sees himself as part of Riverfront, he still considers it his hometown. His father had died in an accident when Frank was a teenager, and his mother never remarried and never left Riverfront.

Frank identifies himself as a WASP (this is an exceptional case), and his parents' backgrounds fall into this category. His father studied at one of the Ivy League Universities and moved here to be a professor at Teacher's College. His mother's side of the family goes back to the original settlers in New England. His maternal grandfather was a county judge in a neighboring county. His family was one of the well-established, well-to-do families in town.

Riverfront at that time was a town of probably about eight or nine thousand people. The distinguishing feature was that it was known as a Polish town. It was also known as a fairly rough town. It was known as a town with more taverns and bars per block than any other town in Wisconsin of comparable size. It was also known as a town that had one of the really fine traditional farmers' markets. Most housewives, like my mother, would go down there to buy some fresh produce. And then, the other distinct feature, of course, was the presence of a college. That college was small. It had only about eight hundred students. The presence of students and of faculty was really a kind of a counter-balance for the fairly rough character that was established otherwise in people's minds. So, it had a peculiar character of being a college town and of being a farmer-lumber town with a kind of rough heritage.

The coexistence of professional class and working class lives influenced the way in which Frank grew up. He describes the town's social structure in the 1930s as consisting of two groups: a small "ruling class," to which his family belonged, and everyone else, who had no power. Frank prefers to use the term *caste* rather than *class,* although he thinks no one else would use such a term to describe an American society in which democracy is a dominant ideology.

Basically, there are a few well-to-do families, namely the faculty of the college, doctors, lawyers, and fairly prominent business people and factory-owners. And those families constituted basically, not just a social class, but a social caste. I'm sure nobody else did agree with the caste, but sociologically speaking I think it resembles a caste, because, in the first place, it was basically endogamous. No one in that class would marry outside basically, and marriages occurred either in town endogamously, or out of town with people of similar social status. Though there were some Catholic people who owned major businesses and who belonged to this caste, the caste group did tend to have a very strong Protestant, WASP orientation in general character.

The group was quite distinct from the rest of people according to Frank (Figure 12).

Your surname, and the church that you belonged to, and the profession of your father, and the membership of your father in fraternal organizations were signs of belonging to this group. Everybody's father in this group belonged to the Masonic Lodge. They were also members of other fraternal organizations such as Lions Club, Elks Club, and Kiwanis.

There was a sharp difference in wealth between this "ruling class" and the rest of the town. For example, everyone in the ruling class owned a car when owning a car was still unusual. They all lived in several blocks along two parallel streets, Main Street and Cowper Street, between the east end of downtown area and the college, a section of Riverfront City which still has many large, well-constructed houses. Frank does not talk about other ethnic groups, such as the Germans and Scandinavians in town, but often contrasts the lives of his group with those of the Polish people.

The Polish, they were poor. Oh my God, they were poor. Boys came to school with lunches with one big slab of bread covered with a quarter inch of lard. That was their lunch. They didn't have nice clothes; they had to wear the same clothes to school that they had on the farm. They didn't have cars. They didn't speak very good English.

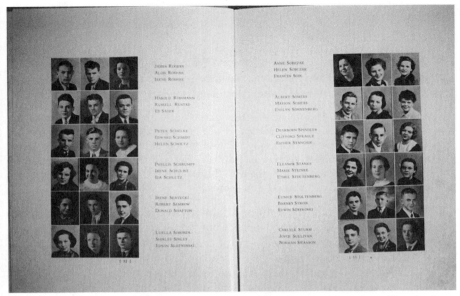

Figure 12. A 1936 high school yearbook. Frank Woodland, one of our interviewees, is on this senior class page.

Their parents hardly spoke English at all. They lived in poor little dirt farms out there where no one could really make a living.

Social activities for Frank essentially took place within the ruling class. For example, members invited only each other to their birthday parties.

It was very important for all of us, I think, that friendships were entirely within a small group of, say, 20 people. I don't think I knew with any degree of intimacy more than 20. I might have known 30 young people. But, of that 30, I probably didn't know more than 10 very well. And I remember their names today. I can remember where they lived.

Their socialization was closely tied with the schooling they had. Frank's parents sent him to a college-affiliated training school, which was considered progressive for that time. Nearly all of the children who attended the school had family backgrounds similar to his. In retrospect, Frank believes that there were "special socialization and cultural transmission processes" operating in this group. As Ueda (1987) described, high school graduates did not fail to lead successful social lives in those years.

They were prepared from childhood with a superior education, a special recognition, a special attention, and reinforcement and went to a high school that had special teachers, special programs, special privileges, and that went on. Many of us went to the Teacher's College, as it was called then, for 2 years, and then went on to the University of Wisconsin or some other universities. Now, as a consequence, I doubt very much that there was a single member of that group, which for me was a cohort group of about 30, who didn't become successful in life. They became doctors, lawyers, businessmen, engineers, and what have you.

Frank recalls a great separation between Protestants and Catholics at that time, as well. Not only was interreligious marriage regarded as unacceptable, but also close friendships between faiths were considered unwise.

> My mother strictly prohibited me from going out with a Polish girl because you wouldn't want to get anything started. I might get so involved with a Polish girl, I might get involved with her sexually. The very thought of a Polish girl getting pregnant, and then, therefore, forcing me to marry her and thereby having to become a Catholic was utterly abominable for her. To become a Catholic, for Protestants, was equivalent to the end of the world, you know.

Frank's parents were philanthropic. Many times, they kept young Polish boarders who wanted to go to high school but were unable to do so for economic reasons. Frank grew up with them. One of them, Susan (now age 71), did domestic work for the Woodlands in exchange for room and board in order to attend high school. However, in general, there was no interaction between his group and the Catholics, especially Polish Catholics. The only kinds of relationships they had, according to Frank, were "fundamentally either adversarial or exploitative." In Frank's memory, fighting was common between the youth of his group and the Polish youth. Members of his group felt vulnerable to the Polish youth.

> In winter, we went to the skating rink, which was in the vicinity of the high school. But you had to be very careful because the skating rink was one place you would very likely get hurt. I don't mean because you fall down. But, if you just got on the wrong side of some of the Polish kids, you could get beaten up. And the Polish kids never just came up and fought one to one. You have really three or four Polish on you. So you rarely go there alone. We would try to find two or three other people. Then we would go as a group. And we would avoid any incident, you know, you wouldn't run into anybody, you wouldn't accidentally trip on somebody; you wouldn't look at somebody too long and make comments, because, you see, those people would beat us up. It is as though we carried a caste emblem right in the middle of our forefront. They knew who we were. We didn't know who they were. There were too many of them. We definitely had very strong defensive orientation. In fact, in back of our house was Madison Street where the Polish world began. And so it was very close by.

Sometimes fighting was a daily occurrence:

> There was a point when I was attending the training school a block and half from home, where finally my father had to convoy me to school every day, because otherwise I would get beaten up either going to or from school.

The adversarial relationship stemmed from the fact, in Frank's analysis, that his group, which was predominantly WASP, was of the "ruling class" but distinctly in the minority in terms of numbers.

> Basically, as I reconstruct, it was a class and caste struggle, where the usual rules of caste difference don't apply because it is a democracy, and that won't go. But, they

recognized the special privilege and treatment that we were getting. And, they were extremely envious and hostile towards us as a consequence.

Frank emphasized the importance of the caste in Riverfront's past. For him, the history of the city is a process of "evolution and desegregation," characterized by "the considerable breakdown or even total eradication of the caste line that existed at that time."

Frank Woodland's tales are more analytic and interpretive than any of our other interviewees. No one pointed out the existence of the ruling class as clearly as he did, although we received many hints about it from others. His tales gave us a valuable perspective on social and cultural change in Riverfront during the 20th century, especially between the 1930s and 1980s. Frank Woodland was also helpful in that he introduced us to several people who belonged to or associated themselves with the ruling class. We present those individuals next.

William Taylor (age 80) lives with his wife on Cowper Street close to the university. He was not Frank's cohort, but a friend of his parents; therefore, William can recall Frank's childhood. William says that his ancestors came from England, he was born in a small town in southern Pine County, and his family moved to Riverfront when he was a child. William married Beth Maynard (age 80), who was born in a town near Milwaukee, where he met her. Despite living in Riverfront for many years, he claims that his knowledge of the town is very "limited":

> See, I am a Methodist and a teetotaler. Most people in Riverfront are Catholic, and they drink. Oh, my, how they drink! See, I don't go to taverns, so I don't know much about what's going on.

We sincerely doubt that William knows little about his town. It is interesting that he differentiates the people of Riverfront based on whether they are Protestant or Catholic, and he also draws a line between drinkers and nondrinkers. William worked for the post office until his retirement. He has long been a piano teacher and still gives private lessons to students. He plays mostly classical music, although he is very fond of jazz. He says he does not like polka; it isn't really music for him. Churches of different denominations still ask him to play the organ. However, because he does not like polka, he never plays at wedding receptions, for which local musicians earn extra income. He has accepted invitations from private homes to give small piano recitals or "soirees" as he calls them.

In our interview, William described the north side of Riverfront as "Polish territory," an area he was not supposed to enter during his youth. Although he did not always explicitly say so, he tended to dissociate himself from several things having a strong association with Polish immigrants, such as Catholicism, taverns, and polka dancing.

Mary Schultz (age 93) also was born into a Yankee family in this town. We met her at her apartment in "North Side," where she lived alone. Her great grandfather on her mother's side was one of the pioneers who migrated with his family from Vermont in the 1860s. The old deed records kept at the Riverfront Register's Office indicate that her great grandfather and her grandfather bought farmland in the town of Bishop in the 1860s. Like many other Yankee pioneers, they were buried in a small, old cemetery located on the boundary between Village of Bishop and City of Riverfront. She proudly told us that she is a member of DAR (the Daughters of American Revolution), a status symbol for Yankee families. Those who know her respectfully call her Mrs. Schultz.

Her father's people were also pioneers from back East who settled in the Riverfront area. Both her paternal great-grandfather and grandfather worked as lumber men and migrated from Maine, according to the 1850 census. In the 1900 census, we find that her father worked at one of the furniture retailers as a store manager. Mary married Professor James Schultz, and they raised two sons and one daughter in Riverfront. One of the sons is an acquaintance of Frank Woodland. It was mainly through the college that Mary came to know Frank and also William Taylor, who joined a glee club at a time when Mary's husband was its president.

After her husband passed away, Mary continued to live in their house by herself. Her two sons left the town to become professionals, and her daughter, who married a professional, lives outside of Wisconsin. Several years ago, her children wanted her to move to an apartment so that she could manage daily life on her own with a helper who comes every other day. She has led an independent life and has been actively engaged in philanthropic organizations, including the Women's League.

North Side is clearly marked in Mary's memory, as it is in William Taylor's:

> When I was a girl, my parents told me never go to North Side, because it was considered dangerous. But, in my 90s, I actually live on the North Side!

She says it with laughter, acknowledging that the old meaning of North Side no longer applies. This change took place as the old boundary between elite and nonelite groups blurred in the town's evolution, as Frank Woodland explained. Although the place where she lives now is on the north side, it is not the same area she thought of as "North Side," where many Polish people lived. It was sparsely populated for years and only recently developed with apartment complexes. In fact, her apartment is very close to a townhouse we looked at during our house hunting. The area is still surrounded by open spaces. Landowners probably decided to construct apartment buildings as an investment and for meeting the demands of the older Riverfrontans who decided to sell their houses and look for smaller places to live independently, comfortably, and conveniently. The real estate business, especially apartment construction, has been booming in Riverfront, as it has in other American towns and cities (e.g., Perin, 1977).

Thomas Stromborg (mid-60s), another individual whom Frank Woodland had introduced as a member of his cohort, has no Yankee background but rather a Scandinavian one:

> I was born in Riverfront. My family has been in this community for a long time. My great-grandfather came to this country from Norway. He first settled in near Milwaukee. Subsequently, he bought a farm which is located on the county line between Pine County and Eastlake County, east of here. He came to that area around 1850. The farm continued to be in the family until maybe 15 years ago. His children

went into different fields. One of my great grandfather's children stayed on the farm. He had six or seven children.

Many immigrants from Norway settled in the eastern area of Pine County, one of the Midwestern centers to attract them (cf. Gjerde, 1985). The area is hilly and has abundant small lakes, so it is said to resemble the land in their home country:

> My grandfather left the farm. He was a self-educated man, who also went to business college. He became a registrar of deeds, which is a county position dealing with land-ownership records, and he later became a county judge in Pine County for many years, oh, probably 20 to 30 years.

Thomas' family has continued to live in Riverfront since his grandfather's generation:

> My father and my uncle both became lawyers. They went to the University of Wisconsin at Madison. My aunt married a doctor. They lived in the western part of Wisconsin.

Like his father, Thomas also became a lawyer:

> I was brought up in Riverfront. I lived here most of my life, except for few years when I was in the Army, during the Second World War. Then, I went to the law school at University of Wisconsin at Madison. I stayed there and worked for another law firm for a couple of years. Then I moved back here to my own hometown and opened my own office. I have lived here ever since.

Thomas married while he was in Madison. One of his children also became a lawyer and works in Riverfront as well.

We also met James and Beth Evans (both in their mid-60s), who know the Woodlands and the Stromborgs very well. Both the James' family and Beth's natal family (the Wallaces) have been in Riverfront for more than three generations. James became a lawyer, as had his father. Beth's natal family started Wallace Fish Fry Company in Riverfront. James and Beth went to schools more or less in the same period as Frank, Thomas, and the son of Mary Schultz. Even though they belonged to the same cohort, it was difficult for us to understand how they were connected to each other because none of them used the term *ruling class* to describe themselves. When we asked whether there was a recognizable ruling class in Riverfront, both James Evans and Thomas Stromborg recognized that there had been well-to-do professionals, but they said they would not use the term *ruling class* to describe them.

The fact that our interviewees belonged to the same social circle, as Frank Woodland said, became clear to us at Mary Schultz's funeral in 1985, several months after we met her. At the funeral, William Taylor played the organ. Thomas Stromborg introduced us to Mrs. Schultz's sons, Ken and Peter, and her daughter, Andrea, as friends of Frank Woodland. Because Frank Woodland and Mary Schultz's children had left Riverfront several decades ago, the people gathered at the funeral scarcely had day-to-day contact. Despite this, when we saw them together, we felt that their sense of membership to the same circle was still strong.

LIFE HISTORIES OF POLISH-AMERICANS

When talking about their family histories, several people, such as Frank Woodland, William Taylor, and Mary Schultz, described Riverfront as a Polish town and identified the north side of town as "Polish territory." Although Riverfront attracted immigrants from many other parts of Europe, Polish people stand out even today. Part of the reason is that they outnumber people with other ethnic backgrounds. Although exact numbers are hard to obtain, we made an estimate by counting the number of Polish names on marriage announcements in the local newspaper (see Chapter 4 for a more detailed analysis). In 1985, people who may be considered of Polish descent made up more or less 50% of the town's population. One interviewee said, "Until the university expanded, 70% of the town population was Polish. Now, it is more mixed." If this perception is true, it is likely that until the 1960s, the majority of the town's people were of Polish descent.

Polish-Americans are more noticeable partially because their last names usually end with "-ski" or "-cki." Also, many of their names have several consonants run together, without vowels between them, as, for example, Przybylski or Brezynski. A high school teacher said that he cannot identify Polish children among his students other than by last names. In contrast, Irish, German, and Norwegian names do not stand out so much.

According to documents, 50 Polish families in Riverfront founded St. Paul's Catholic church in the mid-1870s. At that time, Poland was not an independent nation and was subdivided among Prussia, Austria, and Russia. The Polish people often identify themselves as "German-Polish" or, in smaller numbers, "Russian-Polish." These terms mean either that their ancestors came from the area in Poland that was formerly German or Russian territory or that they are offspring of a mixed marriage between German and Polish or Russian and Polish. They seem to use the label more often in the latter sense. Polish-Americans are characteristically Catholic; indeed, people often equate "Polish" with "Catholic." Many of our interviewees, such as William Taylor, describe Riverfront as a Catholic town. In fact, the congregations of the two churches in town, St. Paul and St. Ignatius, were originally Polish and are still considered so by some.

In the course of our fieldwork, we met many people of Polish descent and became friends with some of them. We interviewed our Polish-American friends formally, also visited them informally, and occasionally, even went out with them socially. Unfortunately, we encountered non-Polish Catholics much less often than Polish, so we came to know only a few Irish and German Catholics, most of whom were married to Polish people.

Susan Strovinski (age 71), who once lived with the Woodlands, as described earlier, was born in Chicago into the Janikowski family. Her parents came to Chicago from Poland in 1906. They were among many Polish immigrants who came to the United States during the late 19th and early 20th centuries. Usually, such immigrants settled first in a large city like New York or Chicago, and later, some of them moved to rural areas.

My dad and mother came from Poland, from the southern part of Poland. They lived in Chicago. I always say that I was born in Chicago right by the stockyard. That's where the old stockyard used to be, it's gone now. I have a sister and a brother. All three of us were born there. Both my mother and father come from well-educated families. My dad went to high school in Poland and so did my mother. My dad was a teacher.

Susan does not know why her father chose Chicago. She knew that he did not want to go to Pennsylvania because he did not like coal mines. Her parents started their lives from scratch in Chicago:

> My dad and mother did what young people usually did. My dad worked in the [stock]yard and my mother took care of us. They had a cousin or an uncle staying with them. They had a big house. My relatives were living with them. That is the way they built themselves up. Dad was always in business. Then we moved to the southern part of Chicago. Then my dad owned a grocery store there, and later a hardware store.

The Janikowski's neighborhood in Chicago was predominantly Polish:

> We lived in a Polish territory. It's still a Polish territory over there, a Polish neighborhood. But, in that neighborhood, we had some German people, and some Irish people; they had stores. Jewish people had stores, and there was a dry cleaning place owned by Chinese people or Japanese people. I can't tell you which. Their youngsters used to go to school with us. We didn't have any Negroes in our neighborhood.

Like many other immigrant families, her family spoke Polish at home, whereas Susan spoke English at school:

> We spoke Polish at home till we started school. Then, it was bilingual, both Polish and English. We went to the Catholic School, a Polish Catholic school. Besides the usual curriculum, that's where we got our religion, Polish history, and readings in Polish.

Susan is not a typical second-generation Polish-American because she never forgot her parents' language. Thus, she was able to help edit a Polish-language newspaper even after she retired.

The Janikowskis moved to Riverfront in 1927 when Susan was almost 14 years old. They bought a farm in the township of Higgins, 5 miles north of Riverfront:

> Dad always wanted to go on a farm. I don't know why they came to the Riverfront Area. I have no idea. Of course, they tell me that this territory is almost like the territory they came from, in terms of climate and soil and everything. Very similar.

Neighbors at the place where the Janikowskis settled were predominantly Polish, although they spoke different dialects. Susan went to a one-room rural school in Higgins from the fifth to the eighth grade. In those days, rural schools were set up 2 miles apart, and Susan had to walk 1 mile to go to her school. Only one teacher taught from the first grade through the eighth grade. After she finished eighth grade, Susan went to Riverfront and looked for domestic work because she wanted to go to high school. She found her chance as a boarder with the Woodlands.

> I didn't know them before. Just somebody said that Mrs. Woodland was looking for somebody to help her out. They recommended me, and I went there and talked with her. She wanted to know what I knew how to do. Of course, she knew that Polish girls had to know how to cook and how to sew, things like that. So, I told her what I knew

how to do. I told her that I wanted to go to school. That was all right with her. She said okay, and, they took me and treated me as if I was one of their own. I worked for room and board and they always gave me a dollar a week. That was my studying money. In those days, you could buy an awful lot for a dollar. I got all my school supplies. If I was careful, I could save up enough and buy me a pair of shoes. It was big money. Of course, in summertime, they gave me a little more. That I saved up also for school, for books and things like that. The government paid the tuition. That came out of our taxes.

There was only one high school in the area. Children came not only from Riverfront but also from all over Pine County and even neighboring counties. It was a 4-year co-educational high school. If parents did not live in town, but could afford it, they would pay for room and board for their children. Students stayed with their relatives if they had any locally. If their houses were located 2 or 3 miles away, they went to school by bicycle. Susan's house was located about 8 miles away, so she had to stay in town to go to high school.

Susan's typical day at the Woodlands was as follows:

I used to get up at 6 or 7 in the morning. I helped Mrs. Woodland cook the breakfast, and, after breakfast, I cleaned up. If I had time, I washed the dishes. Then, I went to school at 7:30. I got back at 11:30. I stayed at home during the lunch break. That's when I did the dishes, and if beds were to be made, then I made the beds, and did just a little bit of the things that Mrs. Woodland wanted me to do. I went back to school in the afternoon for 2 hours. Then after school, I did all the other things, such as getting the evening meal ready.

To us, her job sounded like a lot of work, especially in addition to studying at school. However, Susan said it was not very different from when she was at home attending a grade school:

No, no. Even when I was at home, we came back home after school and changed clothes, and we always went to the barn to help — you know, to take care of cows and calves. We had the barn, we had milking cows, and learned how to milk. We came back in the evening with a kerosene lamp and did the school work until 8:30 or quarter to 9. We had a radio, a small one. Dad and Mom didn't let us have it because your school work comes first. So, we did the school work and went to bed.

At high school, where people of various backgrounds gathered, social activities were organized according to students' social and ethnic backgrounds.

The high school was a mixture, but people stuck together and formed cliques. I didn't belong to any of them, because I didn't fit in any of them. I had friends in all of them. See, the youngsters from Riverfront, most of them were from the parents who had money. They had businesses. Their children belonged to a certain group. The youngsters from the North Side, the Polish youngsters, they stuck together. The ones who came from St. Paul's [parochial school], they stuck together. They know that I could speak Polish and of course I carried a Polish name, too. So, I had friends there, but I never stuck with any of them.

We asked her to elaborate on what the "clique" was:

They were the youngsters from certain neighborhoods. They got together; they had their own way of doing things. They played their own baseball. They had their own team. Very few of them went into a sport which was a mixture. They had their own territory and with their own group of people, with the same kind of people that they always lived with. They knew each other and they did things with each other. They would go to each other's houses and things like that. The other ones like the youngsters whose fathers and mothers were business people in downtown, well, they stuck together. They had their own parties, own ways of doing things and going to places. The youngsters from North Side couldn't afford a lot of things, because their dads and mothers maybe were working for somebody else, and not making a big money that the business people did.

Susan's description matches that of Frank Woodland. From her, we learned that not only did the "well-to-do" families associate only with others of their own economic status, but also Polish-Americans themselves formed their own groups as well. In high school, Susan could observe different kinds of students, those from non-Polish wealthier families and those from Polish poor families. Because Susan belonged to a Polish family in a rural area and, at that time, lived in with a non-Polish professional family, she probably found herself in contact with both types of students at the same time.

Eventually she married a man from a Polish farm family in the vicinity of her parent's farm. They left the Riverfront area to establish their own family in a larger town. However, several years later, her husband's parents wanted him to return to take over their farm. So Susan resumed the farming life.

Unlike Susan, most Polish youngsters at that time did not go to high school. They usually finished eighth grade and then started working. This was the experience of Anna Belle (age 73), whom we first met at Jefferson Center (a senior center) when we started volunteering in its kitchen. She was born in Poland the second daughter of the Milanowskis. In 1913, when she was 2 years old, she came to the United States with her mother and her 6-year-old sister. Her father and her mother's brother had come to Chicago a year earlier. Her father was 26 years old, and her mother was 23 years old at the time. Anna does not remember anything about Poland, but she has vague memories of a long journey on the boat.

The Milanowskis settled in the southern part of Chicago, in a predominantly Polish neighborhood. Anna went to a Polish Catholic School only until the third grade because, "Mother said, 'you don't need to go to school any more. Stay here and take care of the young ones.'" Because her older sister married young, Anna was the eldest child then. She had to obey her parents, who decided to keep her at home all day to help her mother take care of her younger brothers and sisters. Her mother had given birth to three boys and five girls — one every other year after Anna's birth. The family lived in Chicago for 13 years (Figure 13).

In 1926, when Anna was 16 years old, her family, except her older sister who was married, moved to Woodside about 3 miles west of Riverfront. Her father got a 60-acre farmland in exchange for his house in Chicago. The previous farm owner had wanted to move to Chicago, whereas Anna's father had wanted to live on a farm. He later bought an additional 80 acres from his neighbor.

When we moved from Chicago, we put everything in two cars. All the children and everything we had. When we got to the farm, Mom cried because the house on the

Figure 13. Two of Anna Belle's family pictures: her communion in 1924 (center) and her sister's wedding (lower right). The pictures sat on a table in her apartment at the senior housing project.

farm was so small. See, they had three sons and six daughters. She said, "Where do my children sleep?"

After they moved, another sister was born, but she died immediately after the birth. Anna's father found a job at a paper mill in Riverfront, and her mother raised vegetables and sold them at the farmer's market on the public square in Riverfront. Anna's job was to take care of the household duties and her younger siblings.

> Before Mom came home from the market, I had to clean the house and get the dinner [at noon time] ready. I had to get everything ready. My younger sisters got their life easy. They didn't have to do as much as I did. They also went to school up to eighth grade. I didn't go beyond the third grade.

Even so, she did not say that she felt jealous of her younger siblings. She was a central figure among them and still is so today. In fact, three of her sisters who live in the town remain close to Anna. She seems to provide them with moral support whenever needed, and thus she is still respected by them.

When Anna was 17, she got a job at the local furniture factory polishing its products.

> I lied about my age. I said I was 19 so that I could get the job. Dad and I and our neighbors rode on a buggy driven by a horse to town to go to work. In winter, it was so cold; I wrapped myself tightly in my blanket.

Asked what she bought with her paycheck, she said, "I gave everything to Mom. In those days, parents took it and kept it for them. I didn't get a penny." Other people we interviewed also said that children were supposed to give their paychecks to their parents, especially to their mothers. In their narratives, it appears that the mother had power to control family finances, and the father was the chief authority.

Polish and Scandinavian people in Pine County both say that they chose those places to settle because those areas reminded them of their homelands. They chose farmlands in places where people of the same ethnic group had already settled because they had heard from their predecessors about conditions there. However, looking closely at farmlands surrounding Riverfront, we often find that neighbors' ethnic backgrounds were more mixed than we expected. For example, the Milanowskis' neighbors were Polish, Bohemian, German, and English. Anna uses the term *English* as a general term referring to Yankees or, probably, those who speak English only. She says:

> I remember August Miller. They were English people. When we lived there, my Mom used to rent some land from him, because his farm was big. . . . What's her name, Helen Soika? Her folks and my folks used to rent land together. We had a big field of corn and a big field of potatoes. Then, we dug potatoes together. They took half, we took half.

In those days, neighboring families shared farm work. The most notable example is threshing, which was done cooperatively until the 1950s, when individual families owned combines (harvesting machines). Men and women had different tasks, but all were involved in the annual work. Older children helped the adults, and even people of different ethnic backgrounds worked together.

A crew would transport a quite large threshing machine from one farm to another. Men of neighboring farms would get together and help finish the work, taking turns on the machine. Anna remembers that six neighboring families helped each other do the threshing. Neighborhood women gathered at the farm where threshing was taking place and cooked together. They baked chicken and made chicken soup, boiled potatoes, big loaves of bread, cakes, and pies on a wood stove. They served the men at a big, long table. The women ate together after the men had finished and returned to work. Anna recalls this period as a busy but fun time.

When their children married, parents' decisions were critical in those days. Marriages often occurred between neighborhood families. Anna recalls that the parents of neighboring farms often hoped that their sons and daughters would marry each other so that they could ensure continued cooperation in farming. Because Anna's parents had many daughters, neighbors were eager to have them as brides for their sons. Anna's mother, however, was against the idea because she thought if Anna married one of the boys in the neighborhood, the families that could not have her would be jealous. Also, her mother never allowed her to go out with a neighbor's boy if he was not a Catholic.

In 1931, Anna married Bill Belle, a man of Polish ancestry who worked for a sash-making company. She explains the reasons why her mother approved of Bill for her husband:

Oh, probably because my husband wasn't from a high class, you know, I mean he was a commoner. And whatever my mother put on the table, "Oh, Ma," he called my mother Ma, whatever you put on the table he ate, you know. My mother liked that. You know, he could talk Polish. She liked that, too. So you know they got along well.

Anna's mother used several criteria to judge Anna's future husband: he was a Catholic; he could speak Polish, the language with which Anna's parents felt most comfortable; and he liked to eat whatever Anna's mother cooked, which meant that food was an essential part of the family's lifestyle. He worked in a factory, which meant that he had a steady income, as Anna's father did working at a paper mill. Thus, he and Anna's father belonged to the same social class. Having a common religion, language, and a steady job, as well as being accustomed to foods prepared by his mother-in-law to be, were considered important criteria by the bride's parents.

Some of our Polish interviewees' families settled in the Riverfront area earlier than Susan's and Anna's families. Among them is the Worski family. We interviewed Irene (age 73), one of the daughters of this family. When we met her at Wigilia, a Polish-style Christmas party, she was sitting across the table from us. When she learned that we were visiting scholars from Japan studying the culture of Riverfront, she expressed interest in our project and invited us to her home. Irene's grandfather emigrated with his family from Poland to the United States in 1883 and settled on a farm about 2 miles north of Riverfront. Her father was 4 years old at the time. Later, the family moved to Riverfront, and her father entered business as a merchant-tailor in North Side, not far from Irene's current house.

In this family there were three sons and four daughters. Her father died in 1935 at the age of 56. Since then, Irene's mother lived with four single children, including Irene, for 30 years until she died at the age of 94 in 1976. Irene has since lived with her brother and sisters, and two other married brothers live in different states.

The Worskis live in North Side near St. Paul's Catholic Church. Even now, compared with other Catholic churches in town, St. Paul's parishioners are predominantly Polish-Americans. Consequently, the church has a Polish-style event of blessing the Easter basket on Good Friday morning. People bring baskets, filled with food such as bread, sausage, ham, and decorated eggs to church and place them in front of the altar. The priest blesses the baskets after the mass, and people bring them back home.

Irene's brother, Fred, and sister, Marsha, all went to high school. Fred also attended the Teacher's College in Riverfront and afterward attended a law school in Illinois. Then, he became a civil servant in Riverfront and a fire department chief. Marsha became a head nurse, and Irene worked at the local insurance company and became head of its secretarial section. They are proud that they all reached the highest positions in the section of their workplaces respectively before their retirements.

The closeness of the family to the parish among Polish-Americans is well known, as it is observed in another Midwestern town by Wrobel (1979). The Worski family is also actively involved in the activities of St. Paul's parish all the time. However, Irene did not go to the church's parochial school. At that time, the catechism was still taught in Polish, and she would have had to memorize it all in Polish, which she did not speak. Her parents sent Irene to a parochial school in Minnesota where their relatives lived when Irene reached the school age so that she could get education in English and prepare for the first communion.

When asked whether Polish people were segregated from the rest of Riverfront's citizens in the old days, Irene mentioned a slough as something she remembered being associated with ethnic divisions in town. The city maps of 1874 and 1929 show the old slough, which flowed a few blocks from the downtown area. It divided North Side from the central part of town. We cannot see the slough on any maps published after the 1930s because it was covered during these years. Irene told us that people used to say the old slough divided the Polish people from others. Bridges across the slough connected the downtown area to North Side. When boys from downtown crossed a bridge, boys of North Side fought with them. By and large, memories of the slough and fighting on the bridges remain only in the minds of individuals older than 70 years of age.

As we shall see in the next chapter, the north side of Riverfront did not originate with the arrival of Polish immigrants but existed since the town's beginnings. An 1874 hand-drawn town map depicts houses and a church in the north side and a north/south-bound street in the middle of it. The street begins at the public square and connects the town to northern Wisconsin. When the state highway was constructed in the late 1970s, most people stopped using this road to travel north.

Based on a 1931 city directory, 40% of the names in North Side (exactly the fourth ward) ended with "-ski" or "-cki." In addition to such names, we tried to identify other Polish names, and estimated that 70 to 80% of the residents in North Side at that time were of Polish descent. However, Polish-Americans did not live exclusively in this section of town. We also saw in the directory many Polish names in other parts of town (see Chapter 4).

DIVERSITY OF LIFE EXPERIENCES

Most of the people whose life histories we examined were between 65 and 75 years of age — members of the birth cohort of roughly 1910 to 1920. Although these people grew up in the Riverfront area in the late 1920s and the 1930s, their experiences were diverse. Therefore, we divide them into two groups: old-timers and latecomers, according to the number of years their families lived in the Riverfront area. If we identify those who immigrated to Riverfront and its environs as the first generation, then the interviewees of the old-timers' families are mostly the fourth generation; that is, their great-grandparents came to this area. Some of these first-generation Riverfrontans were, of course, descendants of the immigrants who came to America several generations earlier. In contrast to this group, those of the late-comers' families are the second generation, as in case of Susan Strovinski and Anna Belle, or the third generation, as in case of Irene Worski. As the waves of immigration to America came from different parts of Europe at different times, the residents of the old-timers group trace their ancestry back to England, Scotland, Ireland, Germany, and Scandinavia, whereas residents of the latecomers group trace theirs from Eastern Europe, primarily Poland.

Occupational differences are clear between these two groups. The old-timers held professional and managerial occupations: university faculty, lawyers, doctors, businessmen, and factory owners. On the other hand, the latecomers were farmers, factory workers, and small-shop proprietors. There was a disparity of wealth between the two groups in terms of income, house size, and location in the 1920s and 1930s. There is also a difference in the number of siblings that these people had. The family size of the old-timers was small; most interviewees have two siblings. In contrast, the interviewees of the latecomers group often had more than five siblings. Susan Strovinski's natal family was relatively small compared with other Polish families of the same generation with two children.

When the people we spoke with talked about their experiences growing up in Riverfront and its environs, they all identified themselves using the social categories to which they belong. We could therefore classify them into such groups as religion (Catholic or Protestant), ethnicity (e.g., English, Norwegian, German, Polish), occupation (lawyers, factory owners, or laborers), social class standing (high or low, rich or poor), rural/urban distinction (farmers or townspeople). However, the lesson we learned from the experiences of our interviewees is that religion, occupation, residence, marriage pattern, ethnicity, and education are variously interrelated. As a result, it is too simplistic to divide people of the Riverfront area on the basis of any single criterion, such as ethnicity (WASP versus Polish) or religion (Protestant versus Catholic).

Let us first look at the old-timers, or what Frank Woodland called the ruling class. Ethnically, they are not all Anglo-Saxon. Thomas Stromborg is from a Norwegian family, and Beth Evans' grandmother came from Germany. We know a few people who have an Irish background. Some residents are Lutherans, whereas others are Baptist, Methodist, or Presbyterian. Some of different faiths intermarried. James Evans, a Catholic, married Beth Wallace, a Protestant, and they attend both churches alternately. These residents' houses are now much more scattered in town than before. Their educational pattern is similar.

The old-timers' lives were separate from the latecomers' lives. At the least, social activities, such as parties, visiting, and going out together, were practiced within one's own group. In the 1920s and 1930s, Riverfront still consisted of enclaves of people, existing simultaneously and relatively independently. Asked whether she knew any Polish people as she was growing up, Mary Schultz said:

> If you go to different schools and churches, you don't meet them. My house was in the second ward, and most Polish people lived in the fourth ward. We have different schools. I go to Methodist Church, they go to a Catholic church. Again, you have nothing to do with them.

For Catholic people also, "church" and "school" were not separable, and these institutions divided people of the town. Mark O'Conner (age 65) is a retired journalist of Irish ancestry who had long worked for the *Riverfront Daily Journal*. He told us how Catholic churches have changed over time:

Catholic churches in this town use to be divided according to ethnic group. The congregation of St. John is Irish, St. Thomas is German, St. Paul and St. Ignatius are Polish. But, the situation has changed. Now, the congregation everywhere is mixed. The change happened in the 1960s when the parish boundary was set by the Bishop's order and then you have to belong to the church according to where you live. That means that people not only have to change churches, but also schools, if they go to parochial schools. There was some resistance at the beginning, but, gradually the composition of the congregation has become mixed.

Public high school was supposed to have been ethnically mixed, but it was divided by cliques, as Susan Strovinski had told us. The boundary between different groups was reinforced by daily social interactions. Occasions when the boundary was crossed were usually volatile situations, such as fighting on the street or bridge.

Neighborhoods were still divided along ethnic, religious, and social lines in the 1920s and 1930s in Riverfront, just as in the narratives of Susan and Anna regarding Chicago. Mark O'Connor also recalled such divisions during his childhood in northern Michigan:

The north side of Riverfront was where most Polish lived. The town was like that everywhere. I grew up in a small town in Michigan. There was an Irish corner, Polish corner, German corner, and so on. There were many enclaves of different ethnic groups.

Even though residential patterns and church membership separated people's day-to-day social interactions, there were occasions in which people of different groups crossed boundaries. In such instances, often friendly relationships were established. In such events, people tended to avoid talking about their differences. Mary Schultz had a close friend who was a Catholic of Irish descent, but, as her mother told her, she never discussed religious matters with this friend. Keeping this attitude has perhaps made it possible for them to continue to have a friendship even into their 90s.

The crossing of ethnic boundaries in daily life was often a result either of philanthropy or interdependency. Americans have a tradition of helping the less fortunate members of society. Well-to-do families helped youngsters from families with financial difficulties in their schooling, as we saw in the case of the Woodlands and Susan Strovinski. On the other hand, the farmer's market at the public square represented an interdependent relationship between farmers (mostly Polish) and townspeople (ethnically mixed). Farmers brought in fresh vegetables, crops, eggs, and other produce, and townspeople, such as Frank Woodland's mother, enjoyed going to the farmer's market to buy them. Some farmers delivered directly what they harvested from their fields to houses in town. Women of these houses came to know of such delivery services by word of mouth.

The separation that we discussed earlier in relation to the town's historical landscape raises a question as to whether Riverfront was segregated. Can we say that a certain ethnic group, Polish Americans, were discriminated against? This is a difficult question to answer. The people we spoke with, especially those who are Polish, seemed to be very reluctant to talk about discrimination against them.

Some of them even strongly denied that there was any. We heard one story that Polish students had not been allowed to join any athletic club in high school in the 1930s. However, the person who told us that story, when we were having lunch together in a restaurant, looked around to ensure that nobody was listening. There was a considerable amount of reticence regarding the topic.

Mark O'Connor once told us the following:

> In the past, we had lots of ethnic prejudice. For instance, to refer to Polish people, they used a derogatory term such as *Polander.* Even in the newspaper, around 1870, a heading without an article said, "A Polander was killed in the north side." They didn't even bother to find out who that man was. He wasn't treated as a human being.

However, he stressed the absence of discrimination in town now:

> I don't want you to think that we were discriminating against Polish people, or any other ethnic group. The town had many different enclaves, but, that's because Polish people preferred to live that way, and not because we discriminated against them.

Because Mark had been involved in the publication of the centennial issue of the *Riverfront Daily Journal,* we asked why there was only one article on Polish-Americans out of a 20-page special issue. He replied, "That's because Polish people were rather latecomers here. Though there are many excellent Polish people, their contribution came later than others." Irene Worski also denied any discrimination against Polish people. She said, "There are many Polish jokes, but those who enjoy reading them are Polish people themselves."

Based on the evidence we have gathered, we cannot assert or deny the existence of discrimination against Polish people in Riverfront. Rather than trying to prove or disprove it, we would like to determine what was at stake when Polish people chose their marriage partners and educated their children. Frank Woodland's mother strongly disapproved of her son marrying a Catholic girl. Like her, most Protestants were against marrying Catholics. Avoidance, however, was mutual. Catholics were also against marrying Protestants. Anna Belle's mother forbade her from dating a Protestant boy. We once asked our neighbor, Judy Biza (in her mid-60s) whether marrying a man of Polish descent was important for her. (Her husband John Biza is Polish-American too.) She said, "No, the husband-to-be didn't have to be Polish. He could be German, or Irish, so long as he was a Catholic. Being a Catholic was important for my family." If this is true, it seems religion is a greater criterion than ethnicity. According to Mark O'Connor, interreligious marriages were discouraged until the Second Vatican Conference in the 1960s. There has been a strong ecumenical movement within Catholic churches since then.

Likewise, in sending children to school, Polish-Americans considered it very important to send them to parochial school, despite the fact that they had to pay tuition. Polish-Americans in their 70s often would proudly say, "I sent all my children to St. Paul's school" or "We liked to live in this section of town, because my son can walk to St. Ignatius' School." For old-timers' families, it was important to send their children to a training school affiliated with the college because it was considered progressive. However, for Polish Catholics, like Irish and German

Catholics, it was equally important to send their children to Catholic parochial schools. Irene Worski's case is interesting in this regard. Being a third-generation Polish-American, she is not fluent in the Polish language because her family did not regard it as important to master. At the prospect of having to learn catechism in Polish, her family decided to send her to their relatives in Minnesota. If it had been only for the language difference, we think that they could have sent her to one of the public schools in Riverfront. However, it was imperative for them to keep the Catholic tradition.

It seems to us that at least two different but parallel social structures existed in Riverfront in the 1920s and 1930s — the Protestants and the Catholics. Each had key institutions for socialization: churches and schools. However, what was thought to be important and what people aspired for were likely to be different from each other.

Still, the fact remains that Polish immigrants were latecomers to Riverfront, so there is a disparity of wealth between them and the old-timers. Polish-Americans themselves said that they were poor or that "My folks didn't have money. They had a hard life." However, at the time of our fieldwork, all the Polish people we met were homeowners and had steady jobs as a result of their desires and struggles.

In the next chapter, we examine the historical record to discover Riverfrontans' movement patterns, focusing especially on changes in the north side of town.

CHAPTER 4 / "The North Side Is Polish Territory": Mobility, Stability, and Ethnicity

People migrate both geographically and socially throughout their lives. Such mobility is generally highest among Americans. How do Riverfrontans compare? Do they remain in their hometown, or do they fit the pattern of mainstream America? There are two ways to approach this question. First, we can find and interview individuals who left Riverfront and individuals who left but returned. We can ask them why they left, and, if they returned, why. Among such people was Frank Woodland, a native Riverfrontan (see Chapter 3). What we heard from him was critical to our understanding of migration patterns in this area.

Historical documents are another means of learning about change in the Riverfront population and ethnic composition. In this chapter, we take this approach, focusing only on the north side of town, not merely because it is important to understand how Riverfront became "a Polish town" but also because processing demographic data is time-consuming. Time limitations allow us to use only the north side data from 1870 to 1976 at this moment. Our sources are the U.S. Census' original schedules and city directories.

Before we proceed, it is necessary to sketch out the general population change in Riverfront to provide context for change on the north side. We entered into a computer database all of the available census information for Riverfront and a few surrounding towns from 1850 to 1910 (except 1890, the schedules of which had been destroyed). To analyze the census data, we had to identify the cultural background of each subject, and to do so, we used birthplace. If an individual had listed parents or grandparents, we took their cultural background from those persons. When we traced the parents' or grandparents' lineage, we did so on the father's side, unless it was unknown, in which case we traced the mother's side. When both father's and mother's lineages were available, and only the mother's indicated foreign ancestry, we used the foreign one for the person's cultural background. Using these rules, we determined each person's cultural background.

One of our first concerns using the census data was to decide whether the generally accepted label of "latecomers," which includes Polish people, was applicable to the Riverfront area. Based on our data, there were clearly two migration waves, one in the late 1850s and the other in the 1870s, although people had continuously migrated to the area from the time Riverfront was incorporated as a city in May

TABLE 1   RELATIVE PERCENTAGES OF RIVERFRONTANS BY ESTIMATED NUMBER OF YEARS
          IN TOWN, 1850–1910*

Number of Years	1850	1860	1870	1880	1900	1910
<1%	8.3	1.9	3.7	5.3	1.4	1.4
n	15	8	13	44	31	26
1-10%	73.5	71.4	45.1	54.5	20.9	15.8
n	133	305	158	453	463	301
11-20%	16.6	23.2	41.7	28.9	44.8	17.0
n	30	99	146	240	990	325
>20%	1.7	3.5	9.4	11.3	32.9	65.9
n	3	15	33	94	727	1258
Total %	100.1	100.0	99.9	100.0	100.0	100.1
n	181	427	350	831	2,211	1,910
(N†)	(464)	(1,535)	(1,883)	(4,444)	(9,524)	(8,691)

Source: U.S. Census original schedules.
*Individuals born in Wisconsin are not included in this table because of the difficulty of determining whether the person was born in Riverfront.
†Total population.

1858 until the 1880s (Table 1). The first wave never really ended but abated during the 1860s. The second wave, larger than the first, rose during the 1870s and continued into the 1880s and probably the 1890s. After the turn of the century, migration into Riverfront sharply decreased. Thus, we found that many people who appeared in the 1910 census had lived in Riverfront over 20 years.

Polish immigrants apparently were latecomers to the Riverfront area compared with Canadian, English, German, Irish, Norwegian, and Scottish immigrants, who had arrived already in 1850 with the "early comers": Yankees from the East — predominantly New York, Pennsylvania, and New England. Polish immigrants, however, began to arrive in the area not much later. A substantial number of them were already in town within a decade of the other Europeans, if we recognize "Prussia" in the birthplace column of the census as "Poland." The term *Prussia* was used in the 1860's, 1870's, and 1880's census original schedules (Table 2). Most of those whose birthplace was given as Prussia could be considered Polish because their birthplaces were changed to Poland or German-Poland in subsequent counts. The percentage of Polish (and Prussian) people steadily increased between 1860 to 1910. This is the opposite pattern of Yankee immigrants whose percentage decreased sharply from about 50 in 1850 to 10 in 1910.

Judging from these patterns, it is reasonable to say that Riverfront had a significant Polish population in 1910. Approximately 40% of the town's inhabitants were Polish-Americans. It is also clear that before the Polish incursion, Riverfront was a Yankee town. When did this change occur and how? Between 1880 and 1900, Polish immigrants outnumbered other ethnic groups.

The population of people of Polish background continued to grow steadily between 1900 and 1910, and since then its size has been maintained by their relatively high fertility and by the migration of young Polish people from rural areas. For certain ethnic groups in Riverfront, we calculated the average number of children born to each mother over a 10-year interval. Polish mothers had 6.3 children in 1900 and 6.5 in 1910, whereas Yankee mothers had 4 children in both years; Norwegian mothers had 4.4 children in 1900 and 3.9 in 1910; German mothers had

TABLE 2. RELATIVE PERCENTAGE OF CULTURAL BACKGROUNDS IN RIVERFRONT, 1850–1910

	1850	1860	1870	1880	1900	1910
Austrian	–	0.4 (6)	0.3 (5)	0.9 (41)	0.3 (25)	2.5 (219)
Belgian	–	0.5 (8)	–	0.4 (18)	0.4 (40)	0.4 (36)
Bohemian	–	–	–	1.2 (54)	0.4 (34)	0.5 (42)
Bulgarian	–	–	–	–	–	0.1 (6)
Canadian	10.6 (49)	8.8 (135)	10.0 (189)	7.4 (330)	6.7 (640)	5.6 (489)
Chinese	–	–	–	–	0.1 (5)	0.0 (3)
Danish	–	–	–	0.2 (8)	0.4 (35)	0.4 (32)
Dutch	–	–	0.3 (6)	0.2 (7)	0.1 (10)	0.3 (30)
English	4.3 (20)	4.0 (62)	3.8 (71)	5.7 (255)	4.6 (438)	3.3 (291)
Finish	–	–	–	0.2 (8)	–	–
French	–	0.4 (6)	1.6 (31)	1.2 (54)	0.8 (73)	0.4 (37)
German	3.7 (17)	6.2 (95)	7.5 (141)	9.2 (407)	23.3 (2,222)	18.2 (1,584)
Hungarian	–	–	–	2.1 (95)	2.2 (212)	0.0 (3)
Irish	4.5 (21)	13.2 (202)	14.0 (264)	13.2 (585)	7.3 (700)	5.4 (468)
Italian	–	0.1 (1)	–	–	–	0.1 (11)
Norwegian	0.2 (1)	4.2 (64)	7.2 (135)	6.4 (283)	5.4 (518)	4.1 (352)
Polish	–	0.6 (9)	0.1 (1)	10.3 (458)	21.9 (2,090)	37.5 (3,255)
Prussian	–	5.5 (84)	14.5 (273)	9.0 (398)	–	–
Rumanian	–	–	–	0.1 (4)	0.1 (7)	–
Russian	–	–	–	0.0 (2)	0.6 (53)	–
Scottish	0.9 (4)	1.8 (28)	1.7 (32)	3.3 (145)	1.8 (173)	1.3 (114)
Swedish	–	–	–	0.5 (21)	0.9 (85)	0.7 (64)
Swiss	–	–	–	0.1 (6)	0.3 (32)	0.2 (21)
Sylian	–	–	–	–	0.1 (5)	–
Welsh	–	0.2 (3)	0.5 (10)	0.7 (32)	0.3 (33)	0.3 (22)
Yiddish	–	–	–	–	–	0.8 (73)
U.S.-East	46.1 (214)	33.7 (518)	22.3 (419)	16.5 (735)	11.0 (1,051)	8.7 (759)
U.S.-Midwest	11.9 (55)	6.3 (96)	7.4 (140)	2.2 (98)	5.5 (525)	5.5 (475)
U.S.-New England	15.3 (71)	12.6 (193)	8.1 (152)	8.5 (377)	4.9 (465)	3.0 (259)
U.S.-South	0.4 (2)	1.0 (16)	0.5 (10)	0.4 (17)	0.3 (25)	0.1 (12)
U.S.-West	–	–	–	–	–	0.0 (1)
Total*	97.9 (454)	99.5 (1,526)	99.8 (1,882)	99.9 (4,438)	99.7 (9,496)	99.4 (8,658)

(N† = 464) (N = 1,535) (N = 1,883) (N = 4,444) (N = 9,524) (N = 8,691)

Source: U.S. Census original schedules.
Note: The numbers in parentheses are actual number. "U.S.-East" includes Delaware, Maryland, New Jersey, New York, Pennsylvania, Virginia; "U.S.-MIDWEST" includes Illinois, Iowa, Michigan, Minnesota, Ohio, Wisconsin; "U.S.-New England" includes Connecticut, Maine, Massachusetts, New Hampshire, Rhode Island, Vermont; "U.S.-South" includes states south of "U.S.-East" and "U.S.-Midwest"; "U.S.-West" includes California.
*Total percentage is a sum of percentages in each year.
†Total population.

4.5 in 1900 and 4.9 in 1910. These numbers are almost the same for rural areas for each cultural background except Polish. Polish mothers in Clark, one of the townships on Pine County, had 6.7 children in 1900 and 7.0 in 1910 — more than Polish mothers in Riverfront.

Young Polish people left their parents' farms for Riverfront or other towns to find jobs when they were in their late teens or early 20s. As we shall see, some people, like Chester Stanski and John Biza, did not like farm work and wanted to have their own income. By checking to see whether individuals' names that appeared in the census for a certain year appeared again in the next census, we found that most of the teenagers had disappeared 10 years later. We tried to identify who had moved from Clark to Riverfront using the census record, but we could identify only a small number of people who moved from the farm to town.

Marriage provided another chance for young people to leave the farm. Most of them married persons who had the same cultural background or the same religious orientation. Marriage announcements on the local newspaper gave us the family names of both bride and groom, so we could analyze the extent to which they chose marriage partners with the same cultural and religious backgrounds. We collected 205 marriage announcements from the *Riverfront Daily Journal* for 1899, 332 for 1930, 472 for 1953, and 403 for 1985. We analyzed them, comparing two groups, Polish or non-Polish, because Polish names are more easily identified than names of other nationalities. The percentages of Polish grooms who married Polish brides and Polish brides who married Polish grooms are as follows:

Marriage and Ethnicity	Year			
	1899	1930	1953	1985
Polish groom (n) who married Polish bride	80% (n = 40)	67% (n = 116)	55% (n = 150)	49% (n = 130)
Polish bride (n) who married Polish groom	76% (n = 42)	74% (n = 106)	59% (n = 141)	46% (n = 138)

The percentage of marriage partners with the same Polish background consistently decreased over time, whereas the percentage of marriages between Polish and non-Polish partners increased: 9% in 1899, 20% in 1930, 27% in 1953, and 35% in 1985. These changes in marriage practice among people with Polish backgrounds suggest that they have become less concerned about the continuity of Polish ethnic heritage through marriage.

Of course, the changes did not make Polish names disappear. To the contrary, the percentages of Polish family names steadily increased. Thus, it is not incorrect to say "Riverfront is a Polish town" in the 1980s because many people carried Polish names.

The religious backgrounds of their marriage partners were important for Polish-Americans. To substantiate this claim, we tried to look at patterns of religious affiliation in percentages of Catholic brides who married Catholic grooms and Catholic grooms who married Catholic brides from the data of newspaper marriage announcements. Therefore, we assumed that individuals whose cultural backgrounds were Polish or otherwise eastern European, German, Italian, Irish, French, and Dutch were associated with the Catholic faith. We did so, knowing that different religious orientations exist among these people, because our concern is not to obtain exact numbers but to learn changes over time. We were unable to determine clearly 20 to 30% of the brides' and the grooms' cultural background in each year. As the following table shows, the percentages of marriage partners with the same Catholic faith consistently decreased over time, as in the marriage-ethnicity relationship.

Marriage	Year			
and Religion	*1899*	*1930*	*1953*	*1985*
Catholic groom (n) who married Catholic bride	85% (n = 40)	82% (n = 116)	69% (n = 150)	65% (n = 130)
Catholic bride (n) who married Catholic groom	91% (n = 42)	83% (n = 106)	72% (n = 141)	57% (n = 138)

However, compared with the change in cultural backgrounds of marriage partners, the change in marriage partners' religious backgrounds is more conservative; that is, although people with Polish backgrounds have become less concerned about the ethnicity of their marriage partners, they still remained concerned about their partners' religions. This data fits an attitude, as expressed by Polish-American neighbor Judy Biza, that it does not matter whether bride or groom is Polish as long as she or he is Catholic.

Most of the marriage announcements reported the church in which the wedding ceremony took place. The following table shows the percentages of weddings that took place in a Catholic church.

Wedding at	Year			
Catholic Church (n)	*1899*	*1930*	*1953*	*1985*
Bride is Polish	100% (n = 8)	100% (n = 77)	98% (n = 85)	84% (n = 126)
Groom is Polish	88% (n = 8)	99% (n = 71)	98% (n = 85)	80% (n = 134)

Although the available cases were more limited for this analysis than for the analysis of partners' ethnicity and religion, the results support the claim that the partner's religious orientation is a critical concern in marriage practice among Riverfrontans with Polish backgrounds.

Riverfront was not an isolated town but a crossroads of townspeople and people from smaller towns and farms in the surrounding rural area. In early years, migration patterns of Polish people into Pine County showed that they seemed to prefer farm life to town life. In fact, the first Polish immigrant family settled in the township of Clark in 1857, 1 year before Riverfront was incorporated as a city. Other Polish families soon followed. In 1860, when Riverfront had 9 Polish and 84 Prussian immigrants, Clark had 76 Polish and 54 Prussian immigrants. Connections between Riverfront and the surrounding areas existed from its beginnings, as evidenced by this story: The head of the first Polish family in Clark toured the surrounding area looking for future farmland while his family stayed in Riverfront.

Polish immigrants in Clark, combined with Prussian immigrants, increased their numbers to about 700 during the 1860s. On the other hand, the numbers of those who lived in Riverfront increased to about 270. This difference suggests that Clark was the much-preferred place to live for Polish immigrants in the 1860s, probably because they wanted to live on farms. In the 1880s and 1890s, more than half of the residents of Polish backgrounds in Pine County lived on farms. Since then, however, their numbers increased faster in Riverfront than in Clark. We can safely say that most Polish immigrants who came to Pine County were farmers or became farmers. However, a certain number of them became townspeople as early as a decade after they arrived in the area.

As we have seen, the population of people of Polish backgrounds expanded from the beginning of Riverfront's history and continued to grow as the city grew. We realized this only after examining the census data. It was not evident from what our interviewees told us or from printed material on the town's history. Once we understood the importance of this fact, we asked ourselves how the people of Polish backgrounds became predominant in Riverfront. Riverfront has never been predominated by foreign nationals. Eighty percent of its citizens were U.S.-born in 1850 and in 1910. The number was nearly 70% even at a time of massive migration.

Before we proceed, let us briefly summarize the early history of the town. Before the population of German and Polish immigrants rapidly increased, during the 1870s, "Yankee" town would be the appropriate name to describe Riverfront. Forty-six percent of the entire population had come from eastern states, especially New York and Pennsylvania. Fifteen percent came from New England or had ancestors from there. If people who were born in the Midwest or had lived in this region more than one generation are included in these two cultural categories — U.S.-East and U.S.-New England-more than 70% of the population consisted of migrants and their descendants from eastern states. However, other cultural categories, such as Canadian, English, German, Irish, Norwegian, and Scottish, had already arrived in 1850, although their numbers were still small. These individuals were the "pioneer" immigrants for their respective cultural categories. During the 1850s, the numbers of people in all categories increased; however, in the 1860s, while the numbers of people of foreign cultural categories increased, the numbers of people who moved from eastern states decreased. It is possible that the latter group remigrated to the West in response to the population pressure of immigrants from Europe. However, immigrants from eastern states continued to move to Riverfront as part of the second migration wave of the 1870s (see Table 1).

A fourth ward was created in the 1870s (the year has not been determined), and the creation coincided with the period in which the number of Polish immigrants was increasing (see illustrations on page 54). Riverfront had been divided into three wards at its inception. The new fourth ward was created by dividing the first ward in two. Thereafter, the fourth ward became the area where people with Polish backgrounds concentrated. This ward commonly has been called "North Side" or "Polish territory" as we learned in the previous chapter. How did the fourth ward become a dense Polish enclave? One story, we found written down, offers a good answer. First, several Polish families chose their homes where a Catholic church now stands. Then newly arriving families settled around them. But the story does not explain how they chose this particular area in the first place.

We can assume, however, that there was room in the north side for people to establish themselves. In other words, it had not been developed yet, unlike other sections of Riverfront. The south side had been expanded along streets that were connected to the next town, Bishop, and the east side was already well populated, especially along Main Street.

There was a remarkable geographical feature at the south end of the north side — a slough. As we noted in the previous chapter, it ran a few blocks from and almost parallel to Main Street, and it flowed into the Wisconsin River. This marked the southern boundary of the new fourth ward. Although the boundary did not follow the slough exactly, the fourth ward became geographically and socially separated from other wards. The creation of a new ward was also politically important because people with Polish backgrounds in the fourth ward could have their own aldermen in the city council. Likewise, the "Yankees" in the first ward could continue to have theirs. Otherwise, they would not be able to do so simply because Polish-Americans outnumbered them. According to a 1958 special edition of the *Riverfront Daily Journal,* when Riverfront was incorporated as a city in 1858, "[s]ection 2 of the first chapter defined the boundaries of three wards but authorized the city council to make any changes in the lines of division deemed proper." The change from a three-ward to a four-ward system was, thus, decided by the city council. The city council members must have been very concerned about the emergence of a large mass of Polish-Americans in the first ward. It was probably considered appropriate to draw a boundary along the slough to divide the first ward in two.

The existence of the new fourth ward was clearly reflected in the census records. In 1880, people with Polish backgrounds were already predominant in the fourth ward (about a half of the inhabitants in the ward). Their percentage in the ward rapidly increased to 77% in 1900, and 90% in 1910. The construction of a Polish Catholic church several blocks north of the public square in 1876 attracted more people with Polish backgrounds from outside of Riverfront. At the same time, as we have seen, the relatively high fertility rates contributed to their population increase on the north side. Meanwhile, people with non-Polish backgrounds decreased in number. German-Americans had increased from 1880 to 1900 but decreased in the fourth ward during the 1900s. German-American numbers increased much more than people of other cultural backgrounds, except Polish, in the fifth and sixth ward (the fifth ward was created by taking part of the third ward, and the sixth ward by combining a part of the second ward with another part of the third ward in circa 1890). (See illustrations on page 54.)

The numbers of people with Canadian, English, Irish, and Yankee backgrounds steadily decreased in North Side. It seems that their numbers were no longer replenished with new arrivals, and many did not choose to live in the fourth ward because it was Polish territory. Geographical, social, and political separation might have contributed to the further concentration of Polish people in the fourth ward.

In 1870, before the four-ward system, the "Yankees" were predominant in each of three wards: about one third in the first and second wards, and almost half in the third ward. They were followed by Irish and Prussian in the first ward; by Prussian, Irish, and Norwegian in the second ward; and by Canadian and Irish in

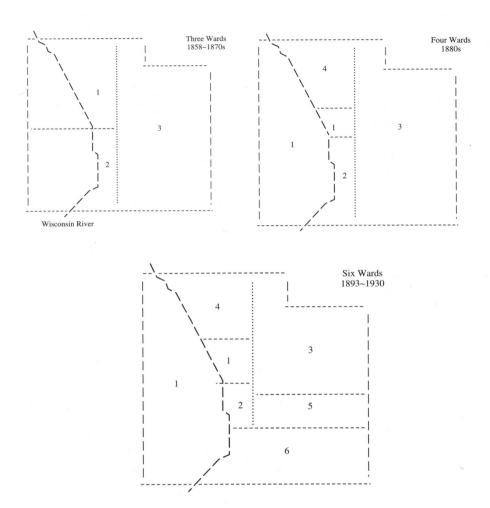

the third ward. Then, in 1880, with the creation of the fourth ward, the "Yankees" still kept the highest percentage in these three wards, whereas in the fourth ward, the "Yankees" were second in number to people with Polish backgrounds. During the 1880s and 1890s, the number of people with German backgrounds grew almost equal to those of the "Yankees." However, unlike people with Polish backgrounds, they lived in every ward except the fourth, and their numbers were the largest or the second largest in respective wards in 1900. This pattern was still seen in the second, fifth, and sixth wards in 1910. However, in the first and third wards, people with Polish backgrounds grew in number to almost rival those of people with German and "Yankee" backgrounds. It was as if they were overflowing the fourth ward and pouring into adjacent wards during the early 1900s.

The process in which Riverfront became a "Polish town" was complex. Even in 1910, if you lived downtown or in a ward other than the fourth ward, you might think that the Riverfront population was a mixture of different cultural backgrounds. Although there were many "Yankees" and German people, you might also have encountered people of Canadian, English, Irish, Norwegian, Polish, Scottish, and other European backgrounds. Residents in the fourth ward did not confine themselves to the ward at all. However, we do not have much data to determine to what extent they remained in their own territory. Therefore, we chose to consult the census data again and also old editions of the *Riverfront City Directory* to see whether individual names appeared in the fourth ward over many years. We discuss the results of this review in the following section. So far, we have been using the phrase *the fourth ward* to refer to North Side. Hereafter, we will simply use *North Side* to avoid confusion.

PATTERNS OF MOVING AND STAYING IN THE NORTH SIDE, 1870 TO 1976

Like residents of other American towns, whether large or midsized, Riverfrontans recognize the parts of the town by using directional terms. We often heard of the south side, north side, and less frequently, the west side, which means the place across Wisconsin River (we have not heard of the east side). As we described earlier, we heard from people of various backgrounds that North Side was considered "Polish territory." It has been the ethnically distinct part of town for those who have lived in Riverfront, whether Polish or not. Newcomers are told about the "Polish territory," and an image of North Side as a "rough" or "exotic" part of town is produced and reproduced. Even present-day high school students of Polish backgrounds have been told stories by their parents of fighting and roughness in North Side and on the border between North Side and the first ward.

Although the image of an exotic and rough North Side has been passed on to the next generation and to newcomers, it is a misperception that North Side is an exotic and rough Polish section. North Side has become less ethnically marked since the 1930s and less so after the end of World War II. In fact, many Polish-Americans began living in other parts of town as early as the first decade of this century (Table 3).

Anna Belle's case is a good example. Like many Polish immigrant families, her family stayed for a while in Chicago in the 1910s after first arriving in the United States and then moved to a farm near Riverfront. Her future husband had lived in town working for a manufacturing factory. He would come to see her by car in the days when people were just beginning to use automobiles. After getting married in 1931, they lived in the third ward, as did many Polish people (nearly 20% of the ward's residents) in 1910 (see Table 3). Anna's husband's family was Polish too, and they moved from a neighboring town to the sixth ward during the 1910s. The family was certainly part of a group of Polish newcomers in this ward. After moving to Riverfront, Anna's father-in-law worked for a newly established paper mill, which needed workers and hired many people with Polish backgrounds to fill the newly created jobs there.

The mobility patterns of people with Polish backgrounds in Riverfront contrasted with those of non-Polish residents of this town. In the 1900s, as we have

TABLE 3. PERCENTAGE OF SELECTED CATEGORIES OF CULTURAL BACKGROUND IN RIVERFRONT BY YEAR (1870, 1880, 1900, AND 1910) BY WARD

	Ward					
	1st	2nd	3rd	4th	5th	6th
1870						
Austrian	0.7 (5)	– (0)	– (0)			
Canadian	8.8 (61)	8.7 (68)	14.1 (46)			
English	4.3 (30)	4.1 (32)	1.2 (4)			
German	8.0 (55)	7.8 (61)	7.6 (25)			
Irish	17.4 (120)	11.1 (87)	12.8 (42)			
Norwegian	6.4 (44)	10.1 (79)	3.7 (12)			
Polish	– (0)	0.0 (1)	– (0)			
Prussian	15.2 (105)	19.3 (151)	5.2 (17)			
Scottish	0.9 (6)	1.9 (15)	3.4 (11)			
U.S. (combined)	36.1 (249)	32.1 (251)	48.9 (160)			
U.S.-East	*19.1 (132)*	*18.3 (143)*	*30.3 (99)*			
U.S.-Midwest	*6.2 (43)*	*8.5 (66)*	*8.6 (28)*			
U.S.-New England	*10.7 (74)*	*5.4 (42)*	*10.1 (33)*			
Total	690	781	327			
1880						
Austrian	1.5 (15)	0.4 (6)	0.3 (3)	1.4 (14)		
Canadian	4.3 (44)	7.9 (109)	8.5 (90)	8.8 (87)		
English	6.7 (68)	6.7 (92)	5.7 (61)	3.4 (34)		
German	11.6 (118)	15.1 (208)	4.7 (50)	3.1 (31)		
Irish	14.0 (143)	12.1 (166)	15.7 (167)	11.0 (109)		
Norwegian	12.4 (126)	7.5 (103)	4.0 (43)	1.1 (11)		
Polish	1.3 (13)	2.7 (37)	0.4 (4)	40.9 (404)		
Prussian	4.8 (49)	9.4 (129)	9.5 (101)	12.0 (119)		
Scottish	2.3 (23)	3.6 (50)	6.5 (69)	0.3 (3)		
U.S. (combined)	33.6 (342)	24.6 (338)	36.5 (388)	14.4 (142)		
U.S.-East	*20.5 (209)*	*14.3 (196)*	*22.6 (240)*	*9.1 (90)*		
U.S.-Midwest	*2.7 (27)*	*1.8 (25)*	*3.1 (33)*	*1.3 (13)*		
U.S.-New England	*10.4 (106)*	*8.5 (117)*	*10.8 (115)*	*3.9 (39)*		
Total	1,018	1,375	1,063	988		
1900						
Austrian	0.4 (6)	0.1 (2)	0.7 (11)	– (0)	0.2 (3)	0.4 (3)
Canadian	7.3 (106)	6.7 (113)	7.4 (119)	4.3 (99)	9.1 (148)	6.5 (55)
English	4.1 (59)	5.4 (92)	6.4 (102)	0.6 (13)	6.1 (99)	8.7 (73)
German	22.1 (320)	33.0 (560)	19.6 (313)	6.5 (151)	35.4 (575)	36.0 (303)
Irish	11.4 (165)	11.1 (189)	7.4 (119)	3.2 (74)	6.8 (110)	5.1 (43)
Norwegian	14.8 (214)	7.7 (131)	4.9 (78)	2.1 (49)	2.0 (32)	1.7 (14)
Polish	8.0 (116)	2.2 (37)	8.9 (142)	77.2 (1,786)	0.1 (2)	0.8 (7)
Scottish	2.3 (33)	3.1 (52)	2.1 (33)	0.1 (3)	2.5 (40)	1.4 (12)
U.S. (combined)	21.9 (317)	24.4 (415)	30.5 (488)	3.6 (83)	28.0 (454)	33.7 (283)

TABLE 3. PERCENTAGE OF SELECTED CATEGORIES OF CULTURAL BACKGROUND IN RIVERFRONT BY YEAR (1870, 1880, 1900, AND 1910) BY WARD — CONT'D

	Ward					
	1st	2nd	3rd	4th	5th	6th
U.S.-East	10.7 (155)	12.2 (208)	16.1 (258)	1.6 (38)	15.2 (246)	17.2 (145)
U.S.-Midwest	5.9 (85)	6.8 (116)	7.0 (112)	0.8 (18)	7.1 (116)	9.3 (78)
U.S.-New England	5.3 (77)	5.4 (91)	7.4 (118)	1.2 (27)	5.7 (92)	7.1 (60)
Total	1,448	1,699	1,600	2,313	1,623	841
1910						
Austrian	0.5 (6)	0.8 (11)	9.5 (143)	– (0)	4.2 (54)	0.7 (5)
Canadian	5.6 (69)	7.0 (92)	10.0 (150)	1.6 (42)	8.2 (104)	4.8 (32)
English	4.1 (51)	4.5 (60)	6.5 (97)	0.4 (10)	3.3 (42)	4.6 (31)
German	21.8 (268)	27.8 (367)	16.5 (248)	2.3 (63)	33.9 (432)	30.8 (206)
Irish	10.0 (123)	8.6 (113)	4.2 (63)	1.4 (39)	7.8 (99)	4.6 (31)
Norwegian	11.9 (147)	6.1 (81)	4.3 (65)	1.4 (39)	1.5 (19)	0.1 (1)
Polish	20.0 (246)	7.3 (96)	18.8 (282)	90.1 (2,431)	10.2 (130)	10.5 (70)
Scottish	2.4 (30)	2.1 (28)	1.4 (21)	– (0)	2.0 (25)	1.3 (9)
Yiddish	1.9 (24)	3.3 (44)	– (0)	– (0)	0.4 (5)	– (0)
U.S. (combined)	16.5 (203)	24.8 (327)	25.2 (378)	1.9 (50)	25.8 (329)	30.7 (205)
U.S.-East	9.2 (113)	11.2 (148)	13.1 (196)	0.9 (25)	14.1 (179)	14.7 (98)
U.S.-Midwest	5.1 (63)	8.9 (118)	8.3 (124)	0.6 (15)	6.7 (85)	10.3 (69)
U.S.-New England	2.2 (27)	4.6 (61)	3.9 (58)	0.4 (10)	5.1 (65)	5.7 (38)
Total	1,231	1,320	1,501	2,697	1,274	668

Source: U.S. Census original schedules.
Note: The numbers in parentheses are actual number. See the note of Table 2 for the states included in each category.
The original three-ward system was changed to a four-ward system in the 1870s, and then it was changed again in the 1880s to a six-ward system. As a result, the area of the fourth ward of 1880 is slightly different from that of 1900, and the area of the third ward was divided into the third and fifth wards.

seen, non-Polish people, especially "Yankees" (U.S.-New England and U.S.-East in Table 3) and people with German backgrounds, decreased in number, which suggests that many moved out of town. To check the possibility that they moved from Riverfront to nearby towns, we looked at the census of Bishop, a neighboring town that is the second largest in Pine County. We found that Bishop did not receive migrants from Riverfront but had experienced the same population change as Riverfront; that is, the dominant group shifted from Yankee to Polish Americans.

Once they moved to the Riverfront area, did people with Polish backgrounds live in the same location for a long time, even more than one generation? How long did they stay in North Side? How long did they live at the same location? To answer these questions, we reviewed city directories and census data to determine how long people lived in North Side. We chose the 1893, 1931, 1954, and 1976 editions of the city directory along with the original handwritten census schedule of 1870 and 1910 so that we had six sets of name lists, approximately 20 years apart. We looked for names that reappeared in subsequent name lists (Table 4).

We found that there were more people than expected who moved within North Side, to other wards, or out of town. However, the percentage of those who appeared only in one name list decreases over 60 years: three fourths in 1893 to one third in 1954. These people must have moved relatively soon, even though some of them might have stayed for about 40 years at the most, for instance, from 1871 to 1909. On the other hand, the increasing percentage of people who appeared in more than one name list suggests that people who settled in North Side remained there as time went by. In fact, the number of people who appeared in three name lists (i.e., remaining about 40 years) increased over time.

People of North Side tended to live longer in the same ward in later years. Between 1893 and 1910, we see a remarkable change in the years that people remained. The chances that those who were living in North Side in 1910 had been there for more than 20 years were greater than those who had lived there in 1893. Likewise, compared with those who were living in North Side in 1910, those who were living there in 1953 were more likely to have been there for more than 20 years.

More interestingly, people of North Side became more mobile within the same area between 1893 and 1910. Then, between 1910 and 1976, about two fifths of people living in North Side experienced at least one address change in their lives. We would need a detailed analysis of this pattern of moving within the same ward before we can understand more clearly why they moved and how they determined their next address. Based on our preliminary analysis, people of North Side seemed to have moved on such occasions as marriage and family building, when their families became too large for their current houses, or when they became widowed (Tables 5 and 6, p. 60).

Here, Adolf Worski's history provides a good illustration. He was born in Poland in 1879, the first child in his family. His parents emigrated with him from Poland in 1883 and stayed on a farm in Pine County. They then moved to North Side with their children in the 1890s and opened a tailor shop downtown. Adolf was also a tailor when he married in 1903 and moved into a house just a block away from his parents' and just a few blocks away from his uncle's (father's brother). His family moved to another residence within North Side in the 1910s or 1920s, probably because they needed a larger house to accommodate their six children. After he died in 1935, his wife and children continued to live together. After Adolf's wife died in 1976, four of his six children continued to live together, never having married.

As this case shows, Polish-Americans seem to prefer living close to their families and remaining in one place. This fits with the stereotypic image of Polish people and, as far as we could discern, holds true for those who remained in North Side. However, what about those who left North Side or even left town? Two of Adolf Worski's three sons left town and moved to other states. These two sons were born in the 1910s, and unlike farm children in those days, they might have been educated enough to become skilled workers or professionals, enabling them to move away.

TABLE 4. NORTH SIDE RIVERFRONTANS WHO APPEAR IN NAME LIST(S), 1870–1976

	[1870]	1893	1910	1931	1954	[1976]
n*	–	458	802	929	1,288	–
Female	–	78	175	134	245	–
Male	–	380	627	795	1,043	–

Appeared only in one name list (MOBILITY)

		1893	1910	1931	1954	
Percentage		75.5	56.9	49.7	34.3	
(n)			(346)	(456)	(462)	(442)
Female (n)		(59)	(105)	(76)	(137)	
Male (n)		(287)	(351)	(386)	(305)	

Appeared in more than one name list within North Side (STABILITY)

		1893	1910	1931	1954	
Percentage		24.5	43.1	50.3	65.7†	
(n)			(112)	(346)	(467)	(846)†
Female (n)		(19)	(70)	(58)	(108)†	
Male (n)		(93)	(276)	(409)	(738)†	

Appeared in three name lists (n)

Year	(1870)	1893	1910	1931	1954	(1976)
			———3———			
				———36———		
					———126———	
					|———131———|

Mobility within North Side

		1893	1910	1931	1954	
Moved during	%	16.1	37.9	42.6	45.7*	
life course	(n)	(18)	(131)	(199)	(387*)	

					1954	
Widowed in the	%	–	–	–	20.0*	
next name list	(n)	(–)	(–)	(–)	(169*)	

Source: Riverfront City Directory for 1893, 1931, 1954, and 1976; U.S. Census original schedule for 1870 and 1910.

*In 1893, 1931, and 1954, *n* is the number of those listed in North Side of Riverfront. In 1910, the total population in North Side was 2,697. Of this, 802 people were selected from a group which can be identified as head-of-family (n = 532 [male = 462, female = 70]) and/or identified in name lists of 1893 and 1931.

†These figures include the number of those who moved out of the city and those who moved out of North Side to other parts of town. The latter is estimated at 10% of the total.

TABLE 5 RELATIVE PERCENTAGES OF U.S.-BORN PERSONS IN RIVERFRONT BY BIRTH PLACE BY YEAR, 1850–1910

Birth Place	1850	1860	1870	1880	1900	1910
East	36.2 (168)	27.2 (417)	16.3 (306)	11.3 (502)	5.5 (520)	4.0 (345)
New England	12.1 (56)	8.9 (136)	4.7 (88)	3.8 (167)	1.7 (161)	1.0 (85)
Midwest	31.9 (148)	35.6 (546)	48.1 (906)	54.1 (2,405)	68.9 (6,562)	74.7 (6,496)
Others	0.6 (3)	0.6 (9)	0.5 (9)	0.2 (9)	0.5 (52)	0.4 (37)
Total	80.8 (375)	72.2 (1,108)	69.5 (1,309)	69.4 (3,083)	76.6 (7,295)	80.1 (6,963)
	(N = 464)	(N = 1,535)	(N = 1,883)	(N = 4,444)	(N=9,524)	(N = 8,691)

Source: U.S. Census original schedules
Note: The numbers in parentheses are actual number. See the note of Table 2 for the states included in each category.

TABLE 6 RELATIVE PERCENTAGES OF U.S.-BORN PERSONS IN RIVERFRONT BY YEAR (1880, 1900, AND 1910) BY WARD

Birth Place	Ward					
	1st	2nd	3rd	4th	5th	6th
1880						
East	13.6 (138)	10.6 (146)	12.7 (135)	8.4 (83)		
New England	3.8 (39)	4.5 (62)	5.8 (62)	0.4 (4)		
Midwest	54.4 (554)	54.6 (751)	56.2 (597)	50.9 (503)		
Others	0.3 (3)	0.1 (2)	0.2 (2)	0.2 (2)		
Total	72.1 (734)	69.9 (961)	74.9 (796)	59.9 (592)		
	(N = 1,018)	(N = 1,375)	(N = 1,063)	(N = 988)		
1900						
East	5.7 (82)	7.2 (123)	6.4 (103)	1.6 (37)	6.3 (102)	8.7 (73)
New England	2.2 (32)	2.2 (37)	2.0 (32)	0.3 (8)	2.3 (38)	1.7 (14)
Midwest	69.8 (1,011)	68.9 (1,171)	70.7 (1,131)	65.5 (1,515)	70.9 (1,151)	69.3 (583)
Others	0.8 (11)	0.4 (7)	1.1 (17)	0.1 (2)	0.7 (11)	0.5 (4)
Total	78.5 (1,136)	78.8 (1,338)	80.2 (1,283)	67.5 (1,562)	80.2 (1,302)	80.1 (674)
	(N = 1,448)	(N = 1,699)	(N = 1,600)	(N = 2,313)	(N = 1,623)	(N = 841)
1910						
East	3.9 (48)	5.6 (74)	4.4 (66)	1.8 (48)	5.3 (67)	6.3 (42)
New England	0.8 (10)	1.9 (25)	1.2 (18)	0.1 (3)	1.9 (24)	0.7 (5)
Midwest	75.4 (928)	73.9 (976)	79.3 (1,190)	72.1 (1,944)	76.0 (968)	73.4 (490)
Others	0.5 (6)	0.5 (6)	0.7 (11)	0.2 (6)	0.5 (6)	0.3(2)
Total	80.6 (992)	81.9 (1,081)	85.6 (1,285)	74.2 (2,001)	83.6 (1,065)	80.7 (539)
	(N = 1,231)	(N = 1,320)	(N = 1,501)	(N = 2,697)	(N = 1,274)	(N = 668)

Source: U.S. Census original schedules.
Note: The numbers in parentheses are actual number. See the note of Table 2 for the states included in each category.

This case also suggests that a family can be traced over three generations in North Side because spouses or children continued to live there even though they had moved from their parents' houses or to amenable residences within North Side or within greater Riverfront. If we trace families as a unit over time, the number of families that remained in North Side for more than four decades would have been much greater than the number of individuals who remained there more than four decades. In fact, the Worski family has lived in North Side for almost a century, since they first arrived there in the 1890s and remained until the middle of the 1980s, although there have been a few address changes.

In answering to the question we asked at the beginning of this chapter, we find that the number of people who live longer in North Side has increased over time. Does this confirm that North Side is an ethnic neighborhood? We would say that the answer is yes, but only in the sense that the majority of residents share a Polish cultural background. Having encountered the rough conditions of North Side in the 1870s and 1880s, many had left by the 1910s. Those who lived in North Side in 1910 tended to remain there longer than those who lived there before 1910. The point is that a massive influx of young Polish people came to Riverfront in the late 1870s, and their children, whether foreign born or not, grew up and married in the 1910s. People of this second generation started families and remained in North Side, often for life. Again, in the 1930s, some members of the second generation started married life at a different house from their parents' but still remained in North Side, and people whom we met are mostly from this generation.

At the time of our fieldwork, people in this generation have been growing old. Of those who appeared in both the 1954 and 1976 listings, about one fifth were widowed by 1976. Without a doubt, such a high ratio of widows or widowers implies that many residents were members of an older generation. Thus, in the mid-1980s, they are entering into advanced old age. Yet, even as members of longtime North Side families get older, such as Adolf Worski's children, young families now are moving into this neighborhood and renting houses to start their own families. Based on this observation, we predict that North Side will become a historical shrine of "the old Polish territory" in Riverfront, while at the same time becoming a nonethnic residential area as older people move into senior housing or pass away and new people move in.

Today, North Side looks neat and quiet, just like other residential sections of Riverfront in the mid-1980s. It is hard to believe that the place use to be regarded as a rough neighborhood. One day, while we were driving in North Side together, Anna Belle pointed out the house where one of her daughters lives:

> When my daughter was getting married, I was worried. I did not want my daughter to get married to a boy from North Side because people over there used to be wild. But my daughter's family lives in a good neighborhood. So I don't worry any more.

In the present era, ethnicity is being redefined, rediscovered, or reinvented as a distinctive feature of towns all over the country. The moving patterns of North Side residents prove to be historically constructed at about the turn of the 20th century in the sense that as non-Polish people moved out, Polish people moved in and reproduced. Eventually, the population of people with Polish backgrounds peaked to almost 90% in North Side; however, at the same time, they also lived in other parts of town. Life among people with Polish backgrounds, whether or not they lived in North Side, became less and less Polish, and consequently, North Side became a little more than a symbol of the Polish experience in Riverfront's history. Although many people with Polish backgrounds still live in North Side, to them, as well as to younger townspeople, it is no longer "Polish territory." It is only the newcomers who may think this part of town as an exotic ethnic zone. We were no exception, at least during the early stage of our field research.

CHAPTER 5 / "This Is Our Way of Doing Things": Ethnic Manifestation and Identity

As noted in the previous chapters, Riverfront has been considered a Polish town by both Polish and non-Polish inhabitants since the end of the 19th century. However, if we had not been aware that the last names of many town residents ended in "-ski," we would not have known that the town was mostly Polish-American. Although a local publishing company still produces a weekly newspaper in the Polish language and has been doing so for more than 70 years, ethnic enclaves no longer exist in Riverfront.

Perhaps the main reason Riverfront does not appear to be a Polish-American town to outsiders is the lack of visible signs, such as Polish restaurants or shops selling Polish ethnic items. In large cities, ethnic foods and souvenir items are numerous and often catch tourists' eyes. Asked why there is no Polish restaurant in Riverfront, one person replied, "Polish food is something you eat at home, not at a restaurant. That is the kind of food my mom used to cook." Another person said, "Oh, there was one before. But, they couldn't make it." "Polishness" seems to be invisible to tourism, embedded as it is in people's daily lives.

During our fieldwork, however, we encountered occasions in which Polish heritage or ethnicity was clearly manifested. On these occasions, Polish food, costumes, and performances, such as folk dance and music, were used to highlight people's ethnic heritage. We should note that these occasions did not always take place in the Riverfront area. They were created 5 or 6 years ago, relatively recently. We are led to ask why that is, as well as who sponsors these events and for what purpose? To answer these questions, we examine events and occasions that represent more or less ethnic features.

EXPRESSIONS, EFFORTS, AND EVENTS

The public square is located at the center of the town and has long been a focal point for residents. On the walls of the buildings that surround the square, human figures in Polish folk costumes are painted. Kataryna Baszka (in her 80s) organized a project in the 1960s to paint these figures as a public expression of Polish heritage. By using visual cultural images, she wanted to emphasize the importance of maintaining a sense of Polish ethnic heritage at the heart of town. Having immigrated to the United States from Poland in the 1950s, Kataryna Baszka is one of the relatively recent arrivals. Educated both in Poland and in the United States, she married a well-educated widower, who later became the editor of the Polish weekly newspaper in Riverfront.

Kataryna enjoys helping other people. She takes her friends shopping, out to eat, to funerals and meetings, and so forth. Because of her language skills, she has been a "liaison" between Polish-speaking and English-speaking people. People hear about Kataryna Baszka and her willingness to help others. She has been asked, even by strangers, to help read letters in Polish. Sometimes she assists those who need help finding a special medicine normally used in Poland. She phones a local drugstore on the public square that an elderly Polish-American pharmacist has operated for years. He keeps a list of medicines printed in Polish for customers who understand only Polish or for those whose relatives or friends in Poland have requested medicine from the United States.

Kataryna's helpful ways extend not only to Riverfront residents but also to people of Polish backgrounds livings in other areas of the United States as well as people living in Poland. She also has been an advocate for Polish-Americans as president of the Riverfront Chapter of the Polish Women's Alliance, a national organization whose original function was to provide its 'members with financial assistance. As Polish-Americans more or less entered the mainstream, Kataryna concentrated her efforts on helping people in Poland. She would send them packages containing daily necessities and medicine.

Perhaps most influential in introducing Polish culture to Riverfront is the local chapter of the Polish-American Congress. The core members of this group are young people in their 20s and 30s who recently immigrated from Poland. The fact that Riverfront was predominantly a Polish community (Sanford, 1908) has attracted both intellectuals and laypeople. Contemporary Polish immigrants, although relatively few, still come to Riverfront and to farms around the area. Unlike immigrants of past generations, they are mostly well educated and, in many cases, political émigrés. In 1982, those new immigrants who found jobs in Riverfront organized a local chapter of the Polish-American Congress. The host organization has a long history and a network of chapters throughout the country.

This local group of young people is trying to discover how their "recent" history in the mother country connects to the Riverfront Polish community's "older" history. For these young people, the political conditions in Poland, especially oppression by the government, was a primary concern during our fieldwork, when Waresa, a political leader, had not appeared in Poland. They hold various group activities to help earlier immigrants understand, or at least be aware of, the plight of people in Poland at that time. For example, they produced "Song & Poetry," a theatrical play held in the basement of the public library. It emphasized the political oppression in their home country. They also engaged in fund-raising activities such as a bake sale in front of a national discount store; and *Wigilia* (a Christmas dinner party in the traditional Polish style) at the Elk's Club downtown; a Polish food booth, offering pierogi (dumplings stuffed with meat or cheese), kielbasa sausage, cabbage rolls, and other delicacies at the Polish Festival held in September in the public square. They emphasize that their proceeds are used to purchase medicine for children in Poland. Some have started working at the Euro-Deli that was recently opened by a medical doctor's wife who is Polish-American. This store specializes in eastern European food, both locally made and imported. In these ways, recent Polish immigrants try to maintain their Polish identity in the United States. At the same time, they try to be accepted by the Polish-Americans who had immigrated some generations before.

Wigilia and Contested Traditional Tastes

We attended *Wigilia* at the Elk's Lodge on January 6, 1985. Susan Strovinski had sent us two tickets for the event, which was very nice of her because one ticket cost $10. We considered the event a great opportunity for our research and therefore made certain to attend. *Wigilia* has not always been celebrated in Riverfront, at least not in its current form. As an annual event, the third of which we were about to attend, it was organized by the Polish-American Congress as a fund-raiser, with proceeds from the event used for medical aid for Poland. When we arrived, Susan Strovinski, an active member of the organization, was busy frying pierogies in the kitchen. Four other women were also busy preparing the food, and we noticed several trays of Polish pastries ready to be served.

Before long, the entire hall was filled. There were two large Christmas trees beside the front stage, and the stage was adorned with paper decorations. Fifteen large tables each had 12 seats, but one seat was always left empty. We were told that it is Polish custom to keep an empty seat at each table so that a traveler, unexpected visitor, or someone who has nowhere else to spend Christmas can always take part. On the tables were plates of marinated herring and fish stew, and at one end of the hall, there was a cash-bar for those who wanted to drink.

The party began with a speech by the editor of the local Polish newspaper. He announced that this was the third *Wigilia* sponsored by the Polish-American Congress. After him, a young man and a young woman, both of whom appeared to be around age 20, took turns explaining Polish customs, such as the tradition of sharing the *oplatek* placed on each table. An *oplatek* is a 3-by-5 inch wafer that is pink and thin. The priest from the Catholic church in Bishop recited a prayer in Polish, and then everyone shared the wafers.

The following is the menu of the *Wigilia* dinner:

In Polish	In English
1. Chleb i buleczki	Bread and rolls
2. Śledzie	Herring
3. Ryba "a la Helena"	Fish "a la Helena"
4. Ogorki i marynaty	Relish tray
5. Barszcz z uszkami	Borsch with dumplings
6. Pierogi z kapusta	Pierogi with sauerkraut
7. Ryż	Rice
8. Ryba z jarzynka	Fish stew
9. Sałatka z ziemniaów	Potato salad
10. Kompot	Fruit compote

11. Świateczne pieczywo   Christmas cakes and cookies
12. Kawa, herbata   Coffee, tea

It is a rule that fish is included in the menu, and no meat should be served. Rice had been listed on the menu but was not served because of the shortage of preparation time. A coffee pot, a plate of herring, and a plate of fish a la Helena had been already placed on the table as we were seated. Dinner began with a relish tray with pickled watermelon, cucumber, radishes, and carrots. A basket of white bread was brought in, followed by a basket of dark bread. Then came potato salad, which we found to be sweet. Borsch with dumplings was actually a red beet soup. A woman sitting across the table from us found it rather tasteless and said, "Americans prefer rich soup. They add sour cream and ham."

The following year, we attended our fourth *Wigilia* (Figure 14). The proceedings and decorations were generally the same as the previous year; however, this time we invited Anna Belle to join us. Anna had come to the United States at the age of 2 (see Chapter 2). We wanted to know what a Polish-American "old-timer" thought of this "traditional" Polish Christmas Eve. To our surprise, the whole event was as exotic to Anna as it was to us. She asked us how much the dinner cost, but because she was our guest, we thought it impolite to tell her the price. Then she asked, "about $3?" She would have been very surprised had she known the dinner was $10 per person. For her, the fact that the proceeds went to Poland meant little. She was familiar with some of the dishes served, such as pierogi and borsch, but emphasized the difference between her own, or her mother's way of cooking, and theirs.

Anna had a similar reaction when we took her to the Euro-Deli for lunch one day. We ordered cabbage rolls, which were cooked in clear soup instead of in tomato sauce. Anna had been accustomed to the latter type, so she was rather disappointed, saying, "I can make better cabbage rolls than these. See the man over there," pointing the clerk behind the counter, "I think he is a Russian. I mean, he came from the Russian part of Poland. My dad is from the German part. We are different. They make cabbage rolls in this way."

We are not certain whether the Euro-Deli employee was indeed from the Russian part of Poland or whether the cabbage rolls are cooked differently in different regions of Poland, but we did find Anna's reaction to "Polish food" interesting. Instead of working as an ethnic symbol to unite Polish-Americans, "ethnic" food seemed to be divisive. When Anna gave Mariko a set of recipes that she had used when her children were still at home, we were surprised to find that these recipes were the ones considered standard American cuisine, the kind found in a Betty Crocker cookbook.

Anna's reaction reminded us of a discussion we had one day with Cheryl Kline, Meal Program Director for the Pine County Commission on Aging. We were talking about ways to organize a proposed International Day at Jefferson Center. Someone suggested making an ethnic dish, "How about borsch, since we have so many Polish people here." The director rejected this idea, saying, "No, it won't work. Borsch is something like beef stew for us. Somebody will say, 'This isn't the way I cook it at my house.' Every house has its own recipe. It won't work.

Figure 14. A scene from the fourth annual Wigilia, *the Polish Christmas dinner party organized by the local chapter of the Polish-American Congress. (Photograph taken in January 1986.)*

It should be something like ham and pea soup. It's easy to make and feeds many people." Cheryl feared that serving "ethnic" food might divide members instead of uniting them. We discuss more about the use of ethnic food at Jefferson Center later in this chapter.

Polish Festival

We attended the second annual Polish Festival, which was held in the public square at the end of September 1985. We had missed the first Polish Festival, which had been held just before we arrived in Riverfront the previous year. It had been held at a park along the Wisconsin River near downtown. Polish Festivals are often held in large cities, like Milwaukee; only in recent years has Riverfront held this type of event. However, it is uncertain whether it will be continued for reasons we will discuss later.

The Polish Festival was sponsored and organized by the Riverfront Chamber of Commerce, which surprised us because we had expected that this kind of event would be sponsored by an ethnically based group. The purpose of the event, however, is to revitalize the downtown area, a motivation with certain commercial implications. The director of the Chamber of Commerce might have thought that the community was predominantly Polish and that the use of their cultural ways would be appropriate for bringing about a renewed sense of community and revitalization of the local economy (Figures 15, 16, and 17).

Figure 15. Members of the local chapter of Polish-American Congress selling homemade Polish food at Riverfront's annual Polish Festival. (Photograph taken in September 1985.)

Figure 16. A local Polish dance group performs at the public square during the Polish Festival, September 1985.

Figure 17. A performance of traditional Polish dance by a group from Milwaukee during the Riverfront Polish Festival, September 1985.

Organizations set up tables under newly installed canopies in the public square, groups such as the Polish-American Congress opened food booths, and farmers sold fresh vegetables. Here again, we found Susan Strovinski working at a booth, and we saw some other familiar faces among the local participants, who brought half-prepared foods and cooked them on-site with electric heaters and cookers. Nonlocal vendors also opened booths. A Polish dancing group, seemingly semi-professional, was invited from Milwaukee to perform on the street, and a local dancing group also participated. One family had apparently traveled from a distant town to set up a booth to sell Polish food.

For the local volunteers working on the festival, the event turned out to be problematic for several reasons. First, it was not well organized. On festival day, there were electrical problems, so people who needed to cook on-site could not begin preparing soon enough before the opening time. Second, the inclusion of outside groups, whether invited or not, was not well received by local participants. People who came just to see the event did not realize that there would be some commercial booths. However, local participants who were working for the booths felt strange about the aforementioned family, who seemed to be professional ethnic food vendors. The fare they sold did not look homemade, but it served commercial purposes. Each piece of their food, especially cabbage rolls, was smaller in size and neater in shape than the local, homemade food, indicating that they must have been commercially prepared. Nevertheless, people bought food from them because the price was reasonably low and because they had prepared enough to serve a large number, whereas local volunteers could not do so. Brown and Mussell (1984) argue that ethnic food contributes to group identity, but in Riverfront, ethnic food seems not to do so. Polish food is regarded as homemade family food, not commercial food; therefore there are no Polish restaurants in Riverfront.

Immediately after the Polish Festival had ended, its primary organizer, the director of the Riverfront Chamber of Commerce, left town to take a position in another town. This change did not help the festival's image at all, and she had left without saying anything to the people involved in the event. The director had tried the idea of using the town's past heritage for the town's future, which is in some cases successfully used in large cities (Wallace, 1956). The director also might have taken an example from the ethnic festivals held at larger cities for her project without taking local contexts into account, perhaps because she was not a native Riverfrontan and not familiar with the local context.

After the festival, some of the local participants realized that their attitude toward their cultural heritage was different from that of the event's organizer. They had been asked to participate in the event through the organizations in which they belonged, and those organizations had been asked to open food booths by the festival organizer. They believed that the festival would be joyful and fun and that it would be a good way for people to experience the richness and flavor of their culture. The local participants worked hard to make the ethnic food, as far as we could tell by tasting it, the locally prepared food was very good. For the local participants, use of the past in the form of the Polish Festival should not include any commercialism or involvement by outsiders. For them, use of the past means bringing a sense of cultural richness from among themselves by preparing good food, dancing, and local music. However, the festival is, by definition, open to the public, and this openness inevitably brings strangers and business-oriented people from the outside.

The Polish Festival inadvertently demonstrated different perceptions of the local community and its past. Nonlocal and business-oriented people might have believed that the local ethnic heritage was long lost or subsumed in modern Riverfront, and they might have thought that the revival of cultural practices makes the community vital. These ideas conflicted with local people's cultural ideas and practices in that the local participants are not comfortable with treating their cultural heritage as part of commercial activity. The Polish Festival shows that commercialism and celebrations of ethnicity do not mix well in the local context.

Church Festivals and Events

Other occasions on which ethnicity is manifested are the church-sponsored festivals and events, which are usually open to the public. They are often held during the summer season but also occur at different times during the year. They are run by church members whose time and energy are donated. The main purpose of these events is fund-raising for the operation of church and church schools and sometimes for donations to local community service organizations. In addition to a main dinner, games such as bingo or craft fairs are often held together, along with food booths. During events held at the Catholic church, usually an enclosed corner is

Figure 18. A church festival at a rural Catholic church, August 1985.

designated for selling beer and snacks. On this occasion, drinking is tolerated and symbolically marked as an essential part of the festival (Figure 18).

The public learns of these church festivals and dinner parties through advertisements in local newspapers. Thus, people who are not affiliated with the church, like ourselves, can know when and where these events are going to be held. The following are examples of the newspaper announcements.

<u>Catholic church</u>
> St. Thomas' Catholic Church Centennial Banquet
> Sunday, November 25, 1984
> We invite all former members and friends of the parish and all current members to come celebrate with us in this banquet of joy and thanksgiving.
> Tickets: $12.00 each

<u>Lutheran church</u>
> Bethany Lutheran Church   LUTEFISK SUPPER
> Friday, Dec. 5 — 4:30-8:30   Adults $7 Under 12 $3
> Preschoolers Free Baked Goods Available

<u>Protestant church</u>
> St. Paul's United Methodist Harvest Fair
> Saturday, October 18
> The fair will feature the Green Thumb, the book Barn, the County Store, the Craft and Christmas Corner, Granny's Attic and, the newest room, the Kids Corner. People also may bid on items during a silent auction.
>
> Luncheon will be served from 11 a.m.-1 p.m. The menu includes hot dishes, salads, rolls, beverages and desserts. The public is welcome and child care will be provided.

From these announcements, we came to know that expressions like "friends of parishioners" and "the public is welcome" are used to emphasize a church's willingness to accept everyone who is interested. Also, by noting the fee for meals, we understand that the main purpose of these events is fund-raising. In Riverfront a full dinner costs from $3 to $4 in family restaurants, so these meals are indeed expensive. Meals are prepared beforehand and then cooked by female church members in the kitchen attached to the hall, which usually is located in the basement. The most notable feature of these events is that the dinner is often served in family style: people sitting at long tables and taking food items from large plates and bowls shared among everyone.

Various food items, including ethnic entrées, are served. For example, at a dinner festival at a Polish Catholic church, the meal consisted of chicken-dumpling soup, duck-blood soup (czarnina), rye bread, pierogi, sausage and sauerkraut, raised doughnuts (ponchka), herring, pickles, potato salad, coleslaw, and coffee. The dinner cost $15 per person. The chicken-dumpling soup, czarnina, pierogi, and ponchka in particular are popular items used in meals represented as "Polish."

One Lutheran church on the border between Pine County and the neighboring county holds an annual event unlike any other Lutheran church in the area. In October 1985, we visited this church, which was located near where many immigrants from Norway had settled. The church held a special dinner called the "Lutefisk Dinner." *Lutefisk* is a traditional Norwegian cuisine: dried cod from the North Sea soaked in a lye solution. Besides lutefisk, the dinner includes meatballs, *lefse* (a soft, unleavened bread made of potatoes and flour, which looks like a thin potato pancake), butter, cranberries, mashed potatoes, coleslaw, pickles, pastries (rosettes, *fattigmann, krumkake,* and *sandbakkelse*), and coffee. Even the paper placemats had illustrations of how to cook lutefisk (Figures 19 and 20).

The Lutefisk Dinner is held not merely for celebration but, of course, for fund-raising. In the *Riverfront Daily Journal,* one of the congregation's historians reported the dinner's background:

> Lutherans have sponsored fund-raising dinners at Northwood for 80 years.
>
> In the early days chicken was served, but since 1915 the main course has been lutefisk. The dinners have only been canceled once or twice — because of a flu epidemic and shortage of potatoes during World War I. . . .
>
> Proceeds of the earliest dinners went toward the cost of building the quaint, white church with its tall spire. Today, the proceeds help maintain the landmark that stands amidst a grove of mature pines.

When we arrived at the dinner, there was a long line of about 100 people waiting in the church's main hall, where regular services are held. More people were coming after us, and the church basement had space to serve only about 60 people at a time. As we waited with our 3-month-old son in Toshi's arms, an elderly man approached us. After commenting on the weather, the church, and the dinner, he asked, "Have you baptized your baby yet?" Apparently he never doubted that we are Christians, just like the apartment owner who asked us which church we attended, or perhaps he believed all the people in this world should be baptized. Before asking this question, he had not asked us what our religion was or even

Figure 19. Kitchen volunteers prepare to serve at the Lutefisk Dinner held at a Norwegian church in Northwood. (Photograph taken in October 1985.)

Figure 20. Lutefisk Dinner served family-style in the church basement. Mariko is on the left. (Photograph taken in October 1985.)

which church we attended. He was a member of this Lutheran church, and he carves gravestones for a living. He is also a lay minister, which explains why several days later, and much to our surprise, he appeared at our door, still recommending that we baptize our baby.

At last the time came for our group of diners to go down to the basement and be served. The two of us were seated at a large table with two other couples who looked to be in their 30s. They commented on our baby, and we talked about the food we were eating. Then, one of the men said, "You know, we eat all this stuff. But, we are not really Norwegians." Another man said, "What do you mean we are not 'really' Norwegians?" "Well, OK. we are Polish. You know what I'm talking about?" Mariko said, "It's OK. We go to church festivals to eat pierogies." "Ha, ha, ha. You got the idea!" This conversation was interesting because in ordinary conversation, people rarely mention their ethnic identities. The fact that we look different must have made him guess that we were there to eat an exotic food. But then, he also realized that the food was not part of his ethnic heritage, either. Church festivals indeed attract outsiders to the church. In this sense, ethnic food could be a medium for eliminating the divisions among people.

A Plan of International Fair at Jefferson Center

Pam Sorenson, the Jefferson Center director, seems to represent the ideal American woman: healthy, joyful, attractive, concerned, educated, and "culturally sensitive." The last attribute is key to our analysis because it is shared by other caregivers in different ways. Pam's cultural sensitivity is demonstrated by the ways she highlights cultural themes and makes them central to the programs that she organizes. For example, each year a large fir tree is brought into the main hall of the senior center in early December, and Pam organizes a Christmas tree-trimming party. The year we attended, Pam asked William Taylor to play the organ for the occasion, and she prepared homemade cookies and drinks. She read Christmas stories and led a group in a discussion of their feelings at Christmas time. In the middle of this party, Pam asked Barsha, one of elderly women, to sing "Silent Night" in Polish. Pam said, "Thank you for sharing, Barsha" after she had finished. "Now, how about Silent Night in German?" Mrs. Henke happened to be there; she speaks English with a German accent. (Toshi knew her from when he rode on a Jefferson Center's bus for the elderly, and he had heard her speaking German.) After she had sung the song, Pam asked us if we would sing "Silent Night" in Japanese. We did, and when had we finished, Pam said, "Isn't it wonderful to listen to the same song in different languages. Thank you everybody for sharing."

Ethnic themes were not always the main focus of programs at the senior center. One afternoon we stayed for awhile talking with staff and volunteers after we had finished in the kitchen. A meeting was to take place in the dining hall, and we were invited to join. It was a meeting regularly held by the meal site advisory council, which consists of four or five volunteers who work at the meal site, including Maggie Smith, meal site manager; Doris Meyher, part-time assistant manager; and Cheryl Kline, director of the meal program. Although her job does not involve meal programs, Pam Sorenson also attended because she wanted to co-sponsor a special event with the meal site people.

At the meeting, Pam proposed "International Day" as a possible event. She said it should be organized as the first fund-raising activity for the senior center programs after the recent budget cut of the Commission on Aging. By "International Day," Pam meant to serve ethnic foods such as lutefisk, because Pam's cultural background is Scandinavian. In subsequent discussions, Mike Sorenka, birthday-cake maker at this meal site (he had told us another time that he is half Polish), suggested that Polish participants serve czarnina, or duck-blood soup, a well-known Polish food. Cheryl responded to this suggestion by pointing out that many prospective participants are Polish-Americans and may not appreciate czarnina being served because the soup tastes differently from family to family.

In a response to Pam's proposal, we offered to participate by bringing some Japanese food. The time was coming when we would have to leave and we wanted to thank people for the help that they had given us during our stay. Elza Gagas, a retired elementary school teacher with a Polish background and a longtime fellow volunteer in the kitchen, confirmed that our intention in preparing our own ethnic foods was to express our thanks to the people of Riverfront. Everyone seemed to understand our motivations; however, again, Cheryl made a very practical point: It would be too much work for us to prepare a complete set of Japanese food for lunchtime, and it also might cost us too much. She also noted that realistically people might not appreciate Japanese food. Therefore, she suggested that we make one kind of Japanese food for either a dessert or appetizer.

The event that eventually took place was called "Strawberry Fair," and the idea of an international theme was dropped. Although people appreciated cultural themes, the idea of sharing culturally specific foods seemed inappropriate for an event at the senior center. Cheryl was correct in saying that the taste of czarnina is different from family to family. Those whom we asked about czarnina-making said, "My mother used prunes a lot." "I don't use lots of dry fruit. If you use lots of dry fruit, the soup becomes too sweet." "People use Kubaba (allspice) here. But people never use it in Poland."

In addition to these intragroup differences, intergroup differences also should be considered. Cheryl certainly knew this, although she did not say so. For instance, although czarnina soup might attract many Polish-Americans, including the elderly, to rural fund-raising events such as dinner festivals or church festivals, it might not appeal to people of non-Polish descent. The following example illustrates this point: Kitchen volunteers were eating, as usual, before the noon meal program began. Bonnie Kelner, a non-Polish volunteer, said, "I don't understand why people eat blood soup," responding to other volunteers' remarks about czarnina. Elza Gagas quickly retorted that czarnina is part of Polish culture. Nobody spoke for awhile. Other Polish-Americans at the table seemed to silently agree with her.

At the senior center, serving ethnic food does not really have the same result as it does at the local university, where a certain number of international students attend. Pam, who is the wife of a university professor, may think that sharing diverse ethnic food at the senior center will have the same positive effects she has seen at the university. However, Cheryl believes that sharing standard American food minimizes differences among participants at the senior center. It is unlike the singing of "Silent Night," where although people sang in different languages, the melody was always the same. In contrast, the same "food" does not mean the same to people of different cultural backgrounds. Sharing common American food is important in the context of caring at the senior center.

AREA MAP OF NATIONALITY AND ETHNIC IDENTIFICATION

We now examine the cognitive maps of ethnicity held by Riverfront residents in order to understand how they situate themselves in the wider geographical context. Area cognition is a good indicator of the self and collective identity. People seem to have a good geographical sense of the central Wisconsin area around Riverfront mainly because they often have relatives in the area, they move around in the area for business and personal needs, and they have access to radio and television broadcasting, which covers the area.

How can we ask about area cognition in interviews? If we want to know what geographical areas people in Riverfront know, we can simply ask them yes or no questions about their knowledge of the towns scattered in the area. We did not ask such questions, however, because we wanted to collect ethnographic data. So, in our interviews we began by sharing town names in the area. We prepared for interviews as follows: First, we compiled a list of 30 town names within a circle, which we arbitrarily drew on a map. The circle was wider north-to-south because we assumed that traffic on a north-south highway is heavier than on an east-west highway. Second, we looked for appropriate terms to ask about characteristics of different towns. *Nationality* is a way of identifying people, at least in the Midwest. So, we decided to use it instead of *ethnicity* or *ethnic background* in conversations and interviews. Finally, we chose people to interview from among those whom we had interviewed or at least met before to ensure having receptive individuals of different cultural backgrounds. It turned out that the four people selected were all elderly people: John Biza (65), Polish-American; Anna Belle (73), Polish-American; Sophie LeRoi (70s), Irish and French-American; and Veronica Lotten (70s), Norwegian-American. When we interviewed Veronica, her husband, who is also Norwegian-American, sometimes participated. All interviewees had lived in the Riverfront area most of their lives.

We followed two procedures during our interviews: (1) To learn whether the interviewees knew anything about the inhabitants of the selected towns, we asked them what kinds of people lived in each town; and (2) to understand how the interviewees characterize the people in selected towns, we let them use their own words. This relates to issues of how people identify others and the kinds of categories they use to do so.

Nationality

Nationality is the word interviewees used to describe their backgrounds. When we asked about their cultural or ethnic background, they responded by saying, "Do you want to know where my folks (or family) came from?" After hearing such responses several times, we simplified our question to, "What is your nationality?"

TABLE 7. NATIONALITIES DESIGNATED BY INTERVIEWEES IN DESCRIBING THE TOWNS

"Nationality"	John	Anna	Sophie	Veronica
Polish	X	X	X	X
Scandinavian	X		X	X
German	X		X	X
English	X	X		
Polish + Scandinavian	X			X
Russian	X			
Dutch	X			
Irish	X			
French			X	
Mixture	X	X		X

or "Where did your grandparents or great-grandparents come from?" Most interviewees answered such questions by using names of European countries. A very small number of them answered by saying, "My nationality? American." This answer usually meant that we could not have a good conversation because we felt we should not ask further about their cultural backgrounds. The different nationalities that our four interviewees described partly overlapped (Table 7).

"Polish"

In our interviews, all four interviewees used the category "Polish." Two of them did so because they considered themselves Polish. The other two referred to "Polish" probably because they knew many Polish-Americans in the area.

John and Anna had almost the same distribution pattern of "Polish" towns on their cognitive maps. This suggests that older Polish-Americans share a clear cognitive map that tells them where people of the same cultural background live. However, it is difficult to say that Anna had a clear image that located the names of towns geographically. On the other hand, John had a good sense of the location of towns on a map, probably because he always consulted maps to locate towns that interested him.

Sophie and Veronica appeared to have a similar cognitive map of "Polish" towns. Sophie's cognitive map covered a slightly wider area than Veronica's and also extended farther to the north and to the south-east than Anna's. Sophie identified "Polish" towns in a few places that were farthest to the northeast, the southwest, and the west of Riverfront. Her cognitive map had the greatest range of the four interviewees probably because Sophie believes that people of Polish descent are scattered all over central Wisconsin.

"Scandinavian"

Scandinavian was not the only word interviewees used to describe the towns in our interviews. They also used Norwegian and Swedish. We lumped these three categories together under the term Scandinavian. Veronica Lotten probably used this term because we gave it to her as an example, instead of the more specific names of Danish, Norwegian, and Swedish when we explained to her the purpose of our interview. John identified "Scandinavian" towns as "Norwegian" and "Swedish." Sophie described only one town located east of Riverfront as "Norwegian." Anna did not use these labels at all.

Veronica and John appeared to have a very similar image of the places where Polish and Scandinavian people lived near each other in Pine County. Historically, Polish people first settled in the central part of Pine County and expanded toward the east. This movement apparently stopped at the county line. Scandinavian people who settled heavily in the neighboring county also had the west end of their settlement just out of their county. As a result, Polish and Scandinavian (mostly Norwegian) enclaves abutted each other. One interviewee in her 30s, a relative newcomer, said she had heard that a specific county road close to her house used to be the clear dividing line between Polish and Scandinavian farms. This is a straight road that runs north and south.

A geological map indicates that such interethnic dividing lines follow the edges of glacial moraines, which also run north and south. Soil conditions are sharply different on either side: sand in the west, the Polish side, and moraine soil in the east, the Norwegian side. Topographic differences are clear, being relatively featureless in the west and hilly in the east. Where the west side has hills, the area in which "Scandinavian" people reside is very much hilly with numerous lakes.

"English"

The word *English* appeared in both Anna's and Sophie's responses. They are friends who talk together at the meal program at the senior center and also phone each other regularly. They might have used the term *English* in their own conversations. However, we interviewed them separately on different conditions: Anna at her home one evening and Sophie in a room at the senior care center. Therefore, we do not believe that they talked with each other about how to answer our interview questions.

It is not surprising that Anna used the term *English*. Other members of Anna's circle of friends also use the word. When Anna said "English," she used it very specifically, and her friends used it as she did. For instance, during a conversation, when Toshi asked what kind of people a certain group are, she responded, "They are more English." On another occasion, she said, "My children are much more English. They are not Polish because they do not speak Polish." Similarly, although John did not use the term *English* to describe the towns in our interview, he mentioned that his only son is not Polish when Toshi asked him whether he thinks of his son as Polish. His reason is also that the son does not speak Polish. In the same manner as Anna, he thought that speaking the language of a specific nationality meant belonging to that nationality. If a person speaks English rather than the parents' or the grandparents' native tongue, this person is considered English according to John's and Anna's ways of thinking.

"German"

All interviewees except Anna used the label *German*. People of German descent are generally predominant in Wisconsin, including its central part. However, this fact was not obvious to us because we have not heard of any "German Festival," "German American Congress," "German-American Veteran's Association," German classes at the public library, or German restaurants (one restaurant served German food but advertised itself as serving "continental" food). This invisibility of all things German gave us the impression that people of German heritage are currently on "backstage," whereas people of Polish heritage are on "center stage," although no Polish restaurants existed in the Riverfront area at the time of our stay, as noted earlier. Consequently, our understanding of "German" immigrants is that they have for the most part merged with the "majority" or mainstream Americans. Nevertheless, we know that there must be differences among them. We saw a few elder individuals speaking German, or English with German accents, and we heard others refer to these people as German.

In our interview, Anna did not use the term *German* to identify townspeople, although she did hold a concept of "German." On another occasion, when we asked her about family names in the neighborhood where her parents had settled, she said, "They are German," and when we talked about the nationalities of her friends, she said such things as, "Her name is German." She also explained differences among Polish-Americans by saying that her father's "side" was Russian-Polish and her mother's "side" was German-Polish. We wondered then what made Anna avoid using the term *German* in answers to our questions about residents of the towns in central Wisconsin. She probably judged ethnicity based on her understanding of the languages that people speak. She does not know of any towns whose inhabitants speak German daily. This reflects the fact that German-speaking people stopped speaking German and began to speak English during World Wars I and II. At those times, "German-ness" dissolved, at least in some people's minds. Superficially, German-Americans seem to be much freer from ethnic jokes and stigmatization than people of other nationalities.

Other Nationalities

Dutch, Russian, and *Irish* appeared only in John's responses, *French* only in Sophie's, and *Welsh* and *Danish* only in Veronica's. Dutch towns were seen as clustering in the southeast of Riverfront. John often mentioned to Toshi that Russian people lived in towns located between Riverfront and the next larger city to the north. He knew this because he had heard it from his father who had worked there when John was very young. He also talked about the Irish when he described his parent's homestead farm. There had been Irish farmers in that neighborhood, but most of them left long ago. In fact, although few in number, farms with Irish names like McGill and O'Brian still exist in the area.

Sophie identified one town to the south of Riverfront as "French." Because we had never before heard of a French community in central Wisconsin, we were curious as to how she knew about it. Among the four interviewees, only Sophie has French ancestry. She said that her background is Irish and French. She may know of towns in which a certain number of French-Americans live. She may have learned this from her parents or their friends, or she may have had encounters with French-American customers when she operated a clothing store in Riverfront.

Veronica and her husband, Malcom, identified two towns as Welsh and Danish, respectively. This couple seemed to know more about the towns to the east of Riverfront than the others. During the interview, they would discuss the nationalities of their acquaintances who resided in the particular town in question. They considered one town Welsh because they knew some individual there who were Welsh. Another town was considered Danish for corresponding reasons. One of our younger interviewees (in her 30s) had been born in one of the counties next to Pine County, the west part of which is inhabited by Scandinavian-Americans, as we have seen. She told us that although many Scandinavian-Americans live in the county where she was born, the number of Danish-Americans is very small.

Bohemian does not appear in any of our interviewees' answers. However, it is a word John and Judy used in conversations with us outside of the interview to designate some immigrants from Bohemia who live in a predominantly Polish-American enclave north of Riverfront. Other interviewees used the word *Bohemian* as well. Anna, for example, used it in informal conversation with us, and some individuals used it when answering our questionnaires at the senior center. We sensed that the label *Bohemian* was sometimes used derogatorily.

During the last couple of decades, a sizable number of Amish immigrants have moved onto farms east of Riverfront. This area used to be considered Polish and Scandinavian farmland, and the adjoining area is still populated by people of these backgrounds. Our interviewees did not use the word *Amish,* but we believe they knew of their presence in the county. To recognize and appreciate Amish culture, a University of Wisconsin–Extension home economist for Pine County organized a special meeting of a group called "Homemakers" one afternoon in October. A woman who was closely acquainted with several Amish women made arrangements for three of them to attend the meeting and bring crafts and foods, talk about their daily lives, answer participants' questions, and finally, to demonstrate how they cook their food. This kind of event, as well as short articles in the local newspaper, including announcements for Amish quilt auctions, gave people the opportunity to learn about the Amish in Pine County. It seems true that Amish people have greater contact with the outside world than Hostetler (1993) has described. When Toshi mentioned to Anna Belle that there are Amish people living in Pine County and asked whether she knew of them, Anna replied tersely that they live on their own and that their life was different from "ours." As far as we know, the Amish have not yet established their own town in Pine County.

Native Americans were not on the list of nationalities in the four interviewees' answers because we did not include names of towns in which they live in the list of town named for the interviews. Of course, the Riverfront area was not always dominated by European-American people. John Biza remembers in his youth seeing a group of horse-riding "Indians," possibly Menominees, Chippewas, or Winnebagos, moving in the trees close to where he lives now. This suggests that they used horses to move, probably between reservations, as late as the late 1950s.

Riverfront residents used the term *migrants* to refer to those who seasonally come from elsewhere to work picking cucumbers at farms in southern Pine County. These migrants are mostly *Mexican* or *Chicano,* but people in Riverfront do not use these words, although they probably knew who the "migrants" were in terms of nationality.

Only the local newspaper columns touched on other nationalities. For instance, it was reported that the number of Vietnamese and Hmong people has increased in Portage County and the surrounding counties because of their recent immigration to the United States. Local newspapers report on these immigrants' lives and their interactions with local people. As a result, the locals know about their presence and also that many Vietnamese eventually relocate to areas with warmer climates. They believed the Vietnamese do not like the cold Wisconsin winters.

Different Perceptions of Self and Others

The four interviewees had different cognitive maps of area towns with respect to their own and others' nationalities, and at the same time, those maps overlapped each other. This overlapping is clearest in the category "Polish," and it is a geographical overlap; that is, although the four shared conceptual understandings of people and place, at the same time, their cognitive map had different shapes. These differences stem from how the interviewees thought about themselves and others.

To understand the factors in differentiating cognitive maps, the cultural background of each interviewee must be considered. The general explanation that people know the most about their own ethnic group conforms to part of the interview data. John and Anna, both Polish, described the greatest number of towns as predominantly Polish; however, the data show variations in other areas, such as the number of nationalities identified and categories of nationalities. Moreover, after putting the data on maps, the distribution patterns of ethnic groups show variations in the association of specific place with specific nationality. These variations suggest that we need another explanation for variations.

The issue we wish to raise is not about which interviewees are smartest or which are able to handle more complex categorical operations in their minds. We want to reveal meanings that are shaped by life experiences and interpretations based on those experiences. Why did John know so many different nationalities, whereas Anna knew only a few? What did *English* mean for Anna and Sophie? What did *mixed* or *mixture* mean for John and Veronica? What was the relationship between *English* and *mixture* for Anna?

To answer these questions, it is useful to examine the domains that anthropology has conventionally studied: gender, work, and kin networks. Gender differences explain to a certain extent differences in knowledge about different nationalities. In communities with traditional sex role expectations, men work outside the home and have more chances to talk with other people — both men and women from different areas. Women who work in the home have fewer chances to talk with different people. Men are more likely know about people in different places through business transactions, whereas women are somewhat limited to family and kin networks. Anna tried to determine the nationality of people in a particular place by thinking of it as the place where her granddaughter lived after getting married. Men, of course, also use these networks. For instance, John learned about people in the north from his father who went there to work. Generally, however, men have more detailed knowledge of people and places. Compare John to Anna and Sophie or Veronica to her husband, who had assisted her in the interview; he was a retired salesman. These men had more chances to move around in their work, at least within central Wisconsin. In short, gender expectations are closely related to differences in work experiences in this community.

The different uses of *English* between Anna and Sophie were probably influenced by the differences in their work experience. Anna tended to categorize everyone in the area surrounding Riverfront as "English." For the same group, Sophie used two categories: "English" and "German." Although Anna worked for several years when as a young woman, she spent most of her life as a housewife. In contrast, Sophie had owned a store for some years in the area. She likely had more chances to interact with German people. Nevertheless, her use of *English* is interesting in understanding the symbolism attached to this word. Why did she use *English* rather than *American,* to represent the mainstream population in American culture?

English people are generally assumed to speak English. This is the basis for Anna's understanding of "self" and "the other." Her self is Polish, and others are English because they speak English, even though she herself is forgetting the Polish language. This sentiment also appeared in Sophie's use of *English.* However, John did not use *English* to describe others, although he admits that his son is not Polish but rather English because he cannot speak Polish. To John, English is penetrating into his understanding of people and place and English-speaking is the practice of people in the mainstream.

What is a "mixture" then? It is a realistic description of the ethnicity of people in Riverfront and its environs. John, Anna, and Veronica try to be honest in answering our questions, and therefore they have difficulty identifying a place with only one or two "nationalities" of people living there exclusively. However, this is the predominant condition of American society. It describes the complexity of towns and small cities. In short, "ethnic" communities and "general American" communities coexist in people's cognitive maps.

NOTES ON SELF-IDENTITY AMONG "POLISH" PEOPLE

Although there are studies of Polish-Americans in Wisconsin and in other states, few have touched on the everyday language they use to describe themselves and others (Buczek, 1980; Fox, 1970; Lopata, 1976; Madaj, 1968; Mikos, 1980; Siekaniec, 1957; Wytrawal, 1961, 1969). We shall examine such language to understand the ways Polish people express their identity and identify others according to their ethnic backgrounds. By focusing on Polish people, we will gain insights into the diversity of ethnic identities among Americans (cf. Royce, 1982).

"German-Polish"

Among the mixed nationalities mentioned by Riverfront residents, "German-Polish" has unique characteristics and is worth noting. As with other nationalities, the category of "Polish" has subcategories, based on regional, linguistic, and politicohistorical differences. These three categories combine to create three major subgroups: "German-Polish," "Russian-Polish," and "Austrian-Polish." These three names derived from the three nations that had occupied three different parts of Poland. We learned these three terms from history textbooks, literature, and university professors. We have not heard the term *Austrian-Polish* used by people in Riverfront. The term *German-Polish* seems to be well known, but *Russian-Polish* is also nearly unknown.

German-Polish may have another meaning: interviewees who describe themselves as such have one Polish-American parent and one German-American parent. Sophie uses double nationalities to describe herself as "Irish-French." Toshi once asked Linda Ronaszak, who lives with Joe Dobczek, whether she was Polish. She instantly said, "Ah, No. I'm German-Polish." She and Joe travel to Los Angeles to visit his sister about once a year. She is probably more aware of the status of "Polish" people in big cities than in Riverfront. Therefore, as a response to Toshi's (a total stranger's) question, she may have chosen the safest label rather than identify herself solely as "Polish." Later, in conversation with Mariko, she talked about her family's Polish ways of doing things, such as cooking, compared with her boyfriend's family, so she could identify herself as "Polish." Also, it is true that one of her parents is German, so she could identify herself as "German-Polish."

"Polack"

John and his wife, Judy, often used the word *Polack* to identify themselves. According to a dictionary, *Polack* is American slang for "a person of Polish descent or birth. An offensive term used derogatorily." Why did they use a derogatory word to refer to themselves? The use of *Polack* by people of Polish descent is not unique to John and Judy. Other Polish-American interviewees also use it, although less often. They apparently know that the word is derogatory in the context of American society. Even on TV, we heard a participant in a game show say "Polack" when she introduced herself. The host then asked her if she liked pierogi and kielbasa, and she smiled affirmatively.

The use of this word by people of Polish descent suggests that the word has meanings that have been shaped in America and also that the meanings have been reshaped by Polish-Americans in response to the meanings non-Polish people associate with it. When using the derogatory word, Polish-Americans seem not to lose their self-esteem but rather to challenge the mainstream culture. This challenge may be constructive in the sense that Polish-Americans may identify themselves as such by appropriating an American-slung word as their own (cf. Goffman, 1963). For those who use the word, the ideas and values in the mainstream culture (e.g., individualism) are in conflict with their own (e.g., family-oriented). At the same time, mainstream culture allows people to express their own ethnic identities. Expressive use of the derogatory word suggests that Polish-Americans are engaging in cultural dialog with the American mainstream. In this sense, ethnic humor prevails as the word's original meaning is transformed (Boskin & Dorinson, 1985).

"Strange" and "Nobody"

Like other ethnic groups in the United States, Polish-Americans are not cut from a single cloth. As we have seen, they originate from different regions of Europe. They also belong to different classes, which generally fit the standard American class structure of high, middle, and low. We can also use occupations as criteria for describing subgroups among Polish-Americans in Riverfront. Occupational types may include professionals, white-collar workers, and blue-collar workers. For example, there are several Polish-American professors at the local university, a few medical doctors, many nurses, school teachers, and factory and office workers. However, most Polish-Americans appear to be employed by mills and factories.

How do Polish-Americans differentiate themselves within the Polish community? "Strange" is one description they use. Joe, the Polish-American landlord of the house we eventually rented, responded to Toshi's question of whether he knew about a certain neighbor by saying, "He is strange." Before that question, Toshi had asked him the neighbor's name. Joe paused before replying that his name was Biza, a Polish name. We would not have given his pause a second thought if he had not said that the man was strange. The neighbor's name was not easily accessible to Joe at the time we asked probably because he did not think about him much. The word *strange* indicates his attitude about this neighbor.

Interestingly, John Biza described Joe as "strange" as well when Toshi had visited him to talk about the neighborhood. Toshi was curious about how John would describe Joe. He knew about Joe's family in the countryside, who lives in the same area as John's brother's family. When Toshi mentioned that Joe shot squirrels in his backyard, John had his own explanation for this. Squirrels once entered Joe's house and devastated some rooms, so Joe tried to shoot them. John believed that Joe's "strangeness" came from his family. John talked about what Joe's uncle once did with his baby. When it was born, the uncle grew angry because it was not a boy and threw the baby outside into the snow. John concluded that the family "got something." John apparently interpreted Joe's behavior in light of his uncle's behavior.

"I am nobody" is another expression for identifying oneself among the Polish-Americans we interviewed. This expression is used in contrast to nobility. John knows that there used to be nobility in Poland and that his immediate ancestors did not come from such a class. Nobilities are acknowledged as such, whereas commoners are referred to as nobody. In the American context, *nobody* means out of the mainstream. These ways of self-identification seem to be the same among other ethnic groups, not only in the United States but also in other countries. However, what makes Polish-Americans in Riverfront unique is that they are the predominant ethnic group in the area; therefore, they seem to be less stigmatized than their counterparts living in larger urban areas such as Boston (Morawska, 1977), Los Angeles (Sandberg, 1974), and Pittsburgh (Bodnar, Weber, & Simon, 1979).

Young Polish-Americans do not even seem to be aware of their "Polish-ness." For instance, senior Polish-Americans consider chicken soup an important part of Polish cuisine, but younger people think of it as a universal food. Of course, chicken soup is not unique to Polish cuisine, but the meaning attached to chicken soup differs between the old and the young. In response to her husband's comment that chicken soup is Polish, Michelle Stanke (a "Polish" woman in her 20s who married an Italian-American from Milwaukee) said, "It's universal." Michelle herself appears to have a slight Polish accent, but she mentioned that her parents have not made Polish food much.

INTERPRETATION

We have examined the occasions and identities in which "ethnicity" is manifested. We have seen costumes, dancing, and food used as symbols of ethnic heritage. When groups — religious and nonreligious — organize events, they use these symbols to highlight their differences, uniqueness, and, indeed, their exoticism as compared with their daily lives. In other words, people use these ethnic symbols strategically to manifest cultural depth and diversity in the community. We have also seen how terms marking nationality and personal categorization are used to identify others and selves among local people. Even derogatory terms are strategically used to situate individuals in the society. Meanings of these terms transform over time, both locally and nationally.

What are the purposes of using these ethnic symbols? One explanation is to strengthen group identity, especially ethnic identity. In the case of Riverfront, do these symbols work to this end, as, for example, among Polish-Americans or Norwegian-Americans? Our answer would be no. As we have seen, the purpose of these "ethnic" occasions is fund-raising in support of an organization's activities. These activities include daily church or school operation, and their aim is providing medical and monetary aid to some group. For example, proceeds of the *Wigilia,* sponsored by the local chapter of the Polish-American Congress, were used to buy medicine to be sent to Poland. Holding the *Wigilia* does not seem to strengthen ethnic identity among local Polish-Americans. If ethnic symbols strengthen anything, it must be the identity of the sponsoring organizations rather than ethnic identity. Many of these organizations, including churches, hold ethnic events, but the participants include people of other ethnic backgrounds. In such events, ethnic symbols are used as attractions to induce people to attend, rather than reinforcing ethnic identity among people. Anyone may be invited, and the events are held for a good cause, that is, helping others.

What about the ambivalence that people showed toward the Polish Festival? The purpose of church festivals and the *Wigilia* is much clearer than that of the Polish Festival. In the latter, there was no sense of helping others. Helping the "Riverfront Community" or even "downtown businesses" may have been a motivation, but that would have been too ambiguous for local people. Even if that were the festival's purpose, highlighting only Polish culture and ignoring other ethnic groups would not be appropriate, given the local ethnic mix. It seemed the outsiders' participation helped heighten alienation among the local people.

CHAPTER 6 / "Your Baby Will Be Half-Polish": Changing Relationships with Riverfrontans

Anthropologists in the field often reach a turning point at which the nature of the relationship with their interviewees changes dramatically. For us, the turning point was the birth of our son. Throughout Mariko's pregnancy, our interviewees' attitudes toward us changed. We became less like strangers and more like friends. The change was most noticeable among the elderly people at Jefferson Center, where we worked as volunteers in the meal program. In this chapter, we describe the events surrounding our son's birth in Riverfront and how this affected our relationships with our interviewees, friends and acquaintances in Riverfront.

OUR INVOLVEMENT AT JEFFERSON CENTER

Every Friday, we volunteered at the Jefferson Center kitchen and helped with their meal program for about 18 months (November 1984 to June 1986). The center's staff was very accommodating to our research efforts and helped us meet many elderly people at the center. As stated earlier, Jefferson Center was managed by the Pine County Commission on Aging to provide the elderly a place to participate in various programs. In the late 1970s, Pine County chose the site of Jefferson School, an old grade school, for the new senior center. By retaining the name of the school, it was expected that elderly patrons could easily locate the center. Jefferson Center also serves as a public community center because of its proximity to Riverfront's downtown area.

As is the case at senior centers throughout the nation, the Jefferson Center meal program was considered the most important of its services for elderly people. It ensured them a nutritionally balanced meal at least once a day, thus helping them maintain independent lives, and provided opportunities to socialize with other elderly people (Fujita, 1984; Myerhoff, 1980). Like other senior centers, no set fee was charged for meals. Instead, patrons would give donations, paying whatever amount they thought was appropriate. In this way, everyone could afford a meal, regardless of income level.

Lunch time is a major activity at Jefferson Center. From 65 to 130 people eat lunch at the center on any given day, and the dining hall occupies almost a half of the center's space. Food is not cooked on-site but is brought in from a local school kitchen. The program staff takes reservations so that Maggie Smith, meal site manager, can order the proper amount of food. Four to six elderly volunteers help Maggie. The meal program operates several meal sites at small towns in Pine County. Each meal site has a manager and volunteers who help serve lunch 2 or 3 days a week, depending on the site's schedule.

From 10:30 a.m. to 1:30 p.m., volunteers work on the following: wrapping eating utensils in paper napkins; setting tables with the wrapped utensils, coffee cups, bowls of butter, and flowers; cleaning up the kitchen; making coffee in a large coffee maker; putting butter on sliced bread and cutting each slice in half; receiving cooked food delivered by one of the Commission's bus drivers; and putting the food into pans to keep warm until serving time. Then they sit down together and eat their own meals before other participants enter the dining room. During this time, Friday volunteers, usually six women, sometimes one man, and ourselves, receive the day's serving assignments from Maggie, for example: Pauline, potatoes; Katie, bread; Elza, fish; Bonnie, pudding; Helen, milk; Toshi, salad; and Mariko, coffee. Volunteers prepare for each position, except for Josephine, the day's hostess, who opens the door to the dining hall and stands there to welcome people.

One volunteer becomes the hostess each day, except when Maggie determines that two hostesses are needed. After eating earlier with the other volunteers, the hostess checks with the center's receptionist to see how many people have made reservations. Then, at 11:45 a.m., she opens the door to the dining hall. The hostess has a few special duties, such as overseeing accommodations for those unable to stand in line up to pick up their trays. In such cases, volunteers bring the trays to the tables where they are seated. Another duty is to greet newcomers, escort them to their seats, and explain how things are organized at the meal site.

The serving window is not yet opened as the hostess begins welcoming people. Volunteers in the kitchen peak through the kitchen door to see the day's participants, noting the number of people and any new faces. Maggie circulates among the participants, smiling and chatting and generally keeping the atmosphere of the dinning hall and kitchen convivial and enjoyable. She wants people to feel at home in this place. Some of the volunteers also circulate, serving regular and decaffeinated coffee and preparing sets of trays for those who request to be served. They serve these trays as Maggie makes announcements from the podium and then asks one of the patrons to "say grace" before the meal. The shutter to the serving window is then lifted; this is a moment when hall and kitchen are united. We are excited because we will soon interact with 80 to 100 people individually over a very short period. It is the beginning of our "real" work as volunteers (Figure 21).

In the dining hall, the table closest to the kitchen is always occupied entirely by men. While waiting for serving to begin, kitchen workers, including ourselves, always check to see if the six men who regularly sit at this table have arrived. Because of their proximity to the kitchen, we can easily talk to these men and therefore get acquainted enough to ask some of them for an interview (see Chapter 9).

Figure 21. Kitchen volunteers preparing to serve lunch at the Jefferson Center. (Photograph taken in December 1985.)

Whenever a regular occupant of this table does not show up, another man fills in the vacant seat. During the entire time we volunteered at the Jefferson Center kitchen, we have never saw a woman sit at this table. The other 12 to 15 tables are occupied either entirely by women or by a mixture of several women and a few men.

As the serving window is opened, the hostess goes to the podium to call on the tables one at a time to get in line, take a food tray, and proceed to the serving counter. After serving all of the diners, the kitchen volunteers remain at their stations, waiting on those who come back for seconds. Before long, diners at the first tables served have finished their meals and begun returning their trays to the kitchen window. Volunteers then rinse the trays and dishes before putting them in a dishwasher, wipe up trays and cups, and generally clean up. After the work, the volunteers record their hours worked on a record sheet, chat a bit with Maggie, and then leave the kitchen at about 1:30 p.m. The hours are totaled once a year and used by the Retired Senior Volunteer Program (RSVP) to acknowledge volunteers' contributions to the program. Those volunteers who have accumulated a certain number of hours, such as 200 or 300, are officially honored. They usually pose for a photograph together, which may appear in the local newspaper.

We came to know many Polish-American women through working at the Jefferson Center kitchen. Among them was Anna Belle, one of our key sources of information. She has volunteered at the meal program since it began at a previous location downtown, before Jefferson Center was constructed. Through Anna, Katie Karenski, her younger sister, and Katie's sister-in-law, Pauline Karenski, also became kitchen volunteers. Katie started volunteering after her husband had passed away. Although Anna was not part of our Friday group, Katie and Pauline were.

Other co-workers, also Polish-American, were Elza Gagas, a retired school teacher, and Anita Karenski. Elza had taught Pauline in the 1920s when one-room grade schools were common all around the county. Anita was the oldest of our group, and Elza often picked her up at her house in North Side. In addition to ourselves and the women, two Polish-American men occasionally helped. One of them was a retired farmer who had never married. The other taught ceramics at the center and baked cakes for the center's monthly birthday party. Other volunteers who worked in the kitchen on the other days of the week were of Scandinavian, Lithuanian, German, and Scottish descent. Most of the volunteers would come to Jefferson Center to have meals on their days off.

In the dining hall, we noticed that people sat in the family style but did not exactly eat in this style. They used a "portion meal" style, in which each partici-pant would take a certain amount of several types of food: meat, vegetables, pack-aged milk, bread, and dessert. Some items were shared with four to six persons at the same table, and these included pots of coffee, butter on plates, and small pots of milk for coffee.

At one time, we suggested to Cheryl Kline, director of the meal program, that diners might be interested in eating in the more traditional family style. Instead of lining up at the serving window and taking an individual tray in the cafeteria style, one big platter of meat, a large bowl of vegetables, and so forth could be placed at each table so that the diners could pass them around. Each person would take a portion from the large plate. We believed that people in the area were familiar with family-style dining because we knew that Maple Day Care Center used the family style for their lunches. Moreover, we knew that local churches in rural areas would organize special ethnic dinners in the family style, as we have seen in Chapter 5.

Director Kline, however, told us that eating in the family style was not a good idea for the Jefferson Center for several reasons. First, in the portion-meal style, putting all food items on every tray ensures that everyone will have a nutritionally balanced meal at least once a day. In the family style, people can take only what they like. The director thought the portion-meal style also made it easier to calcu-late the necessary portions and thus minimize food waste. This method also can accommodate individual needs. People can ask serving volunteers to decrease the amount of a specific food item, or they can take seconds after everyone has been served. Those who require salt- or sugar-reduced items can be accommodated without being conspicuous to others. For purposes of socializing, the family style seems to work better. However, because health and medical conditions among patrons of the senior center vary widely, the portion-meal style is better suited to meet their needs.

PREGNANCY AND CHANGES IN PEOPLE'S ATTITUDES

One Friday in January, we arrived late at Jefferson Center because we had been to the doctor's office. We apologized to Maggie and our co-workers for being late and explained that Mariko had a doctor's appointment.

"Is everything OK?" Maggie asked.

"Yeah, we are going to have a baby!" Toshi announced.

Jean showed her excitement by making a big smile and a big gesture with her arms. Pauline, Katie, and Elza also expressed their joy upon hearing our news. Pauline and Katie looked particularly happy.

"You'll enjoy it," said Elza.

"A-ha! That's why you weren't feeling well," Maggie said. "So, it wasn't the flu!" Her daughter was also expecting a baby about that time.

"Oh, I'm so happy for you!" said Katie.

The previous week at lunch time, Mariko had not felt like having her usual cup of coffee. Katie had remarked, "It sounds like you are pregnant." Mariko was very surprised by Katie's comment and wondered how she could know. Today, Mariko reminded Katie about her comment and asked her how she knew. "Well," said Katie, "We have all experienced it, much, much earlier than you." Pregnancy created a common bond between these elderly Polish women and Mariko. Until now, the differences between us — in age, nationality, language, and custom — were always highlighted. They saw us as foreigners, with whom they regulated what they would share. However, now that Mariko was about to experience something they all had experienced, something profound and fundamental, immediately created a sense of "kinship" between us — a joy that we all could share. Katie even said, "Your baby is going to be half-Polish, because you are with us so much!"

From this point forward, these women became very expressive of their feelings toward Mariko. While we prepared the meal that morning, Pauline and Katie continually were touching Mariko and often hugged her. They were also concerned about Mariko's health. "Doesn't it make you sick?" "How is your nausea?" During cleanup, someone offered to take a heavy basket full of coffee cups that Mariko was carrying, saying, "You might hurt yourself." When they were leaving, Pauline and Katie hugged Mariko again and said, "Take it easy. We are so happy for you."

We found that it is common for people here to ask Mariko who her obstetrician was. In a midsize town such as Riverfront, there were only about five of them to choose from. When we told someone the name of her doctor, the reply was usually, "Oh, he is supposed to be a very good doctor." Mariko wondered whether this was said as a matter of courtesy or because their own and their friends' daughters, daughters-in-law, and nieces had told them about experiences with doctors when they were pregnant. Considering the relatively high fertility rate among Polish-American people, having a baby must be an often-experienced rite of passage. They probably had heard of the doctor even if they did not know much about him personally.

News of Mariko's pregnancy traveled quickly throughout Jefferson Center. The director came over to congratulate us. When telling others the news, Maggie always said, "our baby," rather than "their baby." Ruth Warner, the director of the Commission on Aging, also congratulated us, saying, "Oh, yes, we all are going to change diapers. It is a great place for having a baby, because we have so many experts."

As we stated earlier, the prospect of our having a baby marked a transition in our relationship with the people at Jefferson Center. Before, they had regarded us more or less as strangers or friendly visitors from afar. Now we were almost family. Part of this transition stemmed from the fact that our child would be born in the United States and therefore would be an American citizen. Indeed, Mariko overheard a conversation between two elderly women: "You know, the child will be an American," one said to the other. Because the child would be an American citizen, the separation by nationality between our family and the local citizens was no longer as clear-cut.

Katie, a Polish volunteer, said, "He [our son] will become 'half-Polish' because we spend so much time with "us." "Us" included Katie and her Polish-American friends. She did not hesitate to say it, even in front of Maggie Smith, a non-Polish meal site manager. "Half-Polish" implies that a person can become "Polish" to a certain degree. In other words, a certain amount of "Polish-ness" can be obtained by simply being among Polish people. Talking face-to-face, telephoning, visiting their homes, checking out a new restaurant together, exchanging small items such as clothing, and playing games (e.g., Bingo) are among the things we would do with our Polish-American interviewees to get a sense of who they are. It was an essential part of our fieldwork. Although the ethnographer's ideal goal may be eventually to become "half-Polish," our own fieldwork did not help us to become so as much as it helped our son to be seen in this way.

Here we see another meaning of the concept "half-Polish." If a person whose parents are Polish lives among Polish people from the beginning of life, this person would become fully Polish. On the other hand, if a person whose parents are not Polish starts life among Polish people, that person would become partially Polish and at the same time keep his or her own parents' identity, which, in our son Hosaki's case, is Japanese. This reflects the importance of associating with other Polish-American people in childhood. It also reflects a tendency among people of Polish descent to advocate for their own cultural identity while at the same time showing respect for and appreciation of other cultural identities. This attitude seems to be a tendency toward ethnic compromise. For example, they accept non-Polish Catholics as marriage partners because they know that the partner will become "half-Polish" sooner or later by living among other Polish relatives.

People were also interested in where Mariko was going to give a birth: here in America or in Japan. We said, "Because we have many friends, we are going to have the baby here." They were happy to know this. "Good, it's better that you two are together. Besides we can see the baby." However, when Toshi said, "Mariko's parents said okay, but my father wants her to return to Japan. He was rather upset when we said she was not coming back," there was a silent moment.

"It must have been difficult to convince him if he was upset," said Elza.

Why had they become quiet, especially after they had expressed such strong joy about our having the baby in the States? We sensed that they had taken our choice of staying here as a sign of our trust in them. They perhaps felt that having us in their family meant they would be a part of the birth of our baby. There would be a new family member, not only for us but for them as well. In any case, the prospect of the birth of our baby restructured both the nature of our relationship with our Jefferson Center interviewees and the nature of their classification of us as foreigners.

Of course, changes in people's attitudes toward us were not limited to the inside of Jefferson Center. Those who had been not particularly friendly started making an effort to talk to us after they had learned about Mariko's pregnancy. Such changes were the most marked in men's behavior toward Mariko. At a reception held at the university campus, we had a chance to speak to the Chancellor. Because his wife was a board member of Jefferson Center, Mariko told him how well she had been treating us. He asked us how much longer we were going to stay in Riverfront. Hearing that our departure was still more than 8 months away, he suddenly said, "So, the baby is going to be born here!" indicating that he had already noticed Mariko's condition. Although we had met the Chancellor before, our conversation was rather formal. As he was leaving the reception, he asked Mariko, "A boy or a girl?" She answered, "Either one is fine."

On another occasion, a board member of the senior day-care center said, "You are going to have a baby here, aren't you?" Then he suggested that if it is a boy, we should name him after the town. Another board member whom we ran into at the county fair said, "Is something growing here?" tapping his own stomach. Before Mariko's pregnancy had became apparent, these men usually spoke to Toshi first, but afterward, they started talking to Mariko in a direct and friendly way.

How are we to interpret these changes in people's attitudes? The intensely positive response to Mariko's pregnancy stems, of course, from the near universal attitude that birth is a happy event about which everyone should rejoice and be congratulatory. It also gives people something to talk about. Other changes are less easily explained. For example, in a community where middle-aged and elderly men usually talk only to other men and rarely to women in social situations, why would these men suddenly become friendly toward Mariko when they learned that she was pregnant? Our interpretation is that, to these men, a woman is a potential sexual partner, and therefore it is appropriate to avoid interacting with married women so as not to risk giving the wrong impression. It is an implicit rule. Pregnant women, however, are excluded as potential sexual partners (cf. Collier & Rosaldo, 1981) and therefore are available for social interaction with men without giving the wrong impression.

BABY SHOWER

The gesture of welcoming our baby culminated in a surprise baby shower for Mariko held in the middle of August, about a month before her due date. Apparently, the event was organized by Maggie, who obtained permission from Ruth Warner, the director of the Commission on Aging, and solicited assistance from among the participants in programs at Jefferson Center. According to Maggie, many people liked the idea and promised to help out. The fact that we were two international students having our first baby with no relatives close by must have been stressed as the shower was being organized.

The dining room was decorated with ribbons and balloons in pink and blue; pink is a symbolic color for a baby girl and blue for a baby boy. The tables and walls were covered with baby toys. A special table was reserved for gifts. Many people brought gifts and donated money to help pay for the decorations, cakes, and game prizes.

The baby shower began after the regular meal program had finished. Participants gathered around the table for gifts. Baby showers are usually organized and attended by women only, but surprisingly, many men participated in our shower. The party got under way with games, and Bonnie presided over the activities. The first game was to guess the spelling of words. Words and phrases related to birth, such as *mother nature,* were used. Next was a guessing game in which people guessed what the baby's sex would be, date and time of the birth, and birth weight. They wrote their guesses on slips of paper, which were collected and stored in a safe place. The person whose answer came closest to the actual outcome would receive a prize. The final guessing game was to guess, much to Mariko's surprise and slight embarrassment, the size of her waist (Figure 22). After participants wrote down their guesses, a string was put around her waist to measure it. A man won this game. These guessing games appeared to be common at baby showers, and they made the party enjoyable for everyone, including the men. If this were not a baby shower held at the senior center, they would have felt rather awkward participating.

After the games, it was Mariko's turn to open the gifts. People were eager to see what was inside each package and to learn who gave each gift. Just after she finished opening the gifts, some of the gift-givers told how they got or made their gifts for her. For example, if it were a crochet blanket, the giver told how long it took to complete. Gifts were either money, which was enclosed in an envelope with a card, or baby items. In the end, we received 59 cards with monetary gifts totaling $90. The gifts of baby items included bibs, socks, booties, caps, sweaters, stuffed animals, underwear, crib blankets, toys, and books. Most of the clothing was in pastel colors or white, suitable either for a boy or a girl.

We were surprised to see that, during gift-giving, two or three women took the responsibility of recording all of the gifts, writing down what was given by whom. The records turned out to be very accurate. These women were excellent record-keepers and must have been accustomed to this kind of duty. Women are known to be the record-keepers in the household, and this event seemed to support that claim.

The Jefferson Center baby shower was quite different from one held at an individual's house. The latter is organized by one of the female relatives of the expecting woman, and the participants are female relatives and friends only. The baby shower at the center, on the other hand, was an event in which both men and women participated. Indeed, it was a unique event — the first baby shower ever held at Jefferson Center and most likely the last, simply because both patrons and staff members are not of child-bearing age. Many of the patrons may have been invited to baby showers held for their granddaughters, but none of them would be likely to sponsor one themselves. The fact that the baby shower, which is an age-related event, was held at a senior center was very unusual.

The unusual nature of this event is indicative of the degree of excitement people expressed about the birth, in a place where illness and death are more common topics of discussion. At the same time that Mariko was pregnant, Sophie LaValle, the manager of the senior day-care center, had surgery for stomach cancer. Her

*Figure 22. Guessing the size of Mariko's waist as a game in her baby shower held at Jefferson Center.
(Photograph taken in August 1985.)*

illness naturally saddened many people, and because of its seriousness, people worried quite a long time. Ellen Bunzak, the director of the senior day-care center, told
us what Madeline McKay, a participant in the day-care program who is past 90, did
for the baby shower. Her parents had been Irish immigrants. She never married
because, according to her, she was too busy taking care of her father and younger
siblings after her mother died when Madeline was very young. Consequently, she
has no living relatives. She comes to the senior day-care center 5 days a week; it is
like a home to her now. After receiving the news of Mariko's pregnancy, Madeline
began knitting a pair of booties for the coming baby because, according to Ellen,
Madeline takes everything that happens at the center as her family event. She has
been very worried about Sophie LaValle, for example, but the news of Mariko's
pregnancy gave her an opportunity to think about something else. "It took her
mind off of Sophie's illness," said Ellen.

It was as if the coming baby belonged to all the members of Jefferson Center.
Individuals who were about to have a new grandchild or great-grandchild constantly talked about their upcoming happy event. But such events were special
only to the individuals involved. The birth of a baby, which is usually a private and
familial affair, is joyous, but it also tends to separate the center's members, particularly those who have families from those who do not. In contrast, the prospect of
the birth of our baby was something the Jefferson Center patrons could share as a
community. It would be everyone's baby! Because all of the center's members
shared the same social distance in relation to us and our baby, the birth became an
occasion for genuine communal celebration. For this reason, the baby shower was

enjoyed by both sexes alike, as well as by married, widowed, and never-married individuals. It provided everyone with an occasion to come together rather than remain separate.

The celebration also provided a means of reciprocation to us for volunteering at the center. In addition, because we were foreigners without relatives living nearby, it was an opportunity for people to show their hospitality to outsiders. The fact that we were students from their point of view, without financial security, increased the value of their hospitality.

The event was planned so that those who were not particularly interested in baby showers could still have a good time. Games and prizes certainly helped increase people's enjoyment and even made attendance a little profitable for some. In that way, it was like the Bingo game and birthday party held at Jefferson Center every month.

The prospect of the birth of our baby created a common ground of interest and concern for patrons and staff members at Jefferson Center, as well as ourselves. It was something we all could share. As a result, we have been brought into the community not only as friends, but even as "quasi-relatives." The baby shower symbolized this incorporation and also functioned as an occasion that united the participants despite differences in gender, ethnicity, and age. The birth of a "communal baby" also crossed boundaries between individual families; in other words, we all became one big family!

CHAPTER 7 / "Don't Spoil Your Baby": Educating a Novice Mother

Throughout Mariko's pregnancy and especially after the birth of our son, many people gave advice on child care, even when we had not solicited it. The advice was not uniform, however, and we started paying attention to the variety of approaches. At some point, we realized that our baby was being "encultured," at least in part, as a Riverfrontan.

CULTURAL MILIEU

Cultural variability, we discovered, occurs within and between cultures. For example, what is considered the appropriate method of birth varies not only from culture to culture but also within a single culture, depending on the historical period examined. Birthing experiences differed among the women we interviewed, depending on their age, ethnicity, and socioeconomic class. Even among medical professionals, what is considered appropriate and safe changes over time. During our time in Riverfront, in the mid-1980s, the dominant birthing method promoted by the medical profession, whenever complications were unlikely, was "natural childbirth" (often called the Lamaze method named after Fernand Lamaze, the French obstetrician and gynecologist who developed the method in the 1950s). This method discouraged the use of any kind of anesthesia or pain-killing drugs during birth. It encouraged a pregnant woman to learn and practice breathing methods to control pain during labor.

A nurse practitioner, who worked with obstetricians, independently offered an evening prenatal class in the lobby of a medical office building. In this class, the nurse practitioner educated pregnant women and their husbands about the stages of labor, emphasizing that birthing is a natural, physiologic process. The idea, of course, was to prepare pregnant women and their partners for the birth experience by providing pertinent information and opportunities to practice Lamaze techniques. The goal was to help the mother be as relaxed as possible during labor. Husbands were encouraged to attend all classes because they were considered important participants in the birthing process. In the prenatal class that we attended, there were 14 women in similar stages of pregnancy; they were all accompanied by their husbands. Husbands were expected to be "coaches" for their wives during labor, encouraging them to use the breathing method and offering comfort during the difficult process. In the Lamaze method, childbirth is considered an outcome of a couple's joint efforts.

There were generational differences in birthing experiences among the women whom we interviewed. Women in their 20s and early 30s, like Mariko, had given birth via the "natural" method. Many of these women's husbands were with them during the birth. In contrast, middle-aged women in their late 40s and 50s said they had been unconscious during labor and had not felt any pain because of anesthetic drugs. For them, the birthing process was easy and painless, but they had not felt any excitement either. In those days, it was unthinkable for the husband to be present in the labor room. Interestingly, elderly women in their 70s and 80s said they had "natural" births, without using any drugs. It is as though the natural childbirth movement skipped one generation and repeated the experiences of the previous generation. The difference between the natural birth of 60 years ago and contemporary natural childbirth is that 60 years ago women usually gave birth at home, whereas contemporary natural childbirth usually takes place in hospitals. Delivering at home is, even if tends to revive, rare in Riverfront.

In our prenatal class, the nurse practitioner encouraged breast-feeding instead of bottle-feeding with formula for several reasons: (1) Mother's milk contains substances necessary for the baby's immune system, and these are not found in infant formula. The immune system protects the baby from various illnesses both major and minor, including meningitis, gastronomic indigestion, and respiratory diseases. (2) Because babies cannot be forced to drink more mother's milk than they want; breast-feeding tends to prevent obesity. (3) Breast milk is now known to be more nutritious than formula derived from cow's milk. For example, it contains more cholesterol, which is necessary for development of the baby's nervous system. (4) The fact that breast-feeding fosters more human contact and undivided attention than bottle-feeding is another reason for encouraging the former. (5) Also, breast-feeding, which requires strong sucking, helps development the baby's jaw muscles, enhancing the development of facial expressions and speech ability. In addition, breast-feeding is beneficial for the mother by helping the uterus contract after birth and burning fat that had been stored during pregnancy.

Methods of feeding a baby also varied and followed a generational pattern similar to that of childbirth methods. The women we interviewed who were in their 70s had, for the most part, breast-fed their babies and favored it over bottle-feeding. They stressed the ease of nursing, which meant no mixing formula and disinfecting bottles — far more economical. When elderly women of Polish descent talked about nursing, they would proudly point out that their milk supplies were abundant. In contrast, the middle-aged women we interviewed, who commonly had bottle-fed their babies, often expressed ambivalence toward breast-feeding. Some would say apologetically, "Well, I didn't have enough milk. Breast-feeding does not always work." Others expressed strong distaste for nursing, describing it as "animal-like" and that civilized people should not do it. They often emphasized the scientific nature of formula: "You know exactly how much the baby is drinking."

In a postnatal class that we attended called "What Now," the leader encouraged "naturalness," that is, respecting the baby's pace rather than enforcing rigid schedules for nursing and sleeping. Also, parents' tolerance for their child's habits of holding a security blanket and sucking the thumb was considered important. Moreover, the medical profession at the time of our fieldwork also was inclined to favor breast-feeding and respecting the baby's pace rather than scheduling feedings. Always, parents, especially mothers, were encouraged to have a great deal of physical contact with their babies.

EDUCATING A NOVICE MOTHER

In the several months after our son was born, most of our conversations with other people revolved around the baby and baby care. Many people, especially women, offered Mariko numerous bits of advice on child-rearing, telling her what was appropriate and what was not. In a sense, they were unintentionally educating a novice mother.

Advice on appropriate behavior often focused on proper social distance between the baby and mother. Many people wanted to hold our baby, and they also encouraged Mariko to give him a lot of hugs and show abundant affection. However, at the same time, they also were uneasy about the mother showing too much closeness to the baby. While encouraging "lots of hugging," they discouraged "spoiling" the child. Striking a balance between close physical contact and separation seems to be an important issue, especially when dealing with a crying baby, making sleeping arrangements, nursing, and handling the baby in public.

Listening to the ample advice women gave us in Riverfront, we cannot help noticing variations based on age, ethnicity, generation, class, and gender. There seems to be no such thing as a single American way regarding child care, but individuals invest great emotion when advocating their own approaches and are quite intolerant of other styles or opinions.

Taking Care of a Crying Baby

After our baby was born, being invited to other people's houses or conducting interviews suddenly became problematic. Should we bring our baby with us, should one of us remain at home with him, or should we leave him with a baby-sitter? Being Japanese, we were reluctant to take the last option. In general, when Japanese parents leave their babies with someone, it is almost always a female relative, such as the wife's mother or mother-in-law. Hiring a baby-sitter is very uncommon. Although most of the mothers we knew in the Riverfront area also relied on female relatives, use of baby-sitters was far more common. Many students baby-sit as a way of making money. By the time our son was born, we knew quite a few people willing to take care of our baby for several hours. Nonetheless, we did not feel comfortable hiring a baby-sitter and preferred taking the baby with us. Our culturally based inclination was that a baby should not be separated from his parents, especially his mother. We figured that if our baby became too fussy, one of us would hold him while the other continued the interview (Figures 23 and 24).

Most of the time, bringing our son to interviews posed no problem. He slept most of the time in the first weeks after he was born. If he did become fussy or start crying, our immediate reaction was to pick him up and hold him until he stopped. Also, we would check his diaper to see if it needed changing, check his temperature to see if he was running a fever, or try to nurse him. In other words, we would try to identify and eliminate all possible causes of discomfort.

Once, when we were invited to a dinner at the home of Beth and James Evans (both their in mid 60s), we could not decide whether we should take Hosaki, our baby, with us. If we had to leave him with a baby-sitter, who would it be? Beth Evans said that they were eager to see the baby and urged us to bring him, so we did. Before dinner, Toshi held the baby in his arms. While we were talking with the Evanses, the baby was awake but quiet. When dinner was served and we were about to take our seats at the table, Toshi was still holding the baby in his arms. Beth said, "Oh, you can leave the baby on the sofa," pointing the couch behind the dinner table. We were quite astonished by her suggestion. At home, we used a baby car seat for his chair at dinner time, placing it near us as we eat. After his neck became strong enough to support his head, we often held him on our laps. The idea was to keep him as close as possible to us, even during meals. It never occurred to us to leave him unattended on a couch. Nevertheless, we tried Beth's suggestion.

Suddenly alone on the couch, the baby started crying, which was not surprising to us. Seeing Mariko go to pick him up, Beth said, "Don't worry. He just wants attention. Besides, you can't eat holding him." So we left the baby on the couch, where he continued crying, never letting up. In fact, with the baby crying so incessantly, no one was able to enjoy the dinner any more. Finally, Beth, realizing that her way of handling the baby was not working, said, "Do it as you always do at home." Her words indicated that at least she recognized cultural differences in handling babies.

We were very intrigued about the way in which Beth Evans interpreted the baby's crying. Being left alone on a cold, strange couch instead of being held in the soft, warm arms of its parent seemed to us a valid reason to start crying. Also, crying for attention seemed to us a valid interpretation. In other words, Beth's judgment about the baby's reason for crying was the same way as ours, but she apparently concluded that his reason was not worth a response. Going to him, picking him up, and comforting him were considered inappropriate at dinner time. The baby should learn to be quiet by himself. Responding to his cries for attention was considered "spoiling him."

To us, Beth Evans' way of handling the baby was no less than cultural shock. We later discussed this incident with Elinor and Frank Woodland, who belong to the same generation and socioeconomic class as Beth and James Evans. Frank Woodland was very interested in our observations, for what Beth did and said were exactly what he was accustomed to. Being familiar with cultural variations in child care, he agreed with us that Beth's reactions were very "American." According to Frank, that is the way an American baby learns to be independent.

Figure 23. An interviewee holding Hosaki, our 2-month-old "half-Polish" baby. (Photograph taken in November 1985.)

Figure 24. Hosaki with the senior center staff. (Photograph taken in December 1985.)

This incident reminded Mariko of another dinner party we attended during our son's second Christmas, when he was 15 months old. He was sitting in a baby chair at a table. Hosaki amused himself by dropping a spoon to the floor. The woman sitting next to him, picked it up for him. After two or three times, she said, "Okay, the next time, you are on your own. I am not going to pick it up for you. I have a back trouble." Given that an infant tends to repeat an action, this woman's response was understandable. Yet, what she said sounded very cold to Mariko, especially when it is impossible for him to pick up the spoon on his own. She could have given him something else to play with. Again, we can see the emphasis on independence, but also, setting limits on the baby's behavior indicates the level of the woman's tolerance. It is an adult-centered, rather than baby-centered, perspective.

Letting the baby manage his crying on his own and becoming accustomed to not being held all the time certainly represent the American approach to baby care. However, we could also see variations among the people of Riverfront. For example, Polish-Americans seem to be more tolerant of a baby's crying. Soon after the Evans' dinner, we were invited to a dinner at the Bunzaks, a Polish-American family. Several of the Bunzaks' relatives were among the 10 people gathered at the table. The center of their attention was Hosaki. Everyone wanted to hold and cuddle him, and the baby was passed around the table from one person to another. The difference between the dinner at this house and the Evans' house was obvious. Here, instead of being excluded from the gathering, he was at the center of it. Most noticeable were differences in the men's behaviors. At the previous dinner party, James Evans had detached himself from anything having to do with the baby, preferring only to talk to Toshi. The dinner had boundaries that separated not only the adult sphere from the baby sphere, but also the women's sphere, which includes the baby, from the men's sphere. At the Bunzaks', on the other hand, Mr. Bunzak (age 54) was just as interested in Hosaki as his wife was. Dinner conversation did not resolve into spheres according to age or gender.

Susan Strovinski (age 71), another Polish-American friend of ours, also showed an attitude toward the baby's crying that was different from that of Beth Evans. When Mariko was talking to her over the phone and Susan could hear Hosaki crying in the background, Susan suggested that they should quit talking. "Your baby is crying," she said. "Go and take care of him. Don't let the baby cry. I don't like letting babies cry. I always ran to my baby when he was crying whatever I was doing." Her words indicated a perspective that was different from the one that advocated letting a baby manage on his own.

Of course, as we noted earlier, Anglo-Americans stress the importance of physical contact by hugging, kissing, cuddling, and talking to the baby; that is, we do not mean to argue that they ignore babies or dislike taking care of them. Our concern here is to point out the differences in how they take care of their children and show them love. Anglo-Americans, when they are taking care of babies, tend to establish separate spheres for adults and babies, thereby creating boundaries between them. The boundary can be seen in terms of space and time; for example, during meal time, they put babies in a basket or a baby chair instead of holding them in their arms or putting them in their laps. The baby is kept separate from the adults. This separation is evident in other practices, such as sleeping arrangements.

Sleeping Arrangements

Like child-care practices, household sleeping arrangements vary from culture to culture (e.g., Caudill & Plath, 1966). In most cultures, it is considered appropriate for the husband and to wife share a bedroom. Whether or not and until what age, children should share the same bedroom with their parents varies considerably. In middle-class American families, as portrayed in television dramas, the children's bedrooms are separated from the parents' bedroom. The typical scene portrays either mother or father reading a book to a child at bedtime to help him or her fall asleep; as soon as the child does so, the parent turns out the light, quietly leaves the room, and closes the door, at least partially. Occasionally, more than two children share the same bedroom.

In Japan, although it is not unheard of for realtors to advertise floor plan showing separate bedrooms for parents and children, it is more common for parents and children to share the same room at night. In the typical sleeping arrangement, futon mats, one set for each person, are placed on tatami (straw floor matting). At about the age of 10, a child may be considered old enough to have his or her own room. Until that time, children's futon mats are placed between those of the mother and father, and it is unthinkable for most Japanese to let a baby sleep in a separate room. In many households, the baby sleeps on the same futon mat as its mother. In some cases, the baby has his or her own baby futon, which is always placed next to the mother's. Because futon mats are placed directly on tatami, unlike beds, there is no danger of the baby falling.

Riverfront parents place their babies in cribs rather than in beds for sleeping, so that the baby will not fall on the floor. The crib is placed in a nursery, a room separate from the parents' bedroom. Letting the baby sleep in the same bed as the mother is strongly discouraged in Riverfront. The common fear is that the baby will be suffocated if the sleeping mother should happen to roll over on top of it. Elder Polish-American women often talk about putting the baby's crib in the same room as the parents. Younger Polish-American women, however, prefer to put the crib in a separate room.

Babies naturally cry at night, especially when newly born. It is rare for them to sleep through the night. They also must be fed every few hours through the night. Because the parents, especially the mother, must get up several times during the night, it would be easier on everyone if the baby slept nearby. If the baby is sleeping in a separate room, as is common in Riverfront, the mother has to get out of bed and go into the nursery to take care of the baby, interrupting her sleep. If, on the other hand, the baby were sleeping next to the mother, she would not have to get up, but simply pat or nurse the baby while dozing.

At first, we tried putting our baby down to sleep in a crib in a room separate from ours. Under this arrangement he often cried, even after being nursed, so we began to put him down in our bed to sleep between us. Under this arrangement, Mariko found that nursing was much easier, and the baby, cozy and warm between his parents, slept better. So, we started in an American way but eventually switched over to the Japanese way.

How do American parents cope with a baby's crying at night? Our prenatal class advised expectant mothers and fathers as follows:

> Don't go into the nursery immediately. Wait to see if the baby stops crying on his own. If not, go and see if something was wrong with him. Check the diapers. See if he has a fever, is hungry, or cold. If you find something wrong, take care of it. If you don't find anything wrong, pat his back gently until he starts falling a sleep again. Don't pick him up, as he may want to be picked up all the time. Pick him up only as a last result.

Here, again, we see a emphasis on meeting the baby's physical needs such as illness or hunger, while ignoring emotional needs such as eliminating loneliness or seeking physical contact and attention. For these needs, the baby is expected to develop coping skills on his own. Parents who respond to a baby's crying by picking him up immediately are thought to be hindering the development of his coping skills.

People's actual experiences taking care of a crying baby diverged from the advice given at the prenatal class. A middle-aged woman now says she regrets following similar advice when her child was a baby. She had let her baby sleeping in a crib placed in a separate room. "I hated nursing in a cold room alone. If I were going to have another baby, I would let the baby sleep next to me. It's much easier at night." A young Anglo-American mother reported that she nursed her baby when she cried and that she and her baby slept together until morning.

The idea of having a baby sleep alone is closely related to the idea of developing the baby's sense of independence. In a postnatal class we attended, the teacher, referring to psychologist T. Berry Brazelton's view, stressed the importance of the baby waking up alone in the morning. She told the class members the following:

> When the baby wakes up, he looks around. Usually there are several moments before the baby starts crying. This is the moment when he figures out his world on his own. It gives time for him to contemplate. That is how his sense of independence is fostered. So, don't pick him up immediately; it is important not to interfere with his contemplation.

Nine months after our son was born, during the summer, we returned to Japan for 2 months. At that time, Mariko told Toshi's mother about what the teacher of the postnatal class had told us and how Hosaki's moment of solitude was considered a positive experience. Toshi's mother, being accustomed only to the Japanese way of sleeping — the baby with the mother — was utterly shocked at the idea of leaving the baby alone in a separate room. She felt very pitiful toward her grandson, who had been left to sleep alone and wake up alone. She interpreted the situation as total negligence on the part of his parents, especially his mother, who was supposed to be taking proper care of the baby. In her view, there was no such a thing as an appreciation of the baby's independence.

It is interesting to see how differently the same phenomenon can be interpreted, depending on one's cultural background. Despite Toshi's mother's interpretation, we were not neglecting our baby, nor were Riverfront mothers who have their babies sleep in separate rooms. Both Japanese parents and American parents love their babies and do what they think is right or what is culturally accepted. It is, in other words, only a different way of loving. However, in following a different path, what they try to achieve also is different. By letting the baby sleep nearby so that they can respond to crying immediately, Japanese parents foster an emotional bond between themselves and their infant. American parents take care of their infants by checking to see if their physical needs are met. However, they also encourage and foster emotional detachment from the parents by sleeping alone, having moments of solitude, and letting the baby manage crying on his or her own.

Nursing

One advantage of bottle-feeding is very clear when the baby is taken out of the home. One can take a bottle almost anywhere. However, nursing outside one's home is more complicated. Under what circumstances can a mother nurse her baby outside the home and have it be considered appropriate? In this respect, we see variation among different generations.

When we visited the Evanses, Beth led Mariko into a separate room when she wanted to nurse. Mariko and Hosaki sat alone in a family room, away from the Evanses and Toshi. She mentioned that in this way, Mariko could have privacy. In other words, to them, nursing is a private act, which should not be done in the presence of others. Elder Polish-American women who nursed themselves also suggested carrying a bottle whenever we took the baby with us, so that Mariko wouldn't have to nurse in public. However, the nursing mother does not have to expose her breast. Indeed, most of the time, people around her do not notice she is nursing. Nonetheless, older people regard it as a private matter not to be done in public.

Among younger women, a very different attitude can be observed. In a "baby exercise" group that Mariko joined, she saw mothers nursing their babies in front of others, and no one paid any attention. Of course, the participants were all women in the same situation; however, among the women of this generation, nursing can take place even when both men and women are in the same room. One day, we visited and interviewed Nancy Miller and her husband, a couple with whom we had taken a prenatal class. During our interview, their baby became fussy, and Nancy decided to nurse her. Even though Toshi was in the same room, she went ahead and nursed. Perhaps because we had just had our first baby, more or less at the same time as the Millers and had attended the same prenatal class, which emphasized natural birth and nursing, they must have felt a rapport with us. Nursing is not a private act, but something new parents (not just mothers) have in common. In a different situation, Nancy might not have nursed her baby in front of others. Nonetheless, we have sensed a difference between generations of Riverfrontans in nursing methods.

Hiring a Baby-Sitter

About a year later after our visit with the Evanses, they invited us to dine with them at a restaurant. This time we planned to leave Hosaki with a baby-sitter. Beth, however, told us to bring the baby along. During the meal, our son became fussy.

We tried to calm him down by giving him water, and so forth. Beth said, "You should bring something he can eat." We had brought a bag of raisins with us, but Hosaki only shook the bag and dropped its contents on the floor. "Not in such a big bag!" said Beth. She then told us about her recent trip to California where she had dinner with some people who had brought their children along. "The children were so fussy and made a mess. But, the father said, 'You are so good today. Have some ice-cream,' and ordered a special dessert for them. I was flabbergasted! What a spoiler! He rewarded the children instead of punishing them!" Because our child was fussy, we felt very uncomfortable listening to this story. The rule of thumb in Riverfront social intercourse seems to be, do not to disturb others. Beth said, "It's okay to bring children as long as they do not disturb others, so that other people do not become upset." When dinner was over, she said, "Well, you should learn to leave the baby with the sitter." Again, we can discern an adult-centered ethic. It is the child who has to adjust to the adult world and not the reverse. Those parents who yield to children are "spoiling" them.

INTERPRETATION

In advising us on baby care, people express what they value and consider appropriate in bringing up a new member of their culture. Such cultural values as "sharing" and "independence" are emphasized. Sharing is emphasized in the practice of "giving lots of love" to the baby in the form of close physical contact with the parents, especially the mother, who is encouraged to pick up, hug, kiss, and hold the baby. Independence is emphasized as an important goal as the baby learns self-control, by managing physical separation from mother, and loneliness, by not disturbing others (adults) in public. Sharing and independence are values that go hand-in-hand in Riverfront, but sometimes they are in conflict. Too much sharing means spoiling the baby's effort to become independent. Then the mother must maintain an appropriate social distance from the baby; she should be close but not too close.

Observing how people in Riverfront responded to Hosaki, we could see that there were innumerable variations in child-rearing patterns, as, for example, in the social distance between mother and baby. Variations can be observed in attitudes toward sleeping arrangements, nursing in public, and managing a crying baby. Moreover, they can be analyzed along generational, gender, and ethnic lines, such as "Polish-American" and "Anglo-American." How do people reconcile such differences? To answer this question, we must pay attention to the way people explain the differences.

In sleeping arrangements, when older Polish people explained why they kept the baby in the parents' room, they explained in terms of economic difficulties rather than as a norm in child-rearing. The Japanese would say that the baby should sleep with parents, especially with the mother, because of the dangers of leaving an infant alone. Parents' income levels were irrelevant. In contrast, a Polish-American woman would say, "All the boys slept in one room, and the girls in another. The baby's crib was placed in the parents' room. Boys slept in one bed — very crowded. We did so because our house was very small. We didn't have rooms for everyone." In this case, poverty was stressed as the reason for such arrangements, not differences in custom. The Polish-American woman would not say, "Well, the Polish think it is important for the mother and child to be close together." Here we can see an acceptance of a general American norm that children, including babies, should sleep separately from their parents. If an accommodation is made, it is because of economic difficulty.

We also noticed that cultural differences are often discussed in terms of economic differences. One Christmas, Mariko was talking with a social worker about how Christmas is practiced in Japan. The social worker asked Mariko what kinds of gifts people exchange at Christmas time. "We don't exchange gifts for Christmas, but in December there is a traditional gift-exchange season called *oseibo*. So, we give gifts to people then." Mariko explained to her that the most common gift is food of some kind, such as cans of ham or oil, packs of dried fish, and boxes of sugar. In other words, food that does not perish easily. The social worker, in turn, described typical Christmas gifts people exchange in Riverfront. Asked whether people gave food, she said, "We used to when we were poor. We don't do it any more. Poor people still give food as Christmas gifts." In the Japanese cultural context, food is considered an appropriate gift regardless of the income levels of the givers. Indeed, many such gifts are fancy and quite expensive. What the social worker had done was to interpret "food as gift" in an American context, which means poverty. She did not take into account that the quality and value of certain kinds of gifts vary from culture to culture.

Likewise, the sleeping arrangement among Polish people is interpreted, by Polish and non-Polish Americans alike, not as an indication of different attitudes toward child care but as an indication of economic difficulty. The prevailing ideology in child care is that independence should be fostered, and an obstacle to achievement of this goal is a lack of money. Polish-Americans also explain their sleeping arrangements in economic terms rather than as differences in culture. Therefore, people seem to accept the dominant ideology of independence; that is, a baby should be encouraged to be independent, especially from its mother. However, within that dominant framework, we can still see the variations in what is considered the appropriate social distance between a mother and her baby.

CHAPTER 8 / "Share!" and "Be Independent!": Socialization and Social Management at a Child-Care and a Senior Center

In this chapter, we examine cultural concepts underlying the early childhood and late adulthood experience in Riverfront. By looking at both ends of the individual's life course, we hope to understand how the American value of independence is taught, learned, and maintained. We want to know why it persists even in contexts where dependency is actively avoided, accepted as inevitable, or even understood as something that is necessary. Given that the idea of independence is valued highly in Riverfront, it is necessary to consider how mutually interdependent relationships are formed.

Early childhood is a period when core cultural values are taught (Caudill & Weinstein, 1969; LeVine, 1984; Masuda, 1969). In the first half of this chapter, we look at the Maple Child Day Care Center with our focus on the process of cultural transmission. Studying educational routines in day-care centers give us a glimpse into that process. Core American values, such as "independence" and "cooperation" might be discernible in such settings (Fujita, 1984; Hsu, 1973, 1981; Rapson et al., 1967; Varenne, 1977). We introduce some Japanese examples for comparison as we try to discern Riverfrontans' ideas, practices, and interactional patterns. Japanese examples are pertinent to our study because "dependency," the opposite of "independence," is considered a predominant ideology in Japanese society (Doi, 1973; Kiefer, 1970).

Caudill and Weinstein (1969) found differences between Japanese and Americans in mother-child interactions at the beginning of socialization, which help explain differences between the two cultures' mother-child relationships in later life. Is there a similar difference in social interactions with individuals outside the family? If so, what kind of interaction characterizes the connections between the two different life stages?

In the latter half of this chapter, we shift our attention to the elderly, specifically Jefferson Center patrons, to examine the same theme of how ideas about independence shape and are shaped by ideas of dependency and sharing/cooperation.

IN SOCIALIZATION

After making arrangements with the director of the day-care center, we began visiting twice a week to observe its activities. Our observation methods consisted of sitting in classrooms and taking notes. We did not expect any problems with the children, but we were anxious about the teachers' responses to our presence; instead of setting up times and dates for observation and specifying the kind of activity we wished to observe, we used an ethnographic observation method rather than a method to which the teachers might be accustomed (cf. Fujita & Sano, 1998; also Spindler & Spindler, 1987, 1993).

Maple Child Day Care Center is located at the east end of Riverfront on the border of the residential area, adjacent to the commercial area. The center was open Monday through Friday, and parents from all over the county brought their children there. Seven classes, organized by age, were formed in September. Once a child reached a certain age, ages 2 up through 5, he or she would move to the next class, depending on the teachers' evaluations of the child's growth and development as well as availability of a vacancy. Parents could choose which days of the week to bring their children to the center. Some children came 2 or 3 days a week, whereas others came 5 days a week. Fees were charged on an hourly basis and were competitive with those of several other day-care centers in Riverfront.

The ratio of children to teachers in Riverfront day-care centers is set by the State of Wisconsin and is almost the same as Kawa Day Care, a day-care center in Tokyo, Japan, that we studied, for younger children (4:1 for 1-year-olds, 6:1 for 2-year-olds, 8:1 for 2½ year-olds, and 10:1 for 3-year-olds). However, for older children at Maple, the ratios are lower than in Japan (13:1 for 4-year-olds and 16:1 for 5-year-olds at Maple as compared with averages in Japan of 25:1 for both 4-year-olds and 5-year-olds).

There are other differences between Kawa and Maple Centers. At Maple, the floor is entirely carpeted, except for the dining hall, but people enter the building without taking off their shoes because bare feet are not allowed by the state regulations. There is no staff lounge at Maple; however, there is a kitchen-dining room. Kawa Center has an independent kitchen and a relatively large hall for recreation but not for eating because they eat in their classrooms.

Maple Day Care has a daily schedule of activities similar to those at Japanese day-care centers. Most activities are performed according to age group, except in the very early morning and very late afternoon, when only a small number of children are present. One distinct difference between Maple and Kawa Centers is opening and closing times: Maple Day Care Center opens as early as 6:30 a.m. and closes at 6:00 p.m., whereas Kawa Center opens at 7:20 a.m. and closes at 6:00 p.m. but remains open until 7:00 p.m. for some children whose parents need extra time to come from their workplaces to pick up their children. Maple's schedule is apparently tailored to fit parents' work shifts, which go from 7:00 a.m. to 3:00 p.m. at many places.

The staff of the Maple Day Care is almost entirely female, except for one male teacher for the 4-year-old class who also is the center's assistant director. A small number of male teachers work part-time at the center. Although few in number, male day-care teachers are an important part of Maple Day Care. Center's staff. Japanese day-care centers are also almost entirely staffed by women, although a small number of men are becoming day-care teachers. The Maple teachers are graduates of 4-year colleges, and its teacher aides are graduates of 2-year junior colleges or 2-year technical schools. In Japan, almost all day-care teachers are graduates of 2-year junior colleges or 2-year special training schools, and there are no full-time but part-time teacher aides. (Hereafter, we use the term *teachers* to refer to both teachers and teacher aides, unless otherwise noted.)

Sharing

Within our first few visits, we realized that the Maple Child Day Care Center had similar activities to those at the Kawa Day Care Center. We tried to be sensitive to what seemed "strange" to us at Maple Day Care. Within our scheduled time, we observed all the types of interactions that occur in a day-care center, paying particular attention to informal conversations and behaviors occurring in transition from one activity to another.

Among the observations that we found "strange" was an admonition that teachers often gave children, especially to 2-year-old and 3-year-old children: "Share." For example, "Share, Brian," or "Share the toys with friends." Japanese people do not use such expressions in the same context as Americans, but they usually say "Play together," or "Lend it to her." On hearing this, we decided our first task was to understand how American teachers use this concept of sharing, the kind of interactions associated with it, and the other cultural concepts connected to it.

Teaching young children to share apparently is a rather new practice in early socialization in America. One informant told us that until several decades ago, Americans used to say "lend" instead of "share." At first glance, in the context of conflict over a toy between children, either by lending or by sharing, teachers can avoid conflict between children. In terms of object transfer, the behaviors of lending and sharing have the same function. Nevertheless, Riverfront teachers and parents consider sharing an important concept for social life. *Sharing* connotes mutual benefit and equality among individuals, whereas *lending* implies that one side has ownership of the object being lent and therefore, a hierarchy rather than an equality exists between the two sides.

Because teachers and parents want children to internalize the concept of sharing and behave accordingly, they say, "Share!" when disciplining children. In Maple Day Care Center, disciplinary methods include verbal directions and "time-out." Teachers give directions such as, "Brian, share. Now Katy's turn," and "Rachel, you shouldn't do that. I don't like this," without any special body language and in the same manner as they normally talk. On the other hand, "time-out" indirectly conveys the value of sharing by placing the problem child in a nonsharing situation. The teacher picks up a noisy child who is disturbing such sharing activities as story-reading time and says the name of the child a few times. If the child calms down, nothing happens. However, if the teacher's verbal signs are ignored, the teacher says, "I give you a time-out." Upon receiving this command, most children leave the group and go to a designated corner of the room to sit down by themselves. They do nothing but sit quietly until the teacher says, "You may join us now." The concept of sharing is directly and indirectly used to encourage children to be cooperative because it is considered a key to organizing groups.

Each month, Maple Day Care teachers ask children to bring a toy from their homes to share with classmates. This is a way of teaching the concept of sharing directly. First, the teacher introduces the child who is going to share a toy and explains what kind of toy it is. Sometimes the teacher asks the child to demonstrate how to use the toy. After the demonstration, the toy is shared among the class-mates. Occasionally, when the other children begin to play with the toy, the one who brought it begins to object. If this happens, the teacher might say to the child, for example, "Sue, you brought this toy to share with other children. Everybody can enjoy playing with it today." In this way, teachers want children to learn how to deal with conflict.

Based on our observations, Maple teachers' use of *share* entails the emphasis of three cultural values. First, there is an emphasis on group identification. When the teacher says "share" to one child in a group situation, she implies that the child is connected to other members of that group and that he or she is a group member. Second, there is an emphasis on cooperation. When the teacher says "Share!" to two children who are involved in a conflict over toys, for example, she wants them to help each other to solve the conflict peacefully. Third, there is an emphasis on equality. When the teacher directs all the children in a group to "share," she implies that each child has an equal ability to be good to every other child.

As we stated earlier, Maple Day Care children do not come every day and therefore do not associate with the same classmates every day. Unlike Japanese children, who see the same classmates every day throughout the year, Maple Day Care children commonly experience changes in classmates. It is important, and even necessary, to teach children to realize that they belong to a group in order for teachers to successfully manage the group. Sharing can evoke a sense of belonging.

To illustrate the second value, cooperation, we use the following example: One child takes a toy from another child. The first child might react by saying, "No! No!" and then saying to the teacher, "She took my toy." The teacher might tell the child, "Wow! You can share!" In other words, the child hears from the teacher's exclamation that he has lost nothing but, rather, has shown his ability to allow another child to use his toy. Invoking the word *share* allows teachers to de-empha-size competition and facilitate self-control.

Efforts to keep children from becoming overly competitive were evident in other activities we observed. For example, in baseball batting, Maple Day Care teachers did not arrange games by dividing the group into opposing teams but let children line up to wait their turn a bat. The teacher always threw a ball to each child in the batter's box while only a few children played defense. These chil-dren joined the line for batting later. For an indoor game, a teacher sets up a chair, a box, and other obstacles in a line. One at a time, children kick a ball through the spaces between the obstacles from one end of the line to the other. In each of these games, one cannot judge whether one child's skills are better than another's by comparing their performances. Thus, competition is downplayed.

In contrast, in Japan, two teams are often formed to compete with each other. For example, when an outdoor recreation period is over, Japanese teachers may form two teams of children and have them race each other into the building to see who is fastest.

While Maple Day Care teachers implicitly convey the value of equality to the children through the sharing concept, that same concept may be used to celebrate the uniqueness of each child. Maple's monthly activity of inviting a child to bring a favorite toy from home to share illustrates this. In addition, teachers have another activity in which a child is asked to tell about his or her recent experiences or to tell a story to other children. This kind of sharing allows children to demonstrate their own uniqueness.

Finally, it should be noted that the concept of sharing is clearly separated from any misbehavior or destructive behavior at the Maple Child Day Care Center. Sharing objects, experiences, ideas, time, and space are distinguished from following or imitating bad behaviors and ideas. This means that children learn how to control themselves according to the situation. Maple Day Care children are discouraged from sharing behaviors that are destructive to the relationship between a teacher and a child or between a group of teachers and a group of children. One example of this is sitting on a teacher's lap. Teachers explain that if they were to pay more attention to a particular child by allowing him or her to sit on their lap, the other children would want the same attention.

Maple Day Care teachers said that one disruptive child can make an entire class chaotic. They explain that if one child starts getting wild — shouting at meal time, for example — other children soon join in, in a sense, "sharing" in the misbehavior. By using "time-out," teachers separate a misbehaving child from the group so that he or she will have the opportunity to think about proper behavior. Maple Day Care teachers often talked about children's short attention spans, which they believe result in much of the misbehavior they see. Therefore, they draw a line between behaving and misbehaving children so that the misbehaving children will learn to distinguish situations in which sharing is appropriate and those in which sharing disruptive behavior is inappropriate.

If sharing were a basic feature of early socialization, we could assume that teachers and parents do not have to teach the concept consciously to their young children. However, as we have seen, Maple Day Care teachers do try to transmit the cultural value of sharing and encourage sharing behaviors in their young charges. This struck us as strange, especially considering that we observed our own son trying to share a toy without intentionally being taught to do so by us or anyone else. After Hosaki began to walk, at the age of 11 months, he would offer a toy to other Riverfront children of the same age whenever he played with them at our friend Michele's house, as well as at a shopping mall. Ironically, our son was never offered a toy from another Riverfront child. He learned how to stand in front of a class and present to other children a favored object before he learned how to insist on the ownership of things. If his offering behavior were encouraged by adults, it would not be necessary to teach young children directly sharing behaviors. We therefore ask, why do Riverfront teachers and parents find it necessary to directly and explicitly teach young children to share?

We now address this question by considering socialization as a part of cultural transmission (Spindler, 1974) and by introducing cultural analysis into a life course perspective (Schweder & LeVine, 1984). We put Riverfront sharing behavior and its meanings into the context of a life course. By doing so, we can see how values emphasized in early childhood are connected to values in later life stages. Continuities and discontinuities between early- and late-life experiences are important for people to contemplate as they assess the meaning of their lives. They are also important for the ethnographic analysis of a community because the community consists of people at different life stages.

By learning to share, Maple Day Care teachers hoped that children would also learn to become cooperative in general. The idea of cooperation is another value taught explicitly in early American education, but what does "cooperation" mean in American cultural contexts? Cooperative society is one of the conventional folk and professional labels that mark Japanese society. Young Japanese children learn that cooperation is essential for a harmonious society (Hendry, 1986; Lewis, 1984). On the contrary, competition is a label that commonly marks American society. Young American children learn that independence is essential for a competitive society. Do Japanese teachers and parents teach their young children how to behave competitively and conceptualize the competitive behaviors? We believe that they do, but in a different way than we observed among teachers and parents at Maple Day Care. Japanese teachers and parents occasionally help children be competitive, not only because they will later need a competitive edge to survive the war of college entrance exams, but also because Japanese see competitiveness as an indication that the child is becoming an individual. Similarly, teachers and parents at Maple Day Care see cooperation as a sign of good citizenship.

Here we arrive at an interim conclusion that teaching the concepts and behaviors of sharing in early childhood enhances development of self-control, cooperation, and group identity, as well as establishing the teacher's social control. Also, emphasis on sharing in the early stages of socialization helps establish a foundation for building a competitive spirit later in life.

In the eyes of foreign ethnographers, the combination of becoming independent and learning to share is a cultural puzzle that needs further analysis. Bearing this in mind, we now examine how children learn independence and how teachers encourage them to do so.

"Independence"

As we have seen, Maple Day Care teachers often use certain concepts to teach other concepts by establishing connection between them, as when the idea of sharing is used to teach equality and cooperation. Likewise, they connect the concept of "independence" to that of "choice." Teachers often stressed the importance of children's "choosing" an activity. Children were often asked to choose one activity from two or three possibilities. The teachers believed that giving the children choices taught them to sort out their wishes and express their desires to engage in an activity without being forced to do so. Therefore, letting children choose is a step toward independence and freedom.

One way teachers exposed their children to a variety of choices was by dividing each class of older children (age 3 and up) into three groups, particularly during morning activities. The teacher would supervise a group of seven or eight children doing one project. Meanwhile, a teacher's aide would supervise another group doing a different project. The rest of the children in this particular class would be assigned to play on their own with toys in the classroom, and the teacher decides which toys those children may play with. After about 15 minutes, the groups rotate so that eventually all of the children will have engaged in all three of the activities provided in the classroom.

By setting up a few activity options in the classroom, teachers seem to encourage children to be independent. However, if we look more closely at the ways in which the teachers control the children's behavior during those activities, we gain a different view of the meaning of "choice" that children experience. The activities from which the children may choose are always set by the teachers, although they emphasize the importance of having choices as a key to learning independence. If the children engage in activities other than those set by the teachers, the teachers are likely to interpret these side activities as distracting other children and will use some disciplinary measure, such as the "time-out."

Maple Day Care teachers also emphasize independence during the meal time by encouraging children to eat on their own. The center serves hot lunches, as Japanese day-care centers do. Meals are served in two shifts in an uncarpeted dining room. The first shift is for the younger children (ages 1 to 2½), and the second shift is for the older children (ages 3 to 5). The teachers regard lunch as a social occasion, and they encourage the children to talk to one another. At the same time, the teachers supervise their table manners.

At lunchtime, seven large rectangular tables, each of which seats 10 people, are set up in the dining room. The children usually sit with their classmates (Figure 25). Teachers also sit and eat with their own children. At the beginning of the meal, they recite a short, nonreligious prayer giving thanks for the food. Meals are served family style, with each menu item served in a large plate or bowl, which the teachers ask the children to pass around. They instruct the children to take small amounts of every item served. If the children want more, they may ask for seconds. If they do not want to take a certain food, the teachers ask them to "at least try it."

At Maple Day Care, no one, not even the youngest child (age 1), is fed. All children are expected to feed themselves. In contrast, Japanese day-care teachers feed even 3-year-olds who are slow eaters. The Maple Day Care teachers think it is important that each child knows how to eat with utensils, regarding this as a step toward independence. Feeding children, even if they are slow eaters, is not considered a good idea because children would soon stop trying and would expect teachers to feed them. In such a situation, some children would also try to gain extra attention. Then, the whole situation would become chaotic (Fujita, 1986).

Maple Day Care teachers do not use what their Japanese counterparts term a "duty system" for their children. Kawa teachers assign daily chores to children, whereas Maple Day Care teachers solicit voluntary help from the children when performing chores. They think it is important that help from the children be volun-

Figure 25.   Lunchtime at Maple Child Day Care Center.   (Photograph taken in May 1985.)

tary rather than assigned. For example, at snack time a teacher might ask, "Who wants to wipe off the table?" Two or three children usually raise their hands, which means that these children have chosen of their own free will to help the teacher, and the teacher recognizes their willingness. Because the children consider helping out a reward of recognition, the teachers see to it that everyone eventually gets a chance to be the helper. However, to maintain the appearance of voluntariness, the rotation is implicit and the children do not know when their turns will come. For the children, helping is implicitly a competition among them.

While the children are eating lunch, the Maple Day Care teachers set up portable cots in each classroom for nap time. Setting up cots is considered the teachers' duty, and therefore no child helps in this task. This is very reasonable in that chaotic situations that could occur with children in the classroom can be avoided. On the other hand, at a Japanese day-care center, teachers enlist the aid of older children to prepare their classrooms for napping. In the oldest group (age 5), for example, the teacher first vacuums the floor, then the children carry their futons (cotton mattresses) from the closet and lay them on the floor. Although not all of the children always help, preparing the room for napping can be seen as a duty shared by teachers and children.

From our observations of class activities, lunchtime, and nap time preparation, it is clear that Maple Day Care teachers encourage children to become self-reliant by (1) giving them limited choices, (2) expecting them to feed themselves, even at the age of 1, and (3) soliciting voluntary help in doing chores. It should be noted, however, that the Japanese teachers encourage children to become responsible, rather than dependent, by assigning duties and sharing certain tasks, such as laying down futons for napping and cleaning the classrooms with the teachers. In other words, Japanese teachers are not overprotective or indulgent.

Maple Day Care teachers rely heavily on verbal instruction, much more so than Japanese teachers. They find it important to explain procedures to the children for whatever activity they are about to undertake. In fact, at the beginning of every morning, the teacher tells her children what they are going to do that day. Then, at the beginning of each activity, the teacher repeats what they are going to do and what she expects from the children. When the teacher is about to give an instruction, all the children are expected to gather around her and sit down. For example, in wintertime, before the 3-year-old class goes outside to play, the teacher gives a series of instructions to the entire group:

> Now, we are going outside and play. Before you go, I want you to go to the bathroom first. Then, come back here and put on your coat and boots. Don't go outside yet. You must line up in front of the classroom and be quiet. If you are noisy, we are not going outside. Then, we go out together. Okay? Now, go to the bathroom.

The teacher waits for all the children to return to the classroom and then says, "Put on your coats and boots." She helps some children put on their coats.

"Now, I want you to line up in front of the classroom." Those children who have put on their coats start lining up and wait for the others. After everyone has lined up, the teacher gives another set of instructions: "Now, we are going outside. When we finish, I want you to come back right away and line up in front of the building, Okay?" Then the teacher leads her children quietly outside. The children seem to wait for the teacher's instructions (Figure 26).

From a cross-cultural perspective, it is clear that the Maple Day Care teachers place much greater emphasis on verbal instruction than Japanese teachers. The latter tend to believe that for young children, it is not sufficient just to tell them what to do. In fact, it is more important to show them by action, either demonstrating the desired action themselves or letting them follow some children who already know how. Maple Day Care teachers, on the other hand, believe it is important for the children understand *why* they are doing what they are doing to avoid simple obedience on the part of the children. In this way, children are supposed to learn that a person should express clearly and independently what he or she wants to say.

We found another example of Maple Day Care teachers' preference for verbal instructions in the ways they deal with fights among the children. At the beginning of the school year, the teachers set up several sessions to talk with the children about "fights" and to establish some rules. They talked about why fighting is bad, how it feels to be hit, and what children should do instead of fighting. This way, the teachers believed that they could minimize the chances of fighting among the children. In contrast, Japanese teachers do nothing until an actual fight occurs and then teach the children involved what is right and wrong in that particular context. According to Japanese teachers, rules are dependent on individual situations. One Japanese teacher even said that she did not teach children not to fight because she believed that fighting within certain limits was a form of communication and an expression of individual emotions, which should not be discouraged.

Picture 26. Playtime at Maple Child Day Care Center. (Photograph taken in May 1985.)

IN AGING

Now, we shift our focus from youth to elderly people. For studying this population, we visited the individuals we met at Jefferson Center while volunteering at the center's kitchen. We also met additional people who turned out to be sources of information at the senior day-care center at Jefferson Center.

People often assume that the elderly are in a second childhood. Such an attitude has multiple implications, the most important being that they are considered to be undergoing the process of socialization a second time. This implies they are again in a stage of dependency, like young children. If this is the case, one wonders how the concept of sharing is understood and practiced among elderly people. Is this concept practiced in the same way as it is by the children of Maple Child Day Care Center, in eating lunch, telling experiences, and bringing favorite objects? Is it a cultural concept for making good social relationships in American society? How is "independence" fostered? We examine these questions by looking at different forms of sharing among elderly people.

Talk as Sharing

Public speaking affords an opportunity to share personal experience. Jefferson Center occasionally offers such opportunities billed as "Friday Breakfast." Beginning at 8:00 a.m., they provide a guest speaker for those elderly people who want to hear a lecture. Lecture topics vary depending on whom the Center is able to obtain. When Pam Sorenson, director of the senior center, approaches someone to give a lecture, she explains that the breakfast format is designed not as a formal educational program but as an opportunity for those who do not want to come into the center for regular programs to attend an interesting lecture in a relaxed atmosphere. For example, local university professors have been invited to talk about beekeeping or experiences in traveling abroad. Members of local organizations, such as the Riverfront Historical Society, talk about their recent activities and projects.

In fact, we were invited to give a talk for this program about 7 months after we had started volunteering at the center. Pam asked us to make a presentation on our project so that patrons might understand why a Japanese couple was living in Riverfront and regularly visited the senior center. Pam added that if we made a presentation, we would get acquainted more easily with different individuals because participants in the morning lecture program were different from those whom we met at lunchtime. The morning participants tended to be those who were looking for a social time with an educational or intellectual element. We do not have demographic data on the socioeconomic backgrounds of those people, but we believe they did not need regular public support or assistance from the senior center for things such as meals and transportation.

Traditionally, anthropologists do not discuss with their interviewees what they have learned from their ongoing research. We agree with this policy because if we were to divulge what we learned from various people in the same locality, we might have invaded a person's privacy in unknown ways. However, we saw this speaking engagement as an opportunity to get to know people in the center better and to provide an interesting presentation. Moreover, we were sure that the senior center staff was interested in our presentation because they wanted to understand more clearly which aspects of the people that our research project targeted. To protect people's privacy, we decided to talk about nothing related to our research in the local area. We made a slide presentation about elderly people and young children in Japan.

After we had finished our Friday morning talk, an audience member approached us to say something cordial and innocent enough, but something that nevertheless caught us off-guard. He said, "Thank you for *sharing* with us." The word *sharing* was being used in a way we had not considered, suggesting that it has more different meanings than we had realized. This realization came as a sort of cultural shock to us, not in the sense that we had encountered some strange sociocultural scene or system, but because a simple statement had made us realize the complexity of the cultural concept of sharing.

Having encountered this fresh experience of sharing at the senior center, we did not at first make any connections between the day-care teachers' use of the word and the senior citizen's use. We thought that this experience was different from our experience at Maple Child Day Care Center because the day-care teachers were using the concept of sharing in an educational context, whereas the elderly person was using it in a statement of acknowledgment of our efforts to edify and entertain. However, we soon understood that the concept of sharing encompasses both usages and both youthful and old-age contexts. We discuss this later in greater detail.

The presentation was well accepted not only by the elderly audience but also by senior center staff. We were rather surprised to hear some of the staff expressing their enjoyment to us directly. We began to feel a new relationship with staff members. We had shared something with local people and the center's staff, and this was exactly what they had wanted to promote. In other words, the staff was advocating the concept of sharing much as the Maple Day Care teachers had.

Visiting as Sharing

Visiting is one of the important behavioral and conceptual words used in American culture. It is not marked but embedded in everyday life. The word is, in fact, an idea and practice "hidden" from outsiders like us. Toshi thought the word strange when we started going to the senior day-care center to conduct participant observations, in which we attempted to forget our roles as researchers and do the same things the participants did, such as morning exercises, craft-making, and eating lunches and snacks together. We also became volunteers to help the staff in their daily programs. However, we did not do the work of full-time staff — giving special assistance to patrons in the center. In this sense, we did not conduct participant observation as staff members. Generally, our roles were like those of senior volunteers. For example, during rest time, after lunch or snack, and during free activity time, we would sit beside a specific individual and try to engage in conversation.

"You had a nice visit with Toshi," Sophie LaValle, one of the full-time staff, said to Beverly after Toshi had finished a conversation with her and moved to a table where other people sat. Beverly smiled, nodding slightly. Toshi did not think that he had "visited" with her. Why had Sophie LaValle said "visit"? Toshi was puzzled, so he asked Mariko, "What does this mean?" Mariko explained that what Toshi had done is called a "visit."

What visit means includes a relationship between two people. Toshi's previous understanding was that people visit a place, such as a friend's house, or visit a group, such as a family, rather than a specific individual. Of course, people can visit an individual. However, in such a visit, Toshi imagined, people have a business-like reason to do so. He had not understood that one can visit an individual with no specific reason.

It became clear that the concept of "visit" means, among other things, enjoying talking with another individual. The conversation Toshi had with Beverly in the senior center was not smooth dialog, as perhaps a business-like visit might have been, and it was not private. Other people could see Toshi's visit because the center was one large room. The staff continually observe participants in this program, and participants can also observe what other participants are doing. In this sense, "visiting" can be public and focused.

Length of time is not always important in this kind of visiting. The visit can be short, such as our visit with Madeline McKay, a regular routine every time we went to the center. Even when we just made a brief stop, we had a visit with her. In this case, we did not speak a lot except to say, for instance, "Hi. How are you?" and "Hosaki (our son) enjoys playing with the toy you gave him." Madeline would respond briefly. Our short visit with Madeline became sort of emblematic of our visit to the center as a whole, to all members — participants, volunteers, and staff. One day, a senior volunteer called Toshi and said, "Have you talked with Madeline, Toshi? She wants to see you," implicitly inviting Toshi to drop by the center.

People perceive a "visit" as a good thing, perhaps feeling that they are doing good by visiting other people. Basically, people visit because they like to do it. Even if they do not like to visit a specific person for some reason, they feel that they are doing a good thing for this person. More important, the concept of "visiting" is related directly to the concept of "sharing." By visiting, people share their individual experiences and feelings.

Telephone Calls as Sharing

When people visit each other by telephone, the process takes on a new dimension. In addition to sharing time and experience, there is also a sharing of "place." This does not mean a physical or geographical location, but a psychosocial location as a basis for conversation. This "place" is defined by the phone connection and is shared in the sense that each party has equal access to the other and that also, no one else does; the conversation is private.

John Biza, a neighbor of ours in Riverfront and a senior citizen, often calls his older sister, Angie Woblenski (age 76). She lives in Oakwood Manor, one of two senior high-rise apartments in Riverfront, just two blocks away from the city center. He has seven brothers and three sisters, all who are living. Although John goes to visit his siblings and other relatives and he is sometimes visited by them, he keeps more frequent contact with Angie and with his wife's brother. At the time we moved to his neighborhood, John lived with his wife, Judy. His only son worked at a hospital in a city 35 miles from Riverfront, and he came to John's house once or twice a month.

One day, we went to a meal site at Oakwood Manor. At lunchtime in the dining hall, a site-manager pointed out a certain lady to us and said that the lady was a sister of our neighbor. We did not know that John's sister Angie lived there, although by that time, we had heard about her from John. Born in 1909 in Pine County, she is 12 years older than John, has never had children, and is a widow. When John's son was small, Angie baby-sat him while John and Judy ran their own gas station.

The next time Toshi saw John, Toshi told him that we had met his sister at Oakwood Manor. John already knew, suggesting there had been communication between Angie and John. When Toshi told him that we wanted to interview her, John said, "Okay, I can ask her because I call her every morning."

Thus, we came to know that Angie and John had telephone visits every morning. Angie told him that she met our son the previous day, according to John. Then, John said to Toshi, "I told my sister about your son." This is true because Angie herself said, "My brother told me about you and your son." According to Angie's story, John surely had told her something more about our son, such as his appearance (big for his age). John also had to check on the day and time that she had medical appointments because he always picked her up and drove her to the doctor's office. He usually waited for her in his car in front of the doctor's office while she was being seen by doctor. Because of injuries sustained as a marine in the Pacific Theater during World War II, John's automobile license plate is marked for the handicapped, allowing him to park his car in the designated spaces, which is beneficial for his sister as well as for himself.

Now we look at another example of telephone visits between siblings, this time between sisters: Katie Karenski and Anna Belle. Anna, whom we introduced earlier, is an elderly woman with whom we built up good rapport during our field research. Like John, she has many siblings: three brothers and seven sisters. One brother and two sisters (the oldest and the youngest) have died already. Anna was born in Poland in 1911, the second female child, and Katie was born 12 years later. Anna's brothers and younger sisters were all born in Chicago, except for the youngest sister, who was born on a farm after they moved from Chicago to the Riverfront area. Anna, Katie, and two other sisters who live in neighboring cities eat out together a few times each year. Anna and Katie see each other almost every weekday at Jefferson Center, where both of them volunteer in the meal program 2 or 3 days a week and come to the center to have a meal on the days they are not volunteering.

Although they usually see each other at Jefferson Center, Katie calls Anna early every morning. Anna said to us, "Katie gets up at 4 or 5 o'clock in the morning and calls me at 5:30 or 6:00. Well, I'm still sleeping when she calls me. . . . I told Katie not to call me before 7:00." Katie lives with her husband who retired from his garage shop and is still doing odd jobs, such as woodwork, painting, and store remodeling. Katie worked as bookkeeper at her husband's shop. She does not drive a car. The life of Katie and her husband is very similar to that of John and Judy.

Katie does not call to check on Anna's health; she does not seem to be interested in monitoring her sister's physical well-being. Indeed, it is not Anna but Katie who has had a few small heart attacks. More likely, Katie regards Anna as company or a member of the same co-aging "convoy" (Plath, 1980). Anna grows old with Katie, living in the same locale and sharing the same experiences.

The calls in both cases we describe are made from younger to older siblings. Age differences between the caller and the person being called are both about 12 years. In both cases, the person being called lives alone in senior housing located close to the city center. Both use the meal program for the elderly provided by the Commission on Aging. Both callers live with their spouses in their own homes at the edge of the city. Also, both callers happen to be handicapped, although neither has immediate problems. Katie has had heart attacks, whereas John still has occasional high fevers as a result of his war wounds. Although there are, of course, many contrasts between Katie's and John's families in terms of family structure, sibling ties, distance between places of residence, life histories, and even age differences taken together seem to create the motivation and the subject matter for daily telephone visits.

People share some of their deepest feelings among close relatives over the phone. It is not unusual for Americans to cry over the phone when they are talking with family members or close friends. One of our elderly interviewees told us that her sister called her and cried while she was talking about one of her daughters who had decided to get a divorce. She added, "Don't tell anybody this, even my sister." We take the liberty of sharing her story anonymously to illustrate the fact that crying is a very private and hidden behavior in American society.

"Family": Revitalizing a Sense of Sharing

Schneider's (1980) analysis demonstrates that the American family is symbolically composed of husband and wife, a unit formed primarily by sexual intercourse. Although Schneider delineates symbolic forms of the American family, he seems not to be concerned with the symbolic use of the family concept in American community. In fact, the concept of family as used in mainstream America has not been treated in anthropological studies but only in studies focusing on relatively closed communities, such as the Amish. Yet it is one of the most powerful symbols in American life, and one that is cultivated in different ways, as the situation dictates. We found this to be the case in the senior center.

The elderly in Riverfront can arrange their own daily, weekly, seasonal, and annual activities by choosing programs provided by the Pine County Commission on Aging. Although the center was built primarily to serve the elderly, Ruth Warner, the commission director, wants it to be a part of the entire community. In fact, as we pointed out earlier, the center is used as a meeting place for clubs and organizations, mostly public and nonprofit, such as the advisory councils of the Meal Program, Foster Grandparent Program, Retired Senior Volunteer Program (RSVP), and so forth.

Many programs share the objective of fostering intergenerational interactions. The staff assumes that providing opportunities to be with younger people improves the quality of life for Pine County's older adults. In fact, some programs offered to generate an extended-family atmosphere in the center. They encourage older adults to share their knowledge and skills with grade school and high school students. In this way, the elderly realize that their wealth of experience is valuable and can be relevant and useful in young people's lives.

In a place such as the senior center, where intergenerational interactions occur, people can easily visualize and revitalize images of family that are still perceived as important. This is a vital role for the senior center to play in the life of the community. The family image is evoked in myriad ways at the center. For example, Maggie Smith said, "I'm playing a mother role." She has multiple roles as the "boss" of kitchen volunteers, before-meal announcer of the center's upcoming events and other information, camera woman for birthdays, monitor of individual patrons' dietary needs, cheer-up person, receiver of complaints, and generally the focus of many patrons' attentions. She does not look like one of the staff of a public program, and she tries not to behave as anything but a member of the center family. Of course, she does not want to make the place family-like in her own image, but a family-like comfortable place as the patrons and staff commonly envision it.

The following programs are offered by the Pine County Commission on Aging and address the goal of offering senior citizens opportunities for intergenerational interactions. They are designed to help erase the age segregation so common in

America. Programs similar to these might be attempted in Japan, but we have not heard of any that are organized and operated as well as in America. The central theme in Japan regarding programs for the elderly is that younger people do almost everything for elderly people (Fujita, 1999). Therefore, it is striking for us to see that the elderly in Riverfront have such an active orientation toward helping other elderly people.

Foster Grandparent: This program is sponsored by the Pine County Commission on Aging. According to a brochure that we collected at Jefferson Center, "Foster Grandparents are senior volunteers who work in area schools with children who have special needs. Being a Foster Grandparent is rewarding for both the volunteer and the child — the personal bond between the two is very special." Bonnie Kelner, who volunteers as a hostess at the meal site in the senior center, goes to a public school as a Foster Grandparent and helps in the classroom as a teacher's aide, preparing instructional materials.

Pen Pals with Grade School Children: Grade school children visit Jefferson Center and have lunch with senior pen pals. Most of the volunteers at the senior center whom we know participate in this program. Before the children's visit, some senior pen pals are busy writing a response letter to their young pen pals, who are classmates at a particular school. A photo sheet with individual portraits of the classmates is circulated among the senior pen pals beforehand. During lunch, young and old pen pals sit together. If a senior pen pal cannot attend the lunch, friends take over the role and meet the young pen pals. In such cases, those senior pen pals can be seen seated with two young ones (Figure 27).

Folk Fair: The RSVP organizes a festival-like event held in the spring and autumn in grade school gymnasiums. The elderly volunteers demonstrate to school children how to make something according to the old ways and then help the children to make the same thing. This event is much like the county fair in the way it entertains the audience. Volunteers decide which older ways of doing things they are going to demonstrate, taking into consideration their abilities, the kinds of things that are appropriate and interesting for such occasions, and something that might be new and unusual to young people. Some demonstrators have special skills, like Mr. Dallek, who has demonstrated proper tool use in woodcrafts. Even individuals who have no special skills can participate. For example, Katie and Pauline demonstrated how to wash clothes with a washing board, and Anna, Martha, and Amanda made ice cream by hand with a little machine. Participation in such programs does not always mean the elderly can do exactly what they want as volunteers. The director of the RSVP decides who shall do what. Anna told us that if she were asked by the director to perform a task, she could not say, "No." Nevertheless, these activities are fun for the participants and also provide good opportunities for them to feel that they are a part of community life.

From the school teachers' viewpoints, the program provides an occasion for the children to learn something outside of the formal educational environment. In fact, the principal of the elementary school made a speech at the beginning of the Folk Fair emphasizing that the children should learn from the older people while having a good time. For the senior center staff, who try to enrich the lives of the elderly, the fair provides opportunities for them to come out of their houses, which

Picture 27. Jefferson Center patrons share lunch with their pen pals from a local grade school. (Photograph taken in February 1986.)

staff regard as isolated islands, go to the center, and connect with the community through the center.

In organizing these programs, the staff regard the concept of sharing as important because it is the first step for the elderly to form active relations with the community.

A Caregiver's View of Sharing

Visiting is intentionally practiced at the senior center by caregivers who are in their middle age. For example, Ellen Bunczak (age 52), a nurse and a director of the senior day-care center, said to Joe, a participant of the program, "How are you, Joe?" Joe did not show his interest in conversation, so then Ellen said, "I am visiting you. Can you tell me something?" Ellen encouraged Joe to act by himself. However, in reality, such interactions between caregiver and participants do not happen much. Caregivers do not have time to visit with all individual participants because they have to perform in their capacities such as contacting doctors, as staff of the senior center, as staff of other related agencies, preparing material for day's programs, and so forth (cf. Foner, 1994).

The staff expected volunteers to become conversational partners with the elderly patrons. They stressed the importance of having someone with whom each participant could converse. Ideally, the senior day-care center is supposed to be a place where elderly patrons can have conversations with other people. From our point of view, it was a reasonable role to assume, particularly as anthropologists who sought opportunities to converse with the people.

Generally speaking, the caregivers did not often use the word *share*, although they expressed concern on various occasions over how to create and organize their services. Therefore, we did not understand the importance of the concept of sharing in the domain of aging until we came to know of some continuities between early socialization and aging in Riverfront. To delineate such continuities, we looked at caregivers' talk and conversation in the context of aging.

Ruth Warner, director of the Commission on Aging, made a speech at the opening ceremony of their "Sanitation Program." This program was planned and organized by the Meal Program staff once a year. Participants were all engaged in the Pine County Meal Program, including the managers and volunteers of seven meal sites from all over Pine County. We were among the participants because we were volunteers at the meal site in Jefferson Center. Ruth used *sharing* and *family* in her speech as she explained the principles underlying the activities organized by the Commission. She talked about her husband and two sons. The family had lived in East Africa for several years until her husband took a position as a vice principal of Riverfront High School several years ago.

In her speeches, Ruth always tried to be informal by using a big smile and speaking in a casual style. Toward the end of her speech, she said:

> . . . in my family, as I am sure it is in your family, the most important thing is, we sit down to eat together, whether or not we've got prawn curry, or whether or not we've got a beautiful roast beef. . . . most important is the sharing we do together as a family talking and laughing and making jokes; we share hugs we get from each other.
>
> Well, the food is important, but the food wouldn't taste good if we didn't have so much fun together. I think that's true in our meal sites, too. It's really important what we eat. It's also very important what the atmosphere looks like when you' re eating. And that's the role that you volunteers play. You can make your meal site, and I think you do, make your meal site a wonderful, warm, loving, caring family situation. You talk with everybody who comes, ask them how they are feeling, how things are going, and you cheer, with some jokes, things that happen, and you have lots of hugs. And that's what makes this meal program really important.
>
> . . . I've really come . . . come to say, the most important is how people feel when they come to a meal site. And I would like to thank you for all you do to make people feel this is the place for welcome and love and care and with lots of hugs. And you're wonderful.

The connections among caring, sharing, and family are clearly shown in Ruth's speech. The main ideas are the goals, not only for herself but also for other staff, especially directors, such as the meal program director, the transportation director, and the senior center director. It is the directors' responsibilities to actualize Ruth's ideas in activities for the Commission on Aging at Jefferson Center and its satellite places all over the county.

MAPLE CHILD DAY CARE CENTER AND JEFFERSON CENTER

We have examined two centers — one for young children and one for the elderly. In this final section, we focus on both centers' meal programs and look more closely at the conceptual framework by which the caregivers organize and run them. What is the shared cultural system that makes the meal program meaningful and understandable? What is the relationship between the cultural system and the stage of the life cycle that one is in? How does the relationship affect the ways of running the program?

To answer these questions, we need to analyze the meanings of recurring symbols that caregivers use to talk about their programs. Caregivers at both Maple Child Day Care Center and Jefferson Center describe mealtime as an occasion to learn to be independent while, at the same time, sharing. Indeed, "independence" and "sharing" are two key symbols that encapsulate caregivers' attitudes (cf. Ortner, 1973). We examine the meanings of these two symbols by comparing the similarities and differences between meal programs at the two centers.

At both centers, independence is emphasized, especially in two areas. One is self-reliance in eating. It is considered vitally important for children to learn how to eat or for the elderly to maintain skills for eating so that they can eat without being fed by caregivers. Another area in which independence is emphasized is that of decision making. Children are taught to express clearly whether they have finished their meals or want to have more. For the elderly, too, it is their responsibility to decide to make reservations for their own meals, to cancel if they need to, or to request special eating arrangements. The only exception to this rule is for those who are unable to eat on their own because of Alzheimer's or other neuromuscular disease. Otherwise, everyone must try to eat on their own regardless of age. This attitude can be contrasted, as stated earlier, with that of Japanese teachers at a child day-care center who spoon-feed slow eaters to expedite the meal. Such a practical consideration is not an acceptable reason for feeding someone in the American cultural context.

Sharing is also emphasized in the meal programs. The caregivers at both centers agree that the meal is the time to relax and to enjoy food and companionship. Teachers at the child day-care center tell us that children tend to talk about their experiences more freely during lunchtime, and they also encourage them to do so. One of the major purposes of the meal program for the elderly is for elderly persons living alone to get out of the house and socialize with other people to alleviate their loneliness and isolation. Efforts are made to make mealtime a communal experience, for example, by having a birthday party once a month.

The caregivers at both the child and senior centers regard independence and sharing as important and central values for their meal program. However, teachers at Maple Day Care think the family-style meal or communal meal is the best way to teach these values, whereas the staff at Jefferson Center adopts a more individualized and less communal style, that is, the cafeteria style, as a way to foster independence and sharing for the elderly. How do we account for the differences in the caregivers' attitudes in relation to the cultural system?

To answer this question, we need to examine the American concept of "person." The person here follows Geertz's use of the term in his article, "Person, Time and Conduct in Bali." The concept of the person is defined as the culturally specific ways in which people of a certain culture define, perceive, and react to —that is, think about — individual persons (Geertz, 1973, p. 362). The concept of the person is a cultural construct. The term does not imply a psychological construct such as "ego," nor does it imply the unit of legal and theological responsibility as the term is usually thought of in a legal context (Rorty, 1976, p. 309).

In American culture, the concept of the "person" is divided into "adults" and "babies." Adults are and ought to be independent, whereas babies are considered dependent. Adults should be able to do everything without receiving help from others. Individual adults are and ought to be, that is, descriptively and normatively, in control of their own lives. Control in this sense covers everything: bodily and mental functions, living environment such as one's home, finance, work, schedule, and so on. What "control" here symbolizes includes self-care, autonomy, and voluntarism. First, adults should take care of themselves. Second, adults should make decisions about their own lives independently. Third, adults should be able to choose things and actions according to their will and should not be forced to do what they do not like to do. Also, adults should live in their own homes, because home is a sphere where their control is realized.

In contrast, babies are thought to be helpless and dependent. Adults should take care of babies, for babies are thought to be unable to exercise control even over their bodily functions. Thus, they are fed, bathed, put in diapers, and clothed. Babies are thought to be incapable of making their own decisions, so adults have to make decisions for them. In short, babies are not in control of their lives.

At both Maple Day Care and Jefferson Center, every effort is made not to treat any person as a "baby." If an older child calls a younger child "baby," Maple Day Care teachers quickly correct the older child by saying, "No, he is not a baby." "Don' t act like a baby" is a standard injunction that teachers use to scold children. Children are taught to become adults as quickly as they can, at least as far as table manners are concerned. At Jefferson Center, caregivers are careful not to infantilize elderly people, including frail people who participate in the senior day-care program. Avoiding feeding people is one way to avoid treating them as babies.

This underlying cultural concept of the person helps us understand how the caregivers view the relationship between themselves and those they provide care for. Caregivers at the two centers we studied want to create a family atmosphere. The American cultural concept of the "family" is based on a nuclear family, which consists of parents and minor children. The relationship between the parents and children in the nuclear family is asymmetrical: Children are under their parents' control. It is the parents' responsibility to teach manners and supervise their children's behavior. This is the model of how the teachers at Maple Day Care interpret their relationship to the children and the model for their conduct. Teachers do not treat children as babies, but they are still minor children who need supervision. Their family-style meal symbolizes this relationship.

The staff of Jefferson Center also tries to create a family atmosphere as we noted earlier. According to the cultural model of the family, however, both the elderly and the staff are "adults." Their relationship is symmetrical. In fact, the staff is careful not to act "bossy" toward the elderly. Because of the equal adult status, caregivers are not free to supervise the elderly's behavior at the table. Without their supervision, however, the caregivers think that serving meals in the family style is unrealistic. The cafeteria style, on the other hand, is a better way to ensure the elderly adults' status without supervision or criticism.

So far, we have explicated the cultural system underlying the activities for the elderly and for preschool children. The key symbols of independence and sharing reflected in both ends of the life course in American society indeed represent core cultural values. As indicated in expressions such as "standing up on our own feet" and "pulling yourself up by your own bootstraps," Americans aspire to be as independent as possible regardless of their age. At the same time, sharing is also emphasized in American daily life.

However, these values are not automatically given to people but rather are learned throughout life. By comparing similar public programs for two different age groups, we have examined in this chapter how people learn these values and how they balance them as well. We have seen how this balance is deeply connected to the stages of the life cycle through which people pass. Preschool children learn to share food with their peers and learn skills of self-sufficiency in eating while under their teachers' supervision. In other words, teachers control the amount of freedom that children can have, which is necessary because they are minors. For example, children are not allowed to leave the table before others, and they are instructed to use certain table manners.

For the elderly, on the other hand, their adult status is strongly emphasized precisely because their current stage in life may make it problematic to maintain independence. The meal program at the senior center aims to bolster their independence. They are treated as adults with maximum control over their lives; therefore, they are free to participate or not participate in the meal program, to sit with people of their own choosing, to eat in the way they wish (so long as it does not harm other people), and to leave the table when they want. The cafeteria style, or a portion-meal style, makes it easier for them to have control over their own behavior without interference from caregivers. The degree of sharing is left to each individual. However, the more their individual needs are emphasized, the less communal experience they share with their peers.

Although there are clear differences between the two ends of an individual's life course, we found that "sharing" is an important idea common to both young and old, going beyond age differences. "School" is the next stage in life following early childhood. "Family" is the last stage before late adulthood. The reason why sharing has expressive power in the two end stages is that here people become aware of how separated they are from each other, and they are conscious of how they might reconnect with each other in everyday contexts. In this sense, we have seen that such concepts as "caring," "school," "family," "visiting," and "sharing" are all products of life's historical consciousness and cooperative efforts, which are acceptable in the Riverfront area. Riverfront therefore provides a context in which people try to create and recreate meaningful community life, and it is also a place that has been meaningful in the past and will be again for those who are trying to make it so.

CHAPTER 9 / "Boys Became Independent": Hard Work and Caring among Men

When we as anthropologists investigate people's concepts concerning childbirth, child-rearing, and caring for the elderly, we tend to circulate among women because traditionally women have been the caregivers and men have been the breadwinners. Is the reason for this based on a stereotypical gender image? Are men's life stages completely different from those of women? We expect "hard-working" to be a dominant cultural value for men. Indeed, through interviews with a dozen Riverfront men, we found that all had worked hard all their lives. Without a doubt, they share one of the prevailing ideals among the American people: the work ethic. However, what about "independence"? Is remaining in the Riverfront area most of one's life compatible with being independent? How about "sharing" and "caring"? Are they essentially cultural values that only women consider important?

When we pose these questions, we are intrigued by the fact that Japanese men are also hard workers because this superficial similarity leads us to a cultural puzzle. It is considered common sense in Japan that men can work hard if their spouses are supportive by taking good care of the family at home. Clearly, they depend on their spouses and family members to be able to dedicate almost their entire lives to their work. Consequently, in the Japanese cultural context, "caring" and "sharing" are emphasized in the women's sphere and de-emphasized in the men's sphere. A Japanese man needs someone to take care of him as well as his family. In this sense, the Japanese notion of hard work is connected to dependency.

On the other hand, the American notion of hard work is connected to independence. In America, people are expected to be self-sufficient, or independent, and work hard to maintain and protect their self-sufficiency and independence. To prove that they are independent, they are supposed to be able to help others, even to the point of taking care of those who can't take care of themselves. How do American men reconcile achieving independence with sharing and caring?

The contrast between Japanese and American concepts of hard work and dependence/independence is so striking to us that we pose a further set of questions regarding aspects of an individual's life course: How do men grow up, build careers, and grow old? How do they associate with their parents, children, relatives, and others? How do they regard marriage, and how do they balance work and family? What are their wartime experiences like? We include wartime experience because we think that it is as much a part of life experience as work has been for the men who served during World War II. It is also important to know how self-identity and ethnic identity are perceived and how they relate to work experience and life history.

In this chapter, we first describe a group of men whom we met at Jefferson Center and then proceed to examining some of their life histories and of others who do not come to the center.

THE "BACHELORS' TABLE" AT THE MEAL SITE

At the Jefferson Center meal site (introduced in Chapter 4), there is a table we call the "bachelors' table" because it is always occupied by six men who are all leading the "single" life: either never married, widowed, or separated (cf. Rubinstein, 1986). It is an ethnically mixed and working class group. Fredy Lemond and Jack Marphy have known each other a long time, ever since they both worked as cabinet makers at a furniture factory. Fredy has a French accent and never loses his smile. He regularly visits his wife who has long been in a nursing home. Jack is small and quiet. He comes to the center in his own car with his sister.

Joe Dobka, Ed Kacheski, and Chester Stanski are Polish-American. Joe and Chester are stout, solid-bodied men, and Ed is slender and quiet. Joe is only in his 50s, but he is eligible for the meal program because of disabilities. He lives with his mother in North Side. He laughs readily, responding to the other men's banter. Ed has never been married; he lives in a small house at the edge of town in a dense forest and also drives to the center in his own car. He had moved into that house 2 years ago to live alone.

Chester Stanski and Ray Goold are widowers in their 80s who live alone in their own houses. Chester was a paper mill worker. He also drives to the center, often offering others rides. One day he arrived at the center with Pauline Karenski, a widow and one of kitchen volunteers. Their good relationship was still continuing when we left Riverfront. Ray Goold is a retired grocery store owner in downtown Riverfront. His gentle manner reflects his long experience with customers. He rides the bus to the center.

The "bachelors' table" came about spontaneously and was accepted by other participants and volunteers, as well as the center staff. It is rather a familiar phenomenon to us because we have worked among elderly Japanese people in similar social situations. In Japan, even married men will sit in a group of other men, separate from their wives. Consequently, we felt at ease talking to these six men.

"IT WAS A GREAT LIFE, THE PAPER MILL"

Nine months after we first met Chester Stanski at the "bachelors' table," we asked him after lunch was over if he would mind our interviewing him. "Sure," he said generously. So, we soon visited him at his home one sunny afternoon after we had finished working at Jefferson Center. As we crossed over the Wisconsin River, we saw a paper mill on the left bank. In a few minutes, we arrived at Chester's house. We noticed Pauline's house several blocks away because we had visited her house several months before. Chester came out to welcome us and invited us inside. Entering his cozy living room, we saw photographs of his son's family neatly placed on a small table. This was Chester's only child. We sat down at a table and talked for 2 hours.

After telling Chester our purposes for studying American culture, we told him that we wanted to learn about his work life in the paper mills. He responded by saying, "That's hard work. I worked there for 33 years. Let me show you what I got for 33 years of working." He showed us samples of paper made at the paper mill from when he worked there. Chester had worked in the mill from 1937 until 1970, when he retired at the age of 65.

"It was a great life, the paper mill," he said. "It was quite a life, but I put in my share of time there. So, you've never been to the paper mill, eh? Quite a thing, quite a thing."

These comments indicate the great impression the paper mill made on him. People work with massive machines, amidst the dynamic movements of huge paper rolls. It is a noisy, dangerous environment, and tensions among workers can run high. More than just a place to work, the paper mill is a town symbol. Located near the city center, it has signified the economic well-being of Riverfront since the late 1910s. According to Chester, 400 employees worked in the mill when he worked there; but the number is half that now. This change took place beginning in 1980 as local industry shifted from manufacturing to service-oriented businesses and public service.

For Chester, hard work was not limited to his steady job at the paper mill. Long before that, he had experienced hard work during his boyhood. He was born in 1905, the sixth of 12 children. Since early boyhood, he helped his parents, along with his five brothers and six sisters, on a farm 8 miles west of Riverfront. In the following dialog, he recalls how it was for children working on the farm:

Chester:	You know, when you get 3, 4 years old, they've got some chores for you, something to do; carrying wood, or maybe water, there wasn't no running water in those days or nothing like that or these automatic stoves that burn oil, everything was wood or something, and we had to pile wood, they had to store wood, and those was our chores. There was always chores for the kids to do.
Toshi:	Milking cows?
Chester:	Yeah, when you got 10, 12 years old, you learned to milk cows.

Life wasn't all hard work on his parent's farm. Every Sunday during the spring and summer, Chester enjoyed playing baseball with friends. The boys would make a baseball bat out of a piece of wood and a ball by winding string around a horsehair core. Girls, meanwhile, played jump rope and learned cooking.

Like many Polish-American parents, Chester's parents were very strict about the work the children were supposed to do. "We got paddled lots of times," he said. "We got paddlings because kids are always into some trouble. We thought it was fun." Even so, the parents told children all kinds of scary stories at night for fun.

Education was not important to Chester's parents. He openly talks about the poor education he received:

> All the education I got is the eighth grade. When I graduated eighth grade, they didn't believe in high schools or anything. The farmers just said, "Keep on working on the farm."

While Chester did not go to school past the eighth grade, he saw that his son did. Leaving the farm and seeking one's fortune in town is a step that young rural people would take in their late teens to express their desire to be independent. However, in old age, people do not explain it in this way, but rather as Chester does:

> I didn't like farming. Never did like farming. When I was 16 years old [in 1921] I left home and I went to Chicago. I worked for International Harvester, a big machinery outfit. They built fine machinery there. Then the Depression came out of 1929. You've heard of that big depression we had in this country. I got laid off. I was one of the younger ones there and I got laid off. I lied about my age to get a job.

In Chicago, Chester earned 32 cents an hour and paid $3.75 per week for boarding. He could eat out because things were cheap at that time.

Job opportunities were scarce in cities of all sizes during the Depression. Any jobs that were available were temporary and unsteady. Farms were in a similar situation. Chester's brother, the third oldest son, was the only one to remain on the farm; the rest of the children left:

> The girls went away, you know, they went to town and worked in a restaurant. Some worked in the hotel, you know. They got jobs. You couldn't keep 12 people on a farm, 'cause that's too many, you know. There isn't enough work, and then the folks couldn't pay us wages. We wanted a dollar for spending money, so we had to get out and go look around.

Chester returned to his parent's farm 2 years after he had been laid off in Chicago. We interpret his coming back as a socially acceptable dependency on his parents, particularly during the Depression. Of course, he did not enjoy being dependent on his parents and immediately began asking around for a job in town. Soon he landed a job with the city driving a snowplow in winter and hauling dirt and other debris in summer. He did not like this job but had to do it for about 10 years because he had his own family to support.

Chester often joined a group of about 10 young men to ride on a Model-T Ford to go to barn dances in the countryside. Each boy paid his share for gasoline. Barn dances were often held at farms and provided opportunities for young men and women to meet. At one such dance, Chester met Rose, his future wife, who lived on a farm in a neighboring township.

To fulfill his destiny as an independent man who can support his own family, Chester needed a steady job. He applied for a sanding job at a furniture company and a yard job at a paper mill in 1937. As he was hoping would happen, he got a call from the paper mill and went to work there for the next 33 years. Getting that job was the turning point in Chester's quest for independence. A year later, he built his home in a working-class neighborhood. To own a house was rather a common occurrence among Polish-Americans. They would buy or build homes soon after they married to show the world that they are steadily employed and lead independent lives.

Hard Work at the Paper Mill

In the beginning, there was no guarantee that the paper mill job would last. New workers had to do yard work first, and during this initial period, they were carefully observed and their attitudes toward work were assessed. Chester needed to pass this "initiation" by showing that indeed he was a hard worker. Naturally, yard workers earned the lowest wages, but if they worked hard enough, they were likely to get promotions before very long. Chester said, "Newcomers have to take that. They watch and they screen them out, see if they're good worker." Chester worked in the mill yard with 8 or 10 co-workers, loading and unloading boxcars and handling the materials used in paper production, such as lime and salt. He wasn't there for long because he soon proved himself to be a capable worker, which landed him a job inside. To get promoted, he did not need special skills and knowledge because his new task was primarily to push buttons — to start up machines and to shut them down.

Chester rose through the factory ranks over the years, although he never reached the highest possible position in the machine room, the "machine tender." What he achieved was "first-hand" in the machine room, the second to the highest position. A machine tender must always walk around and supervise the other machine operators. Chester says, "I don't think I would have cared for the supervisor's job. I didn't want that responsibility. When the horn blew, a guy stepped in from behind me and took over, and I went home. I didn't have no worries. No supervisor's jobs." By saying so, he shows us that he made choices for his life as an independent man.

Paper mills have changed since Chester retired. Jobs there are still considered desirable but difficult to get. "Today," he said, "those people make big money. Today young people have a hard time getting jobs. It's terrible. You have to ask people to put in a good word or know somebody, put in a plug; they call that a plug." (The Japanese have a similar expression to describe the use of personal connections to get a job.)

The workplace has also changed in significant ways. It is now less gender-biased because of technological developments. Before, it was strictly a man's world and "pretty rough." Women worked only in the front office. Chester used to chew tobacco while he was working in the paper mill but stopped immediately after he retired. "Now they got women working with the machines." Everything has become easier to handle.

Hardworking Wife and the Need for Child Care

When their child was old enough to be left with a baby-sitter, Chester's wife, Rose, began working at the Wallace Fish Fly Company in downtown Riverfront, a company with an international reputation. The workers, about 30 at the time, were all women, mostly Polish-American. In later years, their numbers grew to about 70. Chester described the work:

> Did you ever see them [women workers] sit and tie those flies? My wife was pretty good at it. I went down there one time and they took me around. She was pretty good, she could tie those flies and put those feathers in. It looked like it was more fun than work. But she had to do hard work, I know she did.

Eventually, the company was sold, and its factory was closed — one of the many business closings in downtown Riverfront during our fieldwork. Local businesses, large and small, have relied on the hardworking men and women of the Riverfront area to succeed as much as the workers had relied on them to succeed.

While both Rose and Chester were at work, Rose's mother cared for their son. "Grandma'd come here, and then I'd take her home that night," Chester said.

"Your wife's mother?" Mariko asked.

"Yeah, my wife's mother. There's nothing like having Grandma take care of the kids, you know."

The role of the mother's mother as child caregiver in Polish-American families has been much appreciated. We know of other such cases even nowadays in Riverfront.

Working Hard While Caring for a Family

Paper mill workers have to adjust family time to work time. Inside jobs are run in shifts so that the machines can go 24 hours a day. A worker's shift schedule changes every week: 7 a.m. to 3 p.m. one week, 3 p.m. to 11 p.m. the next week, and 11 p.m. to 7 a.m. the following week. Chester said he preferred the first shift but did not like the second, and the third shift was not too bad because he could spent time with his wife.

Family was much more important than co-workers in Chester's view. When asked if he went out with his co-workers after work, he said, "Oh no, not with the buddies. I'd go out with the wife and the family. Most of my buddies would like to go to the tavern and I've never been much for that life. I never was much for that life, it wasn't for me. To this day I don't go to the taverns much." Chester seemed to place high value on his family.

Why is family so important? We learned that Chester had taken care of his wife while he was working in the paper mill and after he had retired. Rose had become ill and quit her job when Chester was about 42 years old. In light of this finding, we reinterpret the fact that Chester did not get a supervisory position on the machine floor. Although he explained that he did not want that kind of responsibility, we have to conclude that he did not want it for a very compelling reason: He worked hard each day at the mill and then went home and cared for his infirm wife. For more than 20 years, Chester had to manage two heavy responsibilities; he simply could not take on the extra burden of a supervisory position.

Mariko: How did your family cope with your wife's sickness?

Chester: They were helping a lot, my son and his wife, they were both helping a lot.

Mariko: So he had grown up already?

Chester: Yeah, when she got sick he already had his family. But he'd come and help. But it was rough. Some people go through life, they live to real old age and they never have no trouble. Isn't that a fact? Some people have all kinds of trouble.

Getting help from his son and his son's wife represents the practice of reciprocity among kin relations, part of the Polish family "tradition." As a boy, Chester had helped his parents on the farm; likewise, Chester's son helped his parents at home.

Rose died a year before our interview.

Chester: The last couple of years she was home, it was really, really hard. I had to lift her, and it got too much so I couldn't do it no more. (pause) This is me and my wife.

Chester showed us pictures of himself and Rose when they were courting and after they were married. Back then, he says, he never smoked and never drank. We are puzzled by this comment, for a moment but then realized what he was implying. Even though he has tried to be a good person, he still has difficulty understanding why he has experienced hardship. William Taylor, a piano teacher and teetotaler, expressed similar sentiments when he talking about his life: Men who do not drink identify themselves in contrast with stereotypic images of men in the locality — heavy drinkers.

Although Chester did have hard times in his life, this was not his only experience. Even at the paper mill, he enjoyed pleasant times. One pleasant time occurred every day, when the horn blew indicating it was time to go home. Another pleasant time was payday. Chester got a check every second Thursday. He would go to the bank to deposit a certain amount of it and with the rest he paid his grocery bills — debts incurred mostly at stores on Riverfront's public square, where the farmer's market was located.

Chester considered the market his "garden," where he could get fresh vegetables and fruits, which he prepared himself while his wife was sick. Unlike many townspeople, Chester did not keep his own garden, but he did cultivate a lawn and flowers in his yard. Grass cutting is considered men's work. Chester considered gardening hard work, but nevertheless, women's work. He felt badly for his wife, who liked to garden but could not do it because of her illness.

A Way of Taking Care of Chester's Parents and His Views on Marriage

Our concern about how Chester's parents were taken care of turned out to be related to his view on marriage. We had assumed that his brother who had remained on the parents' farm when all of the other children had moved away, was responsible for taking care of the parents. This was true, but the situation was more complicated than we had realized:

Chester:	Dad died when he was 63. He was farming. He died with a ruptured appendix. And Mom stayed on the farm with a boy and one of the sisters until she was 93. Neither of them didn't have to go away to a nursing home or nothing, which was nice.
Mariko:	Your mom stayed with boy and sister?
Chester:	Yeah, she's gone now, she died shortly after Mom died, she died.
Toshi:	Your sister?
Chester:	Yeah, my sister.
Toshi:	So, your sister-in-law?
Chester:	No, real sister, because the boy who's on the farm isn't married, he's a bachelor.
Toshi:	He was always a bachelor? He never married?
Chester:	No, no.
Mariko:	Your sister stayed there, too?
Chester:	Yeah, she never married. [pause] They weren't as foolish as I was to get married when I was young.
Toshi:	You didn't want to get married?
Chester:	Well, it was the way back then, you know what I mean. Two kids get together, foolish, happens. Oh, what the heck. We had a good life, until my wife got multiple sclerosis. Twenty-one years, then she got so I couldn't handle her. Hold her and the wheelchair. I had to put her in a [nursing] home. She lived there 2 years and 3 months. Yeah, that's bad, that's bad, that's bad, that's bad . . .
Mariko:	Did it happen just like that?
Chester:	No, it came on slow, but it kept getting worse and worse and worse.

Chester associated our concern with how parents are cared for with his concern with taking care of his wife. We did not expect that his reflections would flow in such a manner. Among Polish-Americans, married or not, one must take care of the other family members. This idea contrasts with Yankee people's practices of leaving their parents after growing up.

Joining the "bachelors' table" at Jefferson Center, Chester certainly enjoys himself with the other "bachelors." However, this is not because he has forgotten the hardships associated with his marriage. He knows that being a bachelor does not free him from concerns about other people. Some believe that it does, whereas others do not. But the dichotomy between being married and being single is not so simple as we tend to think.

Education and Work

As we have mentioned, education is more important to Chester than it was to his parents. He is aware of the differences in educational level, and he contends to be content with his own — although telling us that his son is always paid monthly — and admits that getting paid on an hourly basis was his preference. Usually less educated people have hourly paid jobs, whereas people who receive a good education acquire better jobs with a monthly salary. We asked him whether he had wanted his son to get a good education:

> Oh yeah, he went to college [in Riverfront in the 1950s]. Then he started to teach at a country school, one year. And when he told me he was gonna quit, I kinda got excited. I thought, "Oh my God." He said he wanted to take up electrical [work]. I said that if that's the way you feel about it, okay.

His son went to Milwaukee to get more specialized education in early 1950s. This story reminds us that if one wants to become a professional, he or she must leave the small town and move to the larger town, as in the cases of Thomas Stromborg and Professor Woodland.

Ethnic Identity

At the beginning of our interview with Chester, he told us his last name and spelled it for us: "Stanski. S-T-A-N-S-K-I." We assumed from the sound of his name that his background is Polish. Nevertheless, as the interview was concluding, we felt it necessary to confirm this. We asked him if he is Polish. "Yeah," he replied. Then we asked, "Your wife?"

"She was Polish, too" he replied. We also asked him about the people who worked at the paper mill with him:

Toshi:	Were there many Polish people in the mill?
Chester:	Yeah, you know, this is kind of a Polish community, Riverfront. There is a lot of Polish people. Some good ones, some bad ones. [laughing]
Toshi:	How can you tell?
Chester:	I don't know if I was good or bad, but I tried to be good. . . . There was pretty much of a Polish gang in the mill. [A neighboring town] is different. It is more of a German town. Riverfront is more of a Polish settlement. Well you can figure it out for yourselves, right, the city has two Polish churches.

In Chester's self-image, ethnic background is situated in local and regional contexts. As we have noted in earlier chapters, the terms *Polish town* or *Polish community* are often used by both Polish and non-Polish people to characterize the Riverfront. Moreover, as we discussed in Chapter 5, local people know well which towns in central Wisconsin are Polish, German, Scandinavian, or English and which are a mixture of ethnicities. The local people situate themselves within not only the local context but the wider area.

In our reinterpretation of Chester's work life, we determine that working hard while taking care of his spouse was required to become independent. While attempting to be independent, Chester accepted the fact that he did not get the chance to receive a higher education than he did. He accepted help from his son's family; therefore, in Chester's value system, interdependence can be practiced without compromising independence.

"CHARGE AND DELIVERY"

One afternoon in early April, several months after we had met him at the "bachelors' table," we visited Ray Goold (age 88) for an interview at his home in the east side of town. It was so warm that the windows were all open when we entered his house. At this time of year, old snow is usually left piled along the roadsides, but the temperatures sometimes get high, as in early summer. We sat down on Ray's sofa while Ray sat in his armchair, next to which stood a small table. On the table, Ray kept a Sony radio and a reading lamp. Ray's house was neat and simple. He had lost his wife a decade ago.

Like Chester, Ray has been coming to Jefferson Center for 2 years. He started coming because he thought that if he continued sitting in his house alone 24 hours a day, he would lose his mind. Like Chester, even though he lives alone, relatives often come by to visit. In fact, his grandson's family arrived at his house at the end of our interview, and on the previous day, his daughter, who lives 75 miles west of Riverfront, dropped by to visit, bringing homemade cupcakes with her.

At the beginning of the interview, Ray described what he did for a living as "charge and delivery," which means that his customers could charge meat and groceries and have them delivered to their homes from his store. He performed this service while selling meat and groceries in downtown Riverfront at about the same time as Chester was charging groceries in the farmers' market. Ray was engaged in the meat business since his early 20s. Later he became a grocery store owner, remaining in that business until he retired at the age of about 65 in the early 1960s.

Unlike Chester, Ray did not speak of any hardship in his business or personal life. He seemed to be satisfied with what he done with his life and what he had gained from his business. He achieved his goal, which he made at the time of purchasing a store. He had a happy marriage and now has nine grandchildren and 21 or 22 great-grandchildren. The only difficult time he recalled, in relation to his business, was during World War II, when no butter or meat was available to sell. During World War II, his son served in the military for several years. When Ray was 65 years old, just before his retirement, that son died.

Taking care of another person and hard work were connected in Ray's life, as they were in Chester's. The death of his father when he was 5 years old affected his progress toward independence in boyhood, living with his mother. Ray was born to a small family, the son of a mailman, in Pepin, a small town in southwestern Wisconsin. Despite being an adolescent who wanted to strike out and establish his independence, he could not leave his mother alone. Therefore, he had to find a job that would allow him to stay with her. His only brother, 8 years his senior, had continued his schooling and graduated from high school in the 1900s, after which he left Pepin for Milwaukee. This is rather a typical way for young people to become independent. However, unlike his brother, Ray did not choose to take this path when he was 15 years old. Instead, he worked in a general store in his hometown. Like Chester and other of our Polish interviewees, he did not go to high school.

Ray is content with married life. During our interview, he said more than once that he has not quarreled with his wife during their entire marriage. Unlike the way that Chester first met Rose, at a barn dance, Ray met Jane, his future wife, while working at the general store in Pepin. Soon after they met, they were married. She was 18 years old, and he was 19 and a half. Because the law required that the bride be 19 and the groom 21 to marry without parental consent, Ray's mother signed the marriage documents. Jane's life story was similar to his own; she had lost her mother when she was 5 years old and was raised by her grandparents, who lived in the farming area near Pepin.

As it had been in Chester's life, marriage was a turning point in Ray's life. A year after marriage, he got a new job at a meat market in a larger town in central Wisconsin and worked there for 20 years. He had heard about the job from a meat salesman who traveled around in the region.

His mother did not move with his family when he left Pepin. This did not make sense to us because we would feel obligated to live with a widowed mother. If an American couple is independent — free from any obligation to take care of their parents — who else will take care of them? This idea that children are not necessarily supposed to take care of their elderly parents is unfamiliar to us. However, if we look at the interactions between children and parents in America, we find that visits are relatively frequent between them. Ray's family had a lakeside cottage between his house and his mother's. His family and his mother came to this cottage to meet each other every Sunday for several years until she passed away.

Because of the nature of his business, Ray did not have promotional possibilities as Chester had. Rather, he promoted himself as an entrepreneur. While working for someone else's small business, he came to think of making himself more independent to make more money. He heard, again from a meat salesman in 1937, that a meat shop owner wanted to sell his entire business in Riverfront. The owner offered Ray a deal so good that he could not turn it down. When he came to Riverfront, he learned that the business had been doing well, and thus he decided not to change the shop's name.

It was about this time, in the late 1930s, that Chester, Ray, and other "members" of the "bachelors' table" crossed paths in downtown Riverfront. A year after Ray had come to Riverfront, Chester changed his job from city street worker to paper mill worker. He preferred to buy his vegetables and fruits at the farmers' market rather than at regular grocery stores, which might include Ray's. Also, the mother of Professor Woodland, a native Riverfrontan who told us his experiences in this town in the 1930s, went to the farmer's market to buy fresh produce.

"Charge and delivery" services were the key to Ray's success in business. He eventually had six employees and one delivery man, who was a Polish-American. He described his employees as the "best men I have had; women just love them."

He was lucky to have employees who attracted customers for his business. One of them had worked with him at a previous store and wanted to work with him again, so as soon as his new business got off the ground, Ray invited the man to join him. Another employee had been a total stranger. He had approached Ray in his store and asked him directly if he needed another man. This man explained that he worked in a meat-and-grocery business in a neighboring town to which he had to commute every day. He was tired of making the daily journey. Ray said, "Okay, I do need another man."

Ray had wealthy customers who could afford to buy "the best meat in town." Many of them liked to have their meat custom cut, and Ray accommodated them. This service was well received, especially by Jewish people. There used to be many of them in town, and most were store owners. Ray thinks that such customers were protectors of his business because of their patronage.

Another group of customers were employees of a growing insurance company based in Riverfront. In those days, the company headquarters stood one block away from Main Street where Ray's store was located. Three quarters of Ray's business was charge-and-delivery services with these people, which implies that there was a distinction in the 1940s and 1950s between customers who could afford to use the services and those who could not. Even though the farmers' market was busy, it did not affect Ray's business.

Because we knew Polish sausage is one of the popular meats among Polish people, we asked Ray if he made it. He replied shortly, "Yeah, blood sausage." However, he did not talk about related Polish custom, only about the how to make the sausage. "We didn't have big equipment like they do now," he said. "We had to do it all by hand, you might say that."

Polish farmers relied on stores like Ray's, where they could bring their eggs to sell. Ray would examine them under a bright light and buy them if they were fresh enough. In those days, every farmer raised chickens and sold their eggs as a supplemental income, as Bert Wobski and his mother did.

In 1962, a few years before Ray was to retire, his 42-year-old son died of a heart attack. Ray would not talk about what he had felt at the time; he did tell us that when his son died, he did the same thing that he had done when his mother had died: he let his son's wife and four young children live close to him but kept a certain distance in respect for their independence.

Ray has only vague ideas of his ethnicity. He describes himself as "English or Yankee," but he knows that there were many Swede farmers around his hometown. In fact, his wife was a Swede from that area. Ray honored a "Yankee" value by keeping his family small, even though he married very young. He had one boy and one girl — the same family size as his parents.

"I WOULD BE A DUMB POLE HUSBAND"

Unlike Chester and Ray, Bert Wobski (age 65) was not a participant of the meal program at Jefferson Center. He was in a chorus group when we first met at a Christmas party sponsored by a local chapter of the Polish Women's Alliance

(Figure 28). We became interested in his life story because he was the only true bachelor farmer we knew. He was freshly retired and had time to talk to anyone who would listen. One day in March, we made our first visit to his farm 8 miles south of Riverfront. Our second visit was made after we happened to see him again at a Catholic church in Bishop. He remembered us and recognized our new baby. We wanted to record his family tree and asked him if we could drop by for a visit. On the day of our appointment, it was very cold and snowing, so we decided that only Toshi should go because it seemed difficult to take Hosaki along. The following descriptions are based on both the first and second interviews.

A handful of buffaloes raised for commercial use and a big birdhouse sitting on top of a tall pole catch our attention as we enter Bert's farm for the first time. We are also impressed by his house, built in 1904. Inside, there is a long, large table, where a big family can sit together. In fact, at this table, about 16 men, a threshing team and neighborly helpers, ate dinner during threshing days on his farm. The house was originally made as one large room, 18 square yards, where various indoor work was done. It was remodeled and divided into several rooms after World War II, when his father died. By that time the family was able to buy farm equipment, such as combines and threshers. Since then, the farm has done very well.

Bert is a lifetime farmer who now lives alone. He sold his 500-acre farmland when he retired a few years ago. He still owns a piece of land on which the farm house, barns, pasture, and gardens sit, all intact. He now spends most of his time volunteering to help older people who cannot afford to hire handymen for odd jobs and participating in such activities as the Big Brothers Program and the Polish Choir, of which his brother is also a member. He keeps busy but does not miss going to church every day, which he has done since childhood. During interviews, he did not talk about his war experience, so we did not ask.

Listening to Bert talk about historical changes on the farm, we notice that the idea of mutual assistance among farmers has disappeared while they became more independent after World War II. In those years, because farmers did not have their own machinery, a team of threshing machines would be moved from one farm to the next, and farming neighbors helped each other get the jobs done. Women also helped at those times by cooking meals for men. Thereafter, people started borrowing tractors and combines from relatives who farmed close by. Sooner or later each farm started acquiring its own machinery, and the tradition of neighbors helping each other disappeared.

As farm work has become more and more mechanized, fewer and fewer people have been needed on the farm. Young people who dislike hard farm work go to town to get better jobs. Moreover, as many small farms have difficulty surviving, more land is put for sale and is often purchased by neighboring farms. Thus, the number of farmers decreases while the size of a farm grows ever larger. Such historical changes in farming, as experienced by Bert and others in the Riverfront area, are certainly part of general trends in American agriculture.

Some farmers in the 1920s and 1930s had regular connections with townspeople. They did not deal in cash but raised chickens, pigs, and various vegetables such as potatoes, tomatoes, cabbages, beats, onions, beans, carrots, and corns. On

Figure 28. A Polish choral group performs at a Christmas party held by the local chapter of the Polish Women's Alliance. We first met Bert Wobski in this occasion. (Photograph taken in December 1984.)

the other hand, townspeople did not keep livestock, but they often had gardens. Thus, farm families would deliver eggs to townspeople, along with vegetables in the summer. Bert recalls much about such practices. He delivered eggs every Saturday to about 60 customers in Riverfront, including doctors, lawyers, business executives, paper mill employees, and shopkeepers of any nationality: Jews, Germans, Poles, and so forth. He says, "They treated me as part of the family."

His first customer was a lady with a German family name in Riverfront. His customers soon increased through word of mouth. Bert also remembers some episodes of his mother's peddling and selling watermelons and handmade butter at the public square. Townspeople like Chester, Ray, and Thomas Stromborg may have bought food from farmers like Bert and his mother.

Bert's father was born in Ohio, grew up in the South, and came to Riverfront at the age of 17 with his mother and siblings in 1894. After he worked at the coal mines in upper Michigan for a few years, he bought land, where Bert now lives; it had been marshland before it was drained in 1900. Bert says that his father's mother moved into the area after her first husband (Bert's grandfather) had died.

Bert's great-grandparents on his mother's side were among the earliest Polish immigrants who came to the United Sates in the middle of the 19th century. His grandfather on his mother's side was very education oriented and started a local school, which later became the parochial school of a Catholic church in Bishop. He sent his daughter (Bert's mother) to another parochial school of St. Paul's Polish Catholic Church in Riverfront for 2 years in the 1890s, during which time she had to board in town. Bert tells a story about how she once wanted to become a nun, but her father said to her "I need you." In fact, according to the U.S. census of 1900, when she was 15 years old, she still went to school while her younger brother, who was 13 years old, had already started working on the farm. She left home and worked as a cook in Milwaukee until she came back home and met her future husband at the age of 29. The following year, 1915, when the groom was 36, they married. This discussion of the parents' ages at marriage allows us to now consider the marriages of Bert and his brothers.

After the first interview with Bert, we assumed that, among his siblings, Bert was the only one never to have married. However, in the second interview, we discovered we were wrong. While drawing Bert's kinship chart, Toshi asked him which of his siblings were married and about how old they had been at marriage. Their ages at marriage suggest a dynamic relationship among the family members. Before delving further, we needed to know more about Bert's siblings.

Bert and his eight siblings were born 13 months apart, except for one case in which there was an interval of 17 months. He discusses this birth pattern spontaneously, which suggests that his family talked openly about it. It also indicates that his parents had minimized birth, spacing up until their mother turned 40, in order to get the maximum number of children.

Bert is the fifth son and the second youngest child. Like Chester and Ray, he only received an eighth grade education. We wondered why he stayed on the farm after finishing eighth grade, and the reason for this was probably related to his brother's death. It was still during the Great Depression when the eldest brother drowned at the age of 19. Bert was about to finish eighth grade at the time. (Chester was still working for the city street department, Ray had not yet come to Riverfront, and Thomas Stromborg and Professor Woodland were in high school.)

Because Bert's father married late, the brothers were still young and probably had not had an opportunity to leave the farm for town to work like Chester had done. Bert started working full time on the farm after finishing grade school. Several years later, the eldest sister (the second-born in the family) married but suddenly died following the death of her husband. This tragedy brought changes in the family. The other two sisters (then 23 and 18 yeas old) married at about the same time. Also, Bert's father was old enough to retire. A few years later, the elder brother married and left the farm to start his own farm on the northeast side of Riverfront. Bert and his two bachelor brothers remained on the farm with their parents.

If we look at the Wobski farm when the patriarch died in 1950 at the age of 73, we find he is survived by his wife and three single sons. However, we should not despair for them; we should not miss the possibility of late marriage. Indeed, 5 years later the oldest of the three brothers married at the age of 40 and moved out to a neighboring farm that he had purchased from his aunt. Three years later, the next eldest brother also married at the age of 40, and a few years later moved out to another farm out of Pine County.

The partnership between Bert and the married brother farming nearby continued. Bert stayed on the farm with his mother for several years until she died. Bert was in his early 40s at the time. He worked on the farm for another 20 years, alone, although some relatives living nearby helped both of them out.

Noticing that two of his brothers married very late, unlike Ray, Toshi commented on this to Bert. Bert explained that it was not unusual for men to marry late. His father married at the age of 36. In his view, being single at age 40 was not a problem. Toshi asked him whether he ever wanted to marry:

Bert:	Not now. . . . Years ago there was no way. I don't want to marry.
Toshi:	Are you busy?
Bert:	No. I don't like women as much. I talk to them and kid around . . . but I don't want to live with them. . . . Women are argumentative. I don't like argument. I would shut up. If I were married, I would be a dumb Pole husband.

We are inclined to take his explanations why he never married with certain reservations. We tend to believe Susan Strovinski's explanation that children who never married are "too good to parents." It is true of Bert. Although he thinks it is important to relate to others and appreciates mutual interdependency among family members, the concept of "independence" does not accord with his beliefs regarding love and family, which he delineated when talking about current problems with family life in the United States. His parents were good to their children in the sense that they told their children to make their own decisions, including the decisions about whether to stay on the farm.

Unlike Chester's strict parents, Bert's parents encouraged their children to be independent. In fact, at least to us, Bert embodies the idea of independence because he could manage hard farm work for himself. He knows the American ideology of independence and knows how to act as an independent person. In his relatively religious mind, however, he has nourished the idea of the importance of dependency.

Another way of thinking about his not having been married is to consider Chester's comment on the institution: "foolishness." If we take Chester's sense, Bert never married because he was not as foolish as Chester. Both Chester and Bert went to school only through the eighth grade. They are hard workers, and neither one is a drinker. One of the differences between them is their attitude toward farming: Chester clearly dislikes farm work, and Bert, although he did not express his attitude toward it during interviews, was a farmer all of his life. Another difference is that Chester enjoyed seeing girls at barn dances when he was young. Bert, on the other hand, although perhaps not indifferent to the opposite sex, was not "foolish" enough to marry one.

Bert told us, with laughter, that he started to help his parents on the farm at the age of 7, which was 2 or 3 years late in those days. This suggests that his parents did not push him to help, so he probably had no chance to dislike farming. However, he had to face the realities. As we learned earlier, the death of his oldest brother might have made Bert become more interested in helping his parents and recognize the fact that his parents were getting older. The combination of Bert's ideas and preferences and the conditions of family members influenced him to shape his life in such a way that marriage was neither urgent nor important. We conclude that there is no single reason for Bert's staying single. Being too good to his parents is the most plausible reason, but we need to understand how children became "too good to parents" in order to understand other similar cases.

We find that Bert, like Chester, John Biza, and many other educated and noneducated Polish Americans, is conscious about his being Polish and aware of the negative images of Polish people in mainstream American culture. He justified his not being married as a result of the choices that he made at various moments in his life. He seems to want to think that his choices were the right ones, so he has avoided becoming a "dumb Pole husband" but rather is a good Pole, like Chester tried to be.

"THERE ARE POLISH OR NON-POLISH IN THE WORLD"

Neighbors were always part of our immediate environment. We conversed with, listened to, and even watched them. It was not long before we knew that we were part of their immediate environment too. We could have lived completely separate from them, but we chose to meet them and have conversations in our backyards. Topics of conversation usually concerned ordinary matters like the weather, gardening, snow-shoveling, and so forth. Even these matters often gave us insights about people of Riverfront. Our neighbors were predominantly Polish-American, and so we learned about local Polish ways of daily living.

Judy and John Biza (ages 60 and 64, respectively) live in our neighborhood and are our "friendly informants." They can see our culturally bound behaviors, and we can see theirs. Sooner or later, we get a sense of regularity or irregularity in our neighbors' behaviors by noticing, for instance, who is going in and out of the front door, which is not normally used by local people, and how long the light over the neighbors' back door stays on in the evening (when the light is on it means they are gone).

Several days after we settled down in a cozy, remodeled house, we noticed that John was watching our house. In fact, we noticed he often watched our house. We wondered what he was so curious about. Soon after we started chatting with him and Judy, we invited them into our house to get acquainted. We learned from them about our house's previous owners and tenants. We also knew that John had been a marine during World War II and served in the Pacific theater. He knew about Japan because he had been stationed in Nagasaki just after the end of war. This made us realize that he wanted to have a chance to talk to us.

We simply had not expected to meet a person who had been in Japan living next door to us. We soon felt at ease around the two of them because we shared something — a sort of exchange: He had gone to our country, and we came to his. Gradually, we came to know about his experiences during wartime and the story of his life in Riverfront.

Like Chester and Bert, John was from a large Polish-American farm family, and like Chester, he did not like farming. So, as soon as he became old enough to leave home, at the age of 16 or so, he came to Riverfront to find a job. At first he worked at a fox farm, but soon he went to war. He became physically disabled while in service, and after he came back home, he met Judy again, also of Polish descent and a Riverfront native. John worked at several different jobs, such as a salesperson at a department store and then as a gas station owner/operator. He is now retired, but Judy is still working for a clothing store owned by Jewish people, so he drives her to work and picks her up every day.

John was a person whom we could count on hearing from about his feelings and experiences during the war. One day Toshi visited John and Judy, and they voluntarily showed him a Japanese sword that had been carried by a Japanese soldier. John probably had picked it up and brought it back with him to the United States. He asked Toshi to look for any sign of the owner's name on it because he wanted to return it to the bearer's family. Unfortunately, no indication of ownership was found. John had taken good care of it as a sort of "family treasure" for 40 years. Judy knew that he had special feelings toward the sword. The meaning for him seemed to change after he had met us. We sensed that he had become more conscious of his wartime memories.

John is among the few people in Riverfront who witnessed the effects of the atomic bomb dropped in Nagasaki. When he was there, he behaved exactly like our image of a GI stationed in Japan — giving children his chocolate and chewing-gum. One day Toshi asked him how he felt in Nagasaki. He wanted to say something, but the words would not come. He knew that one of the major Catholic churches in Japan was in Nagasaki and was destroyed in an instant. He and his wife were Catholics. They went to mass every Saturday evening to avoid the Sunday morning crowd.

As it is in other midsize towns, the American Legion hall is one of downtown Riverfront's landmarks. John is a member of the American Legion, but he does not attend its meetings. Judy is an auxiliary member and is sometimes asked to make cakes for special occasions. We went to the hall a few times for the Friday fish fry dinner and found it quite crowded, both at the bar and in the dining room. There are veteran's organizations in Japan too, but they do not usually have meeting halls where members and even nonmembers can gather and socialize with each other. John drinks hard liquor but does not go to the club for drinking. Instead he enjoys drinking and smoking at home. Such habits are not good for his health. He still periodically has fevers, probably from a disease he must have contracted in the Pacific during the war. He has a disabled hand and arm, and his health has reminded him of events 40 years ago.

There were a handful of casualties from Pine County during the war, whose names are inscribed on a plaque hanging on the wall of the County-City building. To keep memories of wartime experiences, there is an annual ceremony celebrating Veteran's Day in the public square. We found it impressive that small national flags were put beside tombstones at cemeteries for veterans.

Like other older people, John keeps visiting his relatives and is visited weekly by his only son. Yet he goes on living independently by remaining in his own small house with his wife. His son works at a hospital in another town and comes to visit almost every week. John himself often goes to see his brothers in town and on the farm. He is taking care of his sister by visiting with her over the telephone and driving her to the doctor's office, as we noted in Chapter 8.

John's caring manner is not limited to family members but extends to his neighbors and the town as a whole. He identifies himself as a kind of neighborhood chief. Of course, he does not have any official duties as chief, but he knows who lives where in his neighborhood even though he seldom talks with people. There is no association in our neighborhood, which is located just outside the city limits. John can see through his window what is going on outside his house. The accordion music that we sometimes heard during the summer was, according to him, played by a senior Polish-American, one of our neighbors. Polish people, whether young or old, like their music. John's son has played drums since boyhood and was a member of a band.

To find out what is going on in town, John uses a radio scanner to monitor communications among town agencies such as ambulances, fire fighters, and the police. He always hears his nephew's voice, a dispatcher in the town's radio-communications, through a radio scanner that is placed on a small table by his armchair in the living room. John can sense the rhythm of the town by listening to information of emergency situations, crimes, accidents, and problems in town and its environs. One interviewee said that Polish-American people used a short-wave radio to monitor any news of the Pope.

John can also hear of news and town episodes from Judy, who has long worked for a clothing store downtown. She told us that she knew individuals in almost every part of the county but knows very few people on the west side of the Wisconsin River. It surprised us that she knew one young couple whom we had interviewed. When we told her the name of the couple, she instantly spoke about their parents who lived in the countryside. John is well connected to other people in these ways.

Another source of information for John is a city directory and a county directory. He looks at them to identify anyone being discussed. Like others, he and his wife regularly check newspaper articles about townspeople in the police reports, traffic accidents, obituaries, marriages, and births. They know many things unobtainable by any other means; however, they know they are not the sort of people who show up in newspapers.

Superficially, John is ethnocentric; that is, he likes to joke about it. One day, while drinking Front Beer, brewed in Riverfront, which he always drinks, John asked Toshi, "You know? There are two kinds of people in the world." Toshi answered, "I didn't know." "Hey. I'll teach you. One is Polacks and the other is people who want to become Polack. You see," he said, making a big smile. This shows that he is sensitive to ethnic groupings. In front of us, he does not mind talking about something Polish. In fact, he enjoys using stereotypes of Polish people when he tells his jokes.

"MY CHILDREN BECAME SELF-SUFFICIENT"

As we mentioned in Chapter 3, through our acquaintance with Professor Woodland, we came to know a group of local people who have lived in the Riverfront area since the 1920s. Among those people is Thomas Stromborg, whom we met one day in his office. He was a lawyer in his early 60s. Professor Woodland had told him about us over the phone, which made it easy for us to contact him.

In the beginning, Thomas gave us a good introduction of his family background and the developmental changes of Riverfront. While doing so, he expressed his ethnicity. We did not expect it, but we realized it was inevitable for him to talk about it when explaining the origin of his family name. He knew well about his relatives on his father's side. His great-grandfather came from Norway and stayed for a while in a town west of Milwaukee.

Religious denomination and political orientation were also disclosed without our asking. He talked about them while answering our questions about where he was born and raised, how he found a housekeeper or helper after his wife died in her early 40s in the 1960s, and whether his son worked with him.

As noted in Chapter 3, cultural and religious backgrounds of classmates are of less concern to educated young people like Thomas and Frank Woodland, who belong to a particular social group, or "caste," as Frank describes it. In fact, Frank is surprised to know about Thomas' ethnicity through us. We also had assumed that Thomas had an Anglo-Saxon background because he was Frank's old friend. To keep good friendship with others at school, as we have seen, they did not talk to each other about things related to nationality and religion.

Thomas monitors changes in and around Riverfront. For example, he pointed out the shift of main traffic routes that went through the town: north and south, east and west. The shift certainly reflects a progressive expansion of the town's size. John's office is seven or eight blocks away from downtown Riverfront, but it is on a thoroughfare. He therefore noticed that the amount of traffic on the thoroughfare fluctuated when a side road became the main artery, and the thoroughfare then became a minor side street. John explained that this pattern was repeated on each of the through-traffic roads up to the construction of the freeway out of the east edge of the town.

The major developmental changes in Riverfront were felt more or less directly by many residents of the town, especially those whose houses were located along major streets. They could tell how different Riverfront had become from its past (many years ago) by comparing immediate environmental changes. In fact, like Thomas, John told us about how the freeway construction changed the roads and the private land in our neighborhood.

Thomas also talked about the changing layout of the town. At its east end lies a small village that people sometimes called a "tax shelter." Thomas explains that it is the place where affluent people had lived before the war. After the war, town growth went hand-in-hand with the growth of locally based companies and the local campus of the state university. For example, Brooklyn Insurance expanded and brought in a group of more affluent people to be not only the executives of the company but also medical, legal, and other professionals. Before this, there had been a distinct "territory" known as the "North Side" or "Polish territory" up until the 1930s, and it is still remembered by individuals older than 60 years of age. This old territorial differentiation was based on ethnicity, whereas the new one is based on economic factors. However, contemporary residents were not so affluent as those in the past, according to both Thomas and Ray, who is a resident of the village.

Educational opportunities for Thomas were different from other people we spoke with. Children from educated families in town usually went to the local high school and then to the local campus of the state university. Young educated people had the choice of leaving town and getting further education. After spending about 4 years in military service during World War II, Thomas attended the University of Wisconsin in Madison to acquire legal training. After graduation, he worked for a firm for a couple years in Madison and then returned to his hometown.

Thomas belongs to the fourth generation of an immigrant family from Norway. (Bert is also a fourth-generation Polish-American. Chester is a second-generation Polish-American. His father came to the United States from Poland, but his mother was born in Riverfront.) Thomas' great-grandfather once settled in the southern part of Wisconsin and then moved to the eastern part of Pine County, where, like many immigrants from Norway, he came to settle and start a farm in the middle of the 19th century. One of the sons in the following generation took over the farm, while another, who was Stromborg's grandfather, left the farm and received some education in a city. This grandfather was a sort of self-made man because most of what he knew he had taught himself. He returned to Pine County in the 1870s, not to the farm, but to Riverfront. (In those years, Chester's father came from Poland via New York and Chicago to Pine County to start a farm.) Thomas' father and uncles went to the University of Wisconsin in Madison for legal training, and one of them, Thomas' father, came back to his hometown to settle.

There is a similarity between Chester's and Thomas' families in terms of their timing. It was a son in the third generation of each immigrant family who went to universities: Chester's son and Thomas' father. To generalize, the first generation started farms in Pine County, the second generation succeeded them on the farms but wanted their children to have good educations, and the third generation went to college regardless of their ethnicity and the era to which they belonged.

Nevertheless, we see that some differences between the two cases that were related to cultural background, especially attitudes toward education, work, and family. Chester's parents and relatives (second generation) had no idea that people could go further than the eighth grade in their schooling. Thomas said that his grandfather (second generation) liked to read, which implies that his great-grandfather wanted his children to read and probably gave them books and other reading materials at their farm home.

The second generation in both families left their homes. Chester wanted to get a job and Thomas' grandfather wanted professional training in a larger town. After they came back to Pine County, both sooner or later found steady employment in Riverfront. Both were about 30 years of age. While they started their own families in town, their sons (third generation) went to universities: Chester's son attended the local campus of the state university in the 1950s, and Thomas' father went to the main campus of the state university in about 1900. After the war, the local university expanded rapidly, but it did not provide a variety of majors. Therefore, after Chester's son graduated from the school and taught for 1 year, he left town to acquire more specialized credentials in Milwaukee.

As we have seen, how one finds a spouse is a key to understanding one's attitude toward marriage. Responding to a question about his life history, Thomas spoke candidly about how he had met his wife. They met in Madison when both were working and going to school. It was not an unusual meeting but remarkable even among the educated people of the town in those days. Usually, those who had left and then come back to their hometowns, whose future spouses were from the same area, had met during high school years. Thomas, however, did not stray far from the common practice. His future wife, Joan, was not a complete stranger to Riverfront because her hometown was also in the central part of the state.

Illness and death of family members occurred in Thomas' family as in those of other individuals we have described. Like Chester's wife, Thomas' wife became very ill in her 40s, during the 1960s. Joan had cancer, and Thomas had to take care of her. She received treatment at a clinic in Minnesota, but her illness did not last long. She passed away in a relatively short period, leaving Thomas with three young boys. How he was going to raise those boys alone troubled him deeply. His father had died while he was in military service during World War II, and his mother had died a few years before Joan died.

> I guess you just have to act as both a mother and a father, you know. I did have help. We used to get a housekeeper. Very hard to get help lately. I was successful in different periods to have a housekeeper who would come in and did cooking. But, we didn't have a live-in keeper. . . . As a result I guess my children became quite self-sufficient. They can cook on their own. They can bake a cake. They can cook very well, making their own style. They can learn staff, they had sewn button on, you know, that type of thing. They developed a certain amount of self-sufficiency.

Although his situation was difficult, he tried to show us that it could be viewed another way — optimistically, a way of thinking which fit with the cultural idea of becoming self-sufficient. As far as young children learning to become self-sufficient, a parent should never complain.

Thomas regarded wartime experiences as something everybody of his generation had. Like another person we spoke to from the same cohort, he seems to feel nothing emotionally special for having been involved in World War II. It was simply a duty that you had to perform. In the retirement announcements of the community section in the local newspaper, there are almost always descriptions of military services. The newspaper format for such descriptions amounted to a "standardized" way of talking about wartime experiences. However, we came to know through talking with John, Thomas, and others in town that there are various ways of experiencing war, depending on whether one was on the front lines, where they were stationed, what their rank was, whether they were injured, and so forth.

INTERPRETATION

The life histories of five men of Riverfront — Chester Stanski, Ray Goold, Bert Wobski, John Biza, and Thomas Stromborg — reveal five unique and diverse experiences. Their lives were shaped not only by individual choices but also by ideas and images of gender, ethnicity, and class that are accepted as appropriate locally as well as nationally. These men are certainly hardworking people who found their own paths. They chose a course to take from among various opportunities. They made decisions and tried to achieve certain goals. In the process, they experienced life's various social relationships, activities, events, triumphs and tragedies, actions and reactions, emotions, and ideas. Among the more important experiences were illness and death of family members. By connecting the unavoidable, sometimes unexpected, health conditions to work experiences and by situating these connections in their life stories, they struck a balance among such values as self-sufficiency, hard work, and caring for family members.

Working hard while caring for others is a difficult task, but these men did it successfully and with dignity. Midsize towns like Riverfront and its surrounding area became an arena where this task could be achieved. It is individuals like these who call to mind what is good about American culture, by living its "core" values.

How does hard work while caring for others fit into American mainstream values? We have often heard in Japan that American people easily change their occupations in the course of their lives to take advantage of an opportunity for more money or higher status. This image of so-called upward mobility, however, is misleading. Downward mobility recently has become commonplace, and a lower rate of meaningful employment is now the norm. This path, rather than unlimited opportunity, more often is pushing people to change their occupations. The image is also misleading because it does not account for the fact that significant numbers of people still work for the same company or remain in the same profession in the same town for their entire working lives.

People who do not pursue upward mobility are often considered "losers" in mainstream American culture. Are those individuals who work year in and year out at the same job in the same location also considered losers? We do not think so. It is difficult to believe that anyone would "decide" to become a loser, although they may occasionally have the sense of being one. Rather, we should consider such individuals as dynamic agents continually making decisions and adjusting themselves to changing economic and social contingencies. They situate themselves in the world by engaging in dialogs between contrasting ideas and ideals (Spindler & Spindler, 1990).

Examples of such dialogs can be seen in the life histories of the five men we described: independence and dependency, moving away and returning, social image and self-image of gender and ethnicity, distancing and visiting, helping and being helped, and working hard and having fun. Although we usually attend to the more salient dichotomies, the minor ideas, often as subtle and profound as the major ones, may become hidden, suppressed, or discouraged in specific historical times and places. Consequently, anthropologists should be careful not to overlook them when surveying the cultural landscape.

Epilogue: "Our" Hometown

Like many people who come from a foreign country to America, we lived for a time on one of the coasts before coming inland to settle in the Midwest. Although ours was not a permanent migration to the town we call Riverfront, nevertheless, we built strong relationships with the people we lived among and studied as anthropologists. During our fieldwork, our son was born, and thus our own life course took a significant turn in Riverfront. Throughout these experiences, our relationships with people transformed substantially at key moments: when Mariko became pregnant, when we gave a talk at Jefferson Center, when a baby shower was held at the center for us, and when our baby was born 1 year after we had first arrived in town. We spent another 9 months conducting field research while at the same time starting our family. Then we decided to leave town temporarily for 2 months to return to Japan. We needed this intermission to disengage from our field research and rejoin our families.

We came back to Riverfront, not intending to conduct full-time field research. This time we wanted to lead an ordinary town life as well as an academic life conducting our data analysis and writing. We found a relatively new apartment. Our new neighbors were a Polish nurse who lived alone and three female college students who shared another apartment on the same floor. We lived there for 6 months. Toward the end of this period, both of us were offered teaching positions in our own country, so we left Riverfront again in March of 1987. Just as we had done when we first came to town, only in reverse, we headed in our car for California. This time we had a companion, not our cat but our son. This trip was in certain ways very adventurous because of our new passenger in the backseat and the new snow outside. Eventually, while driving from Nevada to California, we came to realize that one of our life stages was over. A grand circle was finally completed in our minds.

These descriptions about what we had done during the fieldwork and postfieldwork periods tell us that our experiences are no greater or lesser than the experiences of others. Throughout our time in Riverfront, we have carried on cultural dialogs between "them" and "us" and among "ourselves." Some people who recently immigrated from Poland to this area are having exactly the same cultural-dialogical experiences as we had. Many others have parents, grandparents, great-grandparents, or ancestors who had such dialogical experiences when they emigrated from foreign countries to this area and started their own families.

It was not necessary for us to return to live in Riverfront after spending 21 months there for field research. Why did we come back? One important reason was that we judged the town as a good place to start our family. This is probably the same reason many native Riverfrontans who had left later returned to their "hometown." The word, *hometown* means the town where a person was born or raised; however, it carries a different and more important meaning to us. *Hometown* means that the place is good for making a home and raising a family. This aspect rings true with Pam Sorenson's comment when explaining why a young receptionist at Jefferson Center left for Milwaukee to take a new job: "This town is good for families, but not for singles."

The image of Midwestern life depicted in a television drama "Beverly Hills High School" is strikingly negative and contrasts sharply with what is supposedly mainstream culture, the Southern California lifestyle. We watched this dramatic series in Japan, equally distant from California and the Midwest. One of the most interesting scenes to us was when Brenda, one of the regular characters, encountered ambivalent feelings when she returned to her hometown in Minnesota to enter the state university instead of staying with her parents in Los Angeles and going to the University of California. Why did she feel ambivalence? Let us phrase this question more accurately: Why did the producer feel the need to contrast the Midwest with Southern California, as if they were polar opposites? Because many people enjoy this drama and the image of the Midwestern lifestyle, and values depicted there are shared and become influential in many audience members' minds.

While listening to how and in what context people talk about religion, class, nationality, and ethnicity, we found that talking about cultural differences is often a sensitive matter; what we anthropologists perceive as cultural differences is reduced in other people's perceptions as differences in wealth. For example, independence can be realized only after being materially satisfied. Therefore, if one wants to become independent, he or she must leave home for larger towns to get an education and a well-paying job. In this sense, the concept of independence is closely tied with separation from home and immediate family and friends (Figure 29). The fact that working hard while caring is practiced in the Riverfront area shows one way in which people deal with the ambivalence toward independence and separation. They want to be independent but do not want to be separated from family members, relatives, and friends. If they work hard, they can secure their independence economically. At the same time, they try not to lose their caring hearts. These are the features of the Riverfrontans that have been shaped over the last 130 years of history. We believe that Riverfront shares these features with other towns of the same size scattered around the country. We contend that without such towns in the backdrop of American society, independence and competition, which characterize the lives of the inhabitants of large cities, cannot alone represent the ideology of this nation.

In November 1999, 12 years after we left, we revisited Riverfront. During our short stay, we were fascinated not only by meeting familiar elderly people but also by observing changes in the town. The town seems to be shifted from a Polish town to the one whose residents are a mixture of people with European and Asian cultural backgrounds. The signs of European heritage such as wall-paintings of European designs and an European deli store disappeared from the public square, whereas the signs of Asian newcomers, especially Hmong people, have prevailed as we see an Asian market at the public square and several photographs of Hmong youths displayed at a photo shop in the downtown shopping mall. Moreover, 24-hour nationwide large retail stores have recently opened and the consuming behavior among Riverfrontans becomes nearly the same as that in the large cities such as Los Angeles, Chicago, and New York. Our new inquiries rise in our anthropological minds. Our "hometown" would never cease to be attractive to us.

Figure 29. High school students in different paths, being interviewed at our house. He has decided to leave Riverfront to attend a university in a large city, whereas she has chosen the local college in her hometown so that she can be close to her family of Polish background. (Photograph taken in March 1986.)

References

Alba, R. (1990). *Ethnic identity: The transformation of white America.* New Haven: Yale University Press.

Barth, F. (1969). *Ethnic groups and boundaries.* Boston: Little, Brown.

Bodnar, J., Weber, M., & Simon, R. (1979). Migration, kinship and urban adjustment: Blacks and Poles in Pittsburgh, 1900-1930. *Journal of American History, 66*(3), 548–565.

Boskin, J., & Dorinson, J. (1985). Ethnic humor: Subversion and survival. *American Quarterly, 37,* 81–97.

Brown, L. K., & Mussell K. (Eds.). (1984). *Ethnic and regional foodways in the United States: The performance of group identity.* Knoxville: University of Tennessee Press.

Buczek, D. S. (1980). The Polish-American parish as an Americanizing factor. In C. A. Ward, P. Shashko, & D. E. Pienkos (Eds.), *Studies in ethnicity: The East European experience in America* (pp. 153–166). New York: Columbia University Press.

Caudill, W., & Plath, D. W. (1966). Who sleeps by whom? Parent-child involvement in urban Japanese families. *Psychiatry, 29,* 344–366.

Caudill, W., & Weinstein, H. (1969). Maternal care and infant behavior in Japan and America. *Psychiatry, 32,* 12–43.

Collier, J. F., & Rosaldo, M. Z. (1981). Politics and gender in simple societies. In S. B. Ortner & H. Whitehead (Eds.), *Sexual meanings: The cultural construction of gender and sexuality* (pp. 275–329). Cambridge: Cambridge University Press.

Doi, T. (1973). *The anatomy of dependence.* Tokyo: Kodansha International Ltd.

Foner, N. (1994). *The caring dilemma: Work in an American nursing home.* Berkeley: University of California Press.

Fox, P. (1970). *The Poles in America.* (American immigration Collection, series 2). New York: Ayer.

Fujita, M. (1984). The cultural dilemmas of aging in America. Ph.D. dissertation, Anthropology, Stanford University.

Fujita, M. (1986). Independence and sharing: A symbolic analysis of meal programs for the elderly and pre-school children. In *Essays by the second year Spencer Fellows.* Cambridge: National Academy of Education.

Fujita, M. (1999). *Amerikajin no rohgo to ikigai keisei* (Shaping lives after retirement in America: Anthropology of elderly people). Okayama: Daigaku-kyoiku-shuppan. (In Japanese)

Fujita, M., & Sano, T. (1998). Day care teachers and children in the US and Japan: Ethnography, reflexive interviewing and cultural dialogue. In G. D. Spindler (Ed.), *Education and cultural process: Anthropological approaches* (3rd ed.) (pp. 430–453). Prospect Heights, Illinois: Waveland Press.

Garreau, J. (1982). *The nine nations of North America.* New York: Avon Books.

Geertz, C. (1973). Person, time and conduct in Bali. In C. Geertz (Ed.), *The interpretation of cultures* (pp. 360–411). New York: Basic Books.

Gjerde, J. (1985). *From peasants to farmers: The migration from Balestrand, Norway, to the Upper Middle West.* Cambridge: Cambridge University Press.

Goffman, E. (1963). *Stigma: Notes on the management of spoiled identity.* Englewood Cliffs, NJ: Prentice-Hall.

Hendry, J. (1986). *Becoming Japanese: The world of the pre-school child.* Honolulu: University of Hawaii Press.

Hostetler, J. A. (1993). *Amish society* (4th ed). Baltimore: The Johns Hopkins University Press.

Hsu, F. (1973). Rugged individualism reconsidered. *Colorado Quarterly, 9,* 145–162.

Hsu, F. (1981). *Americans and Chinese: Passage to differences.* Honolulu: University of Hawaii Press.

Isajiw, W. (1974). Definitions of ethnicity. *Ethnicity, 1,* 111–124.

Kiefer, C. W. (1970). The psychological interdependence of family, school, and bureaucracy in Japan. *American Anthropologist, 72,* 66–75.

LeVine, R. A. (1984). Properties of culture: An ethnographic view. In R. A. Shweder, & R. A. LeVine (Eds.), *Culture theory: Essays on mind, self, and emotion* (pp. 67–88). Cambridge: Cambridge University Press.

Lewis, C. C. (1984). Cooperation and control in Japanese nursery schools. *Comparative Education Review, 28,* 69–83.

Lopata, H. Z. (1976). *Polish Americans: Status and competition in an ethnic community.* Englewood Cliffs, NJ: Prentice-Hall.

Madaj, M. J. (1968). The Polish community—A ghetto? *Polish American Studies XXIX,* 65–71.

Marcus, G. E., & Fisher, M. (1986). *Anthropology as cultural critique: An experimental movement in the human sciences.* Chicago: University of Chicago Press.

Masuda, K. (1969). *Amerika no kazoku—Nippon no kazoku* (American families and Japanese families). Tokyo: Nippon Hoso Shuppan Kyokai (In Japanese).

Matsuo, B. (1966). *The narrow road to the deep north and other travel sketches* (N. Yuasa, Trans.). London: Penguin Classics.

Mikos, M. J. (1980). Polish in the United States: A study in language change. In C. A. Ward, P. Shashko, & D. E. Pienkos (Eds.), *Studies in ethnicity: The East European experience in America* (pp. 15–26). New York: Columbia University Press.

Moeran, B. (1985). *Okubo diary: Portrait of a Japanese valley.* Stanford, CA: Stanford University Press.

Morawska, E. T. (1977). *The maintenance of ethnicity: Case study of the Polish-American community in greater Boston.* San Francisco: R and E Research Association.

Myerhoff, B. G. (1980). *Number our days.* New York: Simon and Schuster.

Ortner, S. B. (1973). On key symbols. *American Anthropologist, 75,* 1338–1346.

Perin, C. (1977). *Everything in its place: Social order and land use in America.* Princeton: Princeton University Press.

Plath, D. W. (1980). *Long engagements: Maturity in modern Japan.* Stanford, CA: Stanford University Press.

Prosterman, L. (1995). *Ordinary life, festival days: Aesthetics in the Midwestern County Fair.* Washington: Smithsonian Institution Press.

Rapson, R. L., et al. (1967). *Individualism and conformity in the American character.* Boston: Heath.

Rorty, A. O. (1976). A literary postscript: Characters, persons, selves, individuals. In A. O. Rorty (Ed.), *Identities and persons* (pp. 301–323). Berkeley: University of California Press.

Royce, A. P. (1982). *Ethnic identity: Strategies of diversity.* Bloomington: Indiana University Press.

Rubinstein, R. L. (1986). *Singular paths: Old men living alone.* New York: Columbia University Press.

Sandberg, N. C. (1974). *Ethnic identity and assimilation: The Polish-American community: Case study of metropolitan Los Angeles.* New York: Praeger.

Sanford, A. H. (1908). Polish people of [Pine] County. *Proceedings of the State Historical Society of Wisconsin, 55,* 259–288.

Sano, T. (1989). Caring Americans: An ethnography of Riverfront, a middle-sized town in the Midwest. Ph.D. Dissertation, Stanford University.

Schneider, D. M. (1980). *American kinship: A cultural account* (2d ed). Chicago: University of Chicago Press.

Shweder, R. A., & LeVine, R. A. (Eds.). (1984). *Culture theory: Essays on mind, self, and emotion.* Cambridge: Cambridge University Press.

Siekaniec, L. J. (1957). The Poles of Northern Wisconsin. *Polish American Studies XIV,* 1–2, 12–16.

Spindler, G. D. (1974). Schooling in Schonhausen: A study of cultural transmission in an urbanizing German Village. In G. Spindler (Ed.), *Education and cultural process.* New York: Holt, Rinehart and Winston, pp. 230–273.

Spindler, G., & Spindler, L. (1987). In Prospect for a controlled cross-cultural comparison of schooling Schoenhausen and Roseville. In G. Spindler (Ed.), *Education and cultural process: Anthropological approaches* (2d ed.) (pp. 389–400). Prospect Heights, IL: Waveland Press.

Spindler, G., & Spindler, L. (1990). *The American cultural dialogue and its transmission..* With H. Trueba & M. D. Williams. London; New York: Falmer Press.

Spindler, G., & Spindler, L. (1993). Crosscultural, comparative, reflective interviewing in Schoenhausen and Roseville. In M. Schratz (Ed.), *Qualitative voices in educational research.* London; Washington, DC : Falmer Press, pp. 150–175.

Stern, J., & Stern, M. (1983). *Good food: The adventurous eater's guide to restaurants serving America's best regional specialties.* New York: Alfred A. Knopf.

Ueda, R. (1987). *Avenues to adulthood: The origins of the high school and social mobility in an American suburb.* Cambridge: Cambridge University Press.

Van Maanen, J. (1988). *Tales of the field: On writing ethnography.* Chicago: The University of Chicago Press.

Varenne, H. (1977). *Americans together: Structured diversity in a Midwestern town.* New York: Teacher's College Press.

Wallace, A. F. (1956). Revitalization movements. *American Anthropologist, 58,* 264–281.

Wrobel, P. (1979). *Our way: Family, parish and neighborhood in a Polish-American community.* Notre Dame, IN: University of Notre Dame Press.

Wytrawal, J. (1961). *America's Polish heritage: A social history of the Poles in America.* Detroit: Endurance.

Wytrawal, J. (1969). *The Poles in America.* Minneapolis: Lerner.

Index